D0001676

MERCHANTS IN THE TEMPLE

MERCHANTS IN THE TEMPLE

Inside Pope Francis's Secret Battle Against Corruption in the Vatican

Gianluigi Nuzzi

Translated from the Italian by **Michael F. Moore**

HENRY HOLT AND COMPANY

NEW YORK

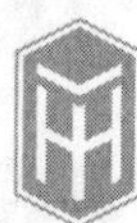

Henry Holt and Company, LLC
Publishers since 1866
175 Fifth Avenue
New York, New York 10010
www.henryholt.com

Henry Holt® and ® are registered trademarks of
Henry Holt and Company, LLC.

Distributed in Canada by Raincoast Book Distribution Limited

Library of Congress Cataloging-in-Publication Data is available.

ISBN: 978-1-62779-865-5

Our books may be purchased in bulk for promotional, educational, or business use. Please contact your local bookseller or the Macmillan Corporate and Premium Sales Department at (800) 221-7945, extension 5442, or by e-mail at MacmillanSpecialMarkets@macmillan.com.

Originally published in Italian in 2015 under the title VIA CRUCIS by Chiarelettere.

First U.S. Edition 2015

Designed by Meryl Sussman Levavi

Printed in the United States of America

1 2 3 4 5 6 7 8 9 10

Contents

ORGANIZATIONAL CHART OF THE VATICAN CITY STATE

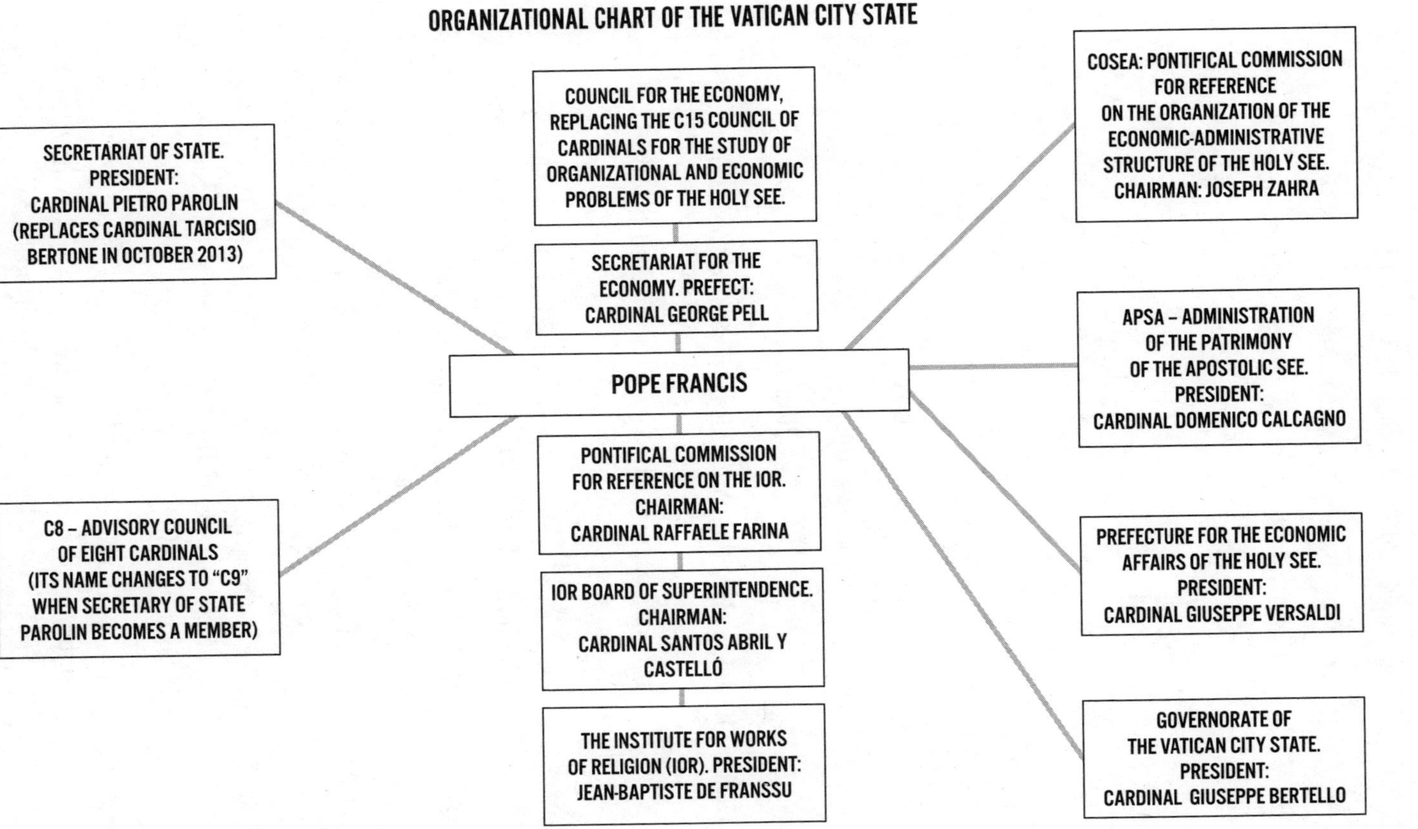

SECRETARIAT OF STATE. PRESIDENT: CARDINAL PIETRO PAROLIN (REPLACES CARDINAL TARCISIO BERTONE IN OCTOBER 2013)
C8 – ADVISORY COUNCIL OF EIGHT CARDINALS (ITS NAME CHANGES TO "C9" WHEN SECRETARY OF STATE PAROLIN BECOMES A MEMBER)
COUNCIL FOR THE ECONOMY, REPLACING THE C15 COUNCIL OF CARDINALS FOR THE STUDY OF ORGANIZATIONAL AND ECONOMIC PROBLEMS OF THE HOLY SEE.
SECRETARIAT FOR THE ECONOMY. PREFECT: CARDINAL GEORGE PELL
POPE FRANCIS
PONTIFICAL COMMISSION FOR REFERENCE ON THE IOR. CHAIRMAN: CARDINAL RAFFAELE FARINA
IOR BOARD OF SUPERINTENDENCE. CHAIRMAN: CARDINAL SANTOS ABRIL Y CASTELLÓ
THE INSTITUTE FOR WORKS OF RELIGION (IOR). PRESIDENT: JEAN-BAPTISTE DE FRANSSU
COSEA: PONTIFICAL COMMISSION FOR REFERENCE ON THE ORGANIZATION OF THE ECONOMIC-ADMINISTRATIVE STRUCTURE OF THE HOLY SEE. CHAIRMAN: JOSEPH ZAHRA
APSA – ADMINISTRATION OF THE PATRIMONY OF THE APOSTOLIC SEE. PRESIDENT: CARDINAL DOMENICO CALCAGNO
PREFECTURE FOR THE ECONOMIC AFFAIRS OF THE HOLY SEE. PRESIDENT: CARDINAL GIUSEPPE VERSALDI
GOVERNORATE OF THE VATICAN CITY STATE. PRESIDENT: CARDINAL GIUSEPPE BERTELLO

Chronology

2013

FEBRUARY 10 Pope Benedict XVI resigns from his office as the Bishop of Rome. As of February 28, the Holy See enters a period of *sede vacante*, when it administered by the College of Cardinals.

MARCH 13 Jorge Mario Bergoglio is elected as the 266th Pope of the Roman Catholic Church and chooses as his name Francis.

APRIL 13 Francis appoints a Commission of Cardinal for the reform of the Roman Curia.

JUNE 24 The Pope establishes the Pontifical Commission for Reference on the Institute for Works of Religion (IOR).

JUNE 27 The international auditors write to the Pope *sub secreto pontificio* detailing the irregularities, inertia, and shady areas in the finances of the Curia.

JULY 3 Francis stands before the hierarchy of the Church in a confidential meeting and delivers a blistering speech on the gravity of the financial situation and the impending risks.

AUGUST 2 The Pontifical Commission for Reference on the Economic-Administrative Structure of the Holy See (COSEA) begins its audit of the Vatican finances.

AUGUST 5 COSEA freezes four hundred bank accounts at the IOR.

OCTOBER COSEA runs into mounting difficulties and does not receive the information it has requested.

DECEMBER 19 Tensions rise over the COSEA audit. A pattern of obstacles, silence, or denial is used to impede the activity of Francis's men.

2014

JANUARY 30 The Secretary of State delivers to COSEA a twenty-nine-page file on the secret accounts.

FEBRUARY 18 The Cardinals learn of all the critical areas uncovered by COSEA.

FEBRUARY 24 Francis appoints Cardinal George Pell as the first Prefect of the Secretariat for the Economy.

MARCH 30 COSEA documents are stolen in the night when burglars break into the safes and strong boxes in the Prefecture's archives.

JULY 8 Francis transfers responsibility for the ordinary section of APSA to the Secretariat for the Economy.

2015

MARCH Hidden microphones are discovered in the offices of the Holy See.

MERCHANTS IN THE TEMPLE

About This Book

The Wounds of the Vatican

It is the afternoon of September 12, 1978. Pope John Paul I, after only eighteen days of his pontificate, discovers that a powerful Masonic lobby with 120 members is active within the Curia. The news is disconcerting. Rather than abiding by the words of the Gospel, cardinals, bishops, and senior clerics are beholden to the vows of the Brotherhood of Freemasons—an intolerable situation. So on September 19, the new Pontiff starts to draft a plan for a radical reform of the Curia.

In the late afternoon of September 28, John Paul summons the Secretary of State, the powerful Cardinal Jean-Marie Villot, to inform him of the changes he wishes to implement. He has prepared a list of senior cardinals to be dismissed. At the top of the list are Paul Casimir Marcinkus, the Monsignor who directs the IOR (short for *Istituto per le Opere di Religione*, the Institute for Religious Works, often referred to as the Vatican bank), and his closest collaborators: Luigi

Mennini and Pellegrino de Strobel. Similar measures will be taken with the Secretary of the IOR, Monsignor Donato De Bonis. These players are too closely associated with the bankers Michele Sindona and Roberto Calvi and as such, they have to be dismissed. They will be asked to leave the Curia the very next day.

Among the other prominent figures to be replaced are the Archbishop of Chicago, Cardinal John Patrick Cody, and the Vicar of Rome, Cardinal Ugo Poletti. Cardinal Villot himself is also slated to be leaving.

John Paul's talk with the Secretary of State lasts for more than two hours, until 7:30 P.M. The next day, at dawn, Sister Vincenza Taffarel finds the Pontiff's lifeless body in his bed. John Paul I has left his last speech on his desk: he was supposed to deliver it to the Procurators of the Society of Jesus, as the Jesuit Order is known, with whom he had an audience the next day, September 30.

It is July 3, 2013, the Feast of St. Thomas the Apostle. As he does every morning, Pope Francis wakes at dawn in Room 201, one of the few suites in Casa Santa Marta, the guest house where he has chosen to live since his election in March. He has refused to move into the sumptuous pontifical apartments, breaking immediately with papal formality. The day seems to be proceeding with absolute normality. In his homily during the celebration of the Mass in the Santa Marta chapel, the Pope uses a powerful metaphor: "We find Jesus's wounds in carrying out works of mercy . . . Let us ask of St. Thomas the grace to grant us the courage to enter into the wounds of Jesus with tenderness."

After the Mass, he has a frugal breakfast. But this will be no ordinary day. Almost four months have gone by since the Conclave that elected him. The time has come to initiate the profound reform promised to Catholics throughout the world.

This is also the start of a war. A war that is still being waged today behind closed doors, in the secret rooms of the Vatican palaces.

This book tells the story of that war—through documents that have never before been made public—offering proof of a gigantic, and seemingly relentless, malfeasance that the Pontiff is challenging with singular courage and determination.

A meeting has been called to discuss the finances of the Holy See. It is a confidential meeting attended, customarily, by the cardinals of the Council for the Study of the Organizational and Economic Problems of the Holy See, and chaired by the Secretary of State of the Vatican, Tarcisio Bertone. The Pope's presence is generally not required at this meeting, but Francis wants to be there. He has something urgent to say to the Church hierarchy, which is assembled in its entirety. At the meeting Francis will bring to light all the wounds of the Vatican, signaling an unprecedented break between the old and the new approach—a rupture whose consequences are still unpredictable.

This Investigation

A live recording was made of the Pope's words during that meeting. By listening to this recording, I became the first journalist ever to have access to what goes on at an insiders' meeting at the Vatican attended by the Pontiff. The investigation begins with the more recent and undisclosed secrets of the Holy See. I will follow the Stations of the Cross as they are contemplated in silence, one at a time, by the Jesuit Pope from Argentina. This is a true battle between good and evil, in which the Pope's men are lined up on one side, while on the other are his enemies, the defenders of the status quo, adverse to any and all change.

Seated around the table with Francis are the fifteen cardinals of the Council. Also in attendance are the leaders of the departments that control the finances of the Holy See: the *Administrazione del patrimonio della sede apostolica* (APSA, for short), essentially the central bank of the Vatican, which also manages the immense real estate holdings of the Holy Roman Church; the Governorate, the body in charge of the museums, commercial activities, contracts for normal and special maintenance of buildings and facilities, the post office, and telephone services; the Prefecture for the Economic Affairs of the Holy See, which oversees all the Vatican offices; and the IOR, the bank that administers assets earmarked for religious works and charity. All the names that count are here.

My knowledge of this meeting is based both on the recording and on the testimony of some of the participants. Through their accounts I was also able to get a visual picture of the faces and expressions, the tensions and dismay. And I was able to ascertain—through this live recording—the resolute position of the Pope, so sweet and affable in public appearances, but steadfast and firm before his closest collaborators. Francis of the big smiles and kind words shows himself to be absolute in his goals and intolerant of the Curia's "human ambition to power," which had also been criticized by his predecessor, Benedict XVI. His words attest to a truth that is quite different from the normal state of affairs described in dry official press releases and flattering news stories—a dramatic, unmentionable sin that was supposed to be kept secret in the Apostolic Palaces.

Exclusive, Never-Before-Published Documentation

I have access to thousands of documents, the most significant of which are reproduced in this book. They show the incredible waste of money by the men who govern the Church. At their worst, these men have engaged in wrongdoing that includes practices closely tied to religious life, such as the procedures for beatification and canonization—a marketplace in which millions of dollars change hands—and the management of the Peter's Pence, the money that is sent to Rome from every diocese in the world, and is supposed to be used to bring relief to the poor, in fulfillment of the Church's pastoral mission and the goals of Francis. And where, you may ask, do these donations go?

This book will reconstruct the facts and erase all doubt as to where the money trail ends.

The people who made this material available to me did so because they are pained by the deeply rooted hypocrisy they see in the Vatican. They cannot stand idly by as these men who know the facts, but refuse to admit the truth, go about their daily business. Every day they observe the huge gap between what Francis has promised and what is being done to hinder his reforms and undermine his credibility.

My previous books, *Vaticano S.p.A.* and *His Holiness*, helped to bring down the wall of *omertà* and silence that has protected the Holy Roman Church for centuries. This investigation continues to seek out the truth at the Vatican, contributing, wherever possible, to flushing out and denouncing the opponents of the revolution of Francis—a revolution which, let us not forget, was born from the unprecedented decision of his predecessor, Benedict XVI, to step down.

This book is not a defense of the Pope but rather a journalistic analysis of the serious problems afflicting the Church today, caused by an ecclesiastical leadership and power circles hostile to change. My intention, once again, is to lend transparency to an authority that has long been obfuscated by narrow, often illegal, interests at odds with evangelical principles. As before, I am not driven by anti-clericalism, but by the desire to acquaint Catholics and non-Catholics alike with the contradictions of the Church—a Church that Francis wishes to reform radically, turning it into a home that is finally open to the needy and the poor and no longer focused on its own privileges and jealous of its own indestructible power.

In May 2012, after the publication of *His Holiness*, the Curia reacted to the book with its traditional obscurantism, trying to hunt down my sources. Shortly after, the arrest of Joseph Ratzinger's butler, Paolo Gabriele—my source for important documents in the book—made headlines. He would later tell friends about his detention in a cell too small for him to even spread his arms. Gabriele was found guilty of theft after a quick trial. He should have been commended for passing photocopies of documents to a journalist and letting the world know what was happening in the Vatican. Instead, he was treated as a criminal.

Paolo Gabriele lost his job and had to leave the house where he had lived with his family. He wanted to make public the incredible difficulties that the Holy Father was facing every day—the same problems that would lead to the Pope's resignation less than one year later. Benedict XVI pardoned his butler. Today we know that he often inquires as to Gabriele's health, whether he has a job, and how his children are doing at school. On Christmas and other occasions, Ratzinger sends presents to his family. But at the Vatican, among the cardinals and senior prelates, the precedent Gabriele created by leaking papers and documents still casts a long and frightening shadow.

1

Pope Francis Issues a Shocking Accusation

On July 28, 2013, a few hours after his customary religious obligations, Pope Francis prepared to go to the Apostolic Palace. As always, he checked his datebook first. "This is what I've always done. I carry it in a black briefcase. Inside is a razor, a breviary, an appointment book, and a book to read."[1] The Pope carefully reviewed his notes. That morning he had a meeting with Archbishop Jean Louis Bruguès, the librarian and archivist of the Holy See. But his most important appointment of the day was a noon meeting scheduled to take place in one of the most inaccessible and mysterious spaces in the Palace: the Sala Bologna, on the third floor, between the papal apartment recently vacated by Benedict XVI and the quarters of the Secretariat of State. The decorations for this sumptuous dining room had been commissioned by Pope Gregory XIII (1502–1585), who wanted frescoes of immense maps and cosmic charts to convey the measure of his ambitious pontificate. Although they had originally been created for the 1575 Jubilee, they were timelier than ever today, in perfect harmony with the designs of Pope Francis. Like Gregory's, Francis's plans were also ambitious and mysterious, inspired by his wish to bring the Church into the world and to fight the Curia's secret dealings and privileges. His was a soft but steady revolution that had already triggered a war without rules or limits. Francis's enemies were powerful, duplicitous, and hypocritical.

The Pope made his entrance to what looked like a miniconclave. The cardinals were waiting for him, conversing quietly in small clusters. The tension was palpable. Cardinal Versaldi, the President of the Prefecture, was present. Off to the side was Cardinal Giuseppe Bertello—a staunch ally of Bertone—who headed the Governorate. Domenico Calcagno, the President of APSA, was also there. All the key players who administer the money and the property of the Holy See were in attendance.

The official order of business was to approve the annual financial report for 2012, but everyone knew that a different issue would be addressed today. Immediately upon his election Pope Francis had announced his intention to reform the Curia. One month later, in April 2013, he had established a group to help him with the governance of the Church: a council of eight cardinals from five continents, created for the purpose of breaking the stranglehold that the cardinals residing in Rome had over the Vatican.[2]

On June 24, the Pope established the Commission for Reference on the IOR, the first commission in history to review the Institute after the many scandals in which it had been embroiled. Although there was already an IOR Supervisory Commission, chaired by Cardinal Bertone, the new Pope wanted more oversight. "The Commission"—announced the Vatican press release—"will gather accurate information on the legal status and various activities of the Institute and . . . shall deliver to us promptly, upon the conclusion of its tasks, the results of its work, as well as its entire archives." In other words, Francis wanted to get a clear picture of the facts and to hear from an impartial new body that reported directly to him.[3]

The Curia was devastated by these moves, but no one had grasped the full scope of the changes: would Pope Francis intervene only superficially, through big media announcements, or would he get to the root of the problems, eliminating the power centers and the infighting? And in these first months of his pontificate, how well did he know the secrets behind the massive circulation of money inside the Vatican?

The cardinals attending the July 3, 2013, meeting with Francis found an immediate answer in the confidential file that they each received with their name on it. Among the papers inside, the most important was a two-page letter that had been sent to the Pope one week earlier, on June 27, from five of the international auditors of the Prefecture. Two of the members expressed the auditors' concerns over the way the Vatican's finances were being managed and decided to take the risk of conveying these concerns to Francis: the loyal Santo Abril y Castelló and the President of the Prefecture, Giuseppe Versaldi. The cardinals were shocked by the letter, a document that has never before been made public. Among other things, it listed the emergency situations that had to be addressed immediately to rescue the Vatican from impending bankruptcy:

> Holy Father,
>
> . . . There is a complete absence of transparency in the bookkeeping of both the Holy See and the Governorate. This lack of transparency makes it impossible to provide a clear estimate of the actual financial status of the Vatican as a whole and of the single entities of which it consists. This also means that no one person can be considered actually responsible for financial management . . . We only know that the data examined show a truly downward trend and we strongly suspect that the Vatican as a whole has a serious structural deficit.
>
> The general financial management within the Vatican can be defined, in the best of cases, as inadequate. First, the budgeting and decision-making processes of both the Holy See and the Governorate are senseless, despite the existence of clear guidelines defined by

> the current regulations.[4] . . . This reality seems to suggest that, at a minimum, the prevailing attitude of the Vatican is best captured by the expression, "the rules don't apply to us." Costs are out of control. This applies in particular to personnel costs but it also extends elsewhere. There are various cases of duplicate activities, where consolidation would instead guarantee significant savings and improve the management of the problems.[5] We have not been able to identify clear guidelines to follow for investments of financial capital. This is a serious limit and it leaves too much discretion to the managers, which increases the overall level of risk. The situation that is applicable to the investments of the Holy See, Governorate, Pension Fund, Health Insurance Fund, and other funds managed by autonomous entities should be immediately improved . . . The managers must clearly shoulder their responsibilities for preparing the budgets and sticking to them in a more realistic and effective way.
>
> We are aware that we have presented strong and sometimes severe advice and suggestions. We sincerely hope that Your Holiness realizes that our actions are inspired by our love for the Church and our sincere desire to help and to improve the temporal aspect of the Vatican. We and all our families beg for Your apostolic blessing, while confirming ourselves as the humble and devout children of Your Holiness.

After reading the letter, Agostino Vallini turned pale. He had been made a cardinal by Benedict XVI and since 2008 had served as the Vicar of the diocese of Rome. He immediately sensed the explosive potential of the documents and invoked the need for confidentiality. These papers "are under papal seal"—he hastened to recall, addressing the Pope—"and we hope they conserve . . . not for our part but, you know . . ."

Vallini's main concern was that nothing be leaked outside the Vatican walls. He was well aware of the impact that this report could have on public opinion. The elderly cardinal turned around slowly to gaze at his colleagues and observed only silence and anxiety. On the surface the reaction was placid, but there were clear undercurrents of tension, dismay, and shock.

The cardinals did not know the full extent of the Vatican's troubled economic situation. Earlier that year, during the congregations for the Conclave in March, they had received information, reports, and numbers, but they were piecemeal and disorganized. A more reassuring picture had been painted instead by the same cardinals who were in charge of the various dicasteries.

None of the members of the Curia were accustomed to the new requirement that information be transparent and openly circulated. Francis probably saw what he had been expecting. As a good Jesuit, he would use the alarming documents he had received from the auditors to make everyone understand that from that moment on, nothing would be the same.

The Holy Father took the floor. He delivered an indictment that would last sixteen interminable minutes, using harsher words than had ever been expressed by a Pontiff to the assembly—words that were supposed to remain secret, protected by the gravity of their contents and the confidentiality demanded of all those who had access to the room. But that would not be the case. Foreseeing the risks that his innovative action would entail—sabotage, manipulations, theft, break-ins, and attempts to discredit the reformers—someone recorded the Pope's charges, word for word.

Dead silence fell over the room as the Pontiff prepared to speak, the clicking on of the recorder going unobserved. On the recording, the sound quality is perfect, and the voice of Francis unmistakable. He is calm and dry but firm and resolute. He speaks in halting but clear Italian, as befitting the Bishop of Rome, leaving long pauses between each item of his indictment.

The silences lend even greater drama to his words. It is evident that

Francis wants every cardinal—including the ones who tolerated bad behavior for years—to realize that the time has come to choose sides:

> We have to better clarify the finances of the Holy See and make them more transparent. What I will say is that to help, I would like to identify some elements that will definitely help you in your reflections.
>
> First. It was universally ascertained in the general congregations [during the Conclave] that [in the Vatican] the number of employees has grown too much. This fact creates a huge waste of money that can be avoided. Cardinal Calcagno told me that in the past five years there has been a 30 percent increase in employee expenses.[6] Something isn't right! We have to get this problem under control.

The Pontiff had already known that most of the new hiring was based on cronyism. The persons in question were employed for vague projects or hired through nepotism or personal connections. It was no accident that, in this small state, rather than have one human resources office, like a private company with thousands of employees, there were fourteen, one for each power center on the organizational chart of the Holy See. Francis denounces this in a lucid crescendo that highlights each of the most alarming situations:

> Second point: the lack of transparency continues to be an issue. There are expenses for which no clear procedures were followed. According to the men who spoke with me [i.e., the auditors who wrote the report and some cardinals]—this comes out in the financial statements. In this connection, I think we have to move forward with the work of clarifying the origins of the expenses and the forms of payment. We have to create a protocol for estimates and also for the last step, payments. [We need to] follow this protocol rigorously. One of the department heads told me: they come to me with the invoice so we have to pay . . . No, we don't. If a job was done without an estimate, without authorization, we don't pay. So who will pay? [Pope

Francis simulates a dialogue with a bursar.] We don't pay. [We need to] start with a protocol and be firm: [even if] we're making this poor clerk look bad, we don't pay! God help us but we don't pay!

C-l-a-r-i-t-y. That's what's done in the most humble companies and we have to do it, too. The protocol for starting a project is the payment protocol. Before any purchase or construction job we have to request at least three different estimates to decide which one is more convenient. Let me give you an example, the library. The estimate said 100 and then 200 was paid. What happened? A little more? Alright, but was it budgeted or not? [Some say] we have to pay for it. No we don't! Let them pay . . . We don't pay! This is important for me. Discipline, please!

Francis goes on to describe the utter superficiality of Vatican bookkeeping. He's angry. Seven times he repeats, "We don't pay." For too long, in an incredibly facile and superficial manner, millions have been disbursed to pay for unbudgeted jobs that were executed without the required oversight and with ridiculously padded invoices. Many have taken advantage, pocketing even the donations of the faithful, the offerings that were supposed to go to the needy. The Pope then addresses the cardinals who lead dicasteries that over the years have mismanaged Church money, the department heads who haven't exercised the necessary oversight. His criticism of them is overt: harsh, direct, scathing, even humiliating. He emphasizes issues that any manager working in even the smallest business should know and understand.

Francis stares Secretary of State Tarciso Bertone in the face. Those who are sitting near the Pope see no signs of the friendship and indulgence that Ratzinger felt for the Italian cardinal that led him to elevate Bertone to the pinnacle of power at the Vatican. No, Francis's gaze conveys the icy admonishment of the Jesuit who came to Rome from the "ends of the Earth." These accusations are an indirect rebuke of Bertone.[7] At the Vatican, in fact, resource management and governance are the responsibility of the Secretariat of State, which had accumulated unprecedented power under Bertone. In the unreal silence that dominates the room, the Pope delivers the final blow by raising the most embarrassing issue:

> It is no exaggeration to say that most of our costs are out of control. This is a fact. We always have to check the legality and clarity of contracts with the utmost attention. Contracts can be very tricky, right? The contract might be clear but in the footnotes you find the fine print—that's what it's called, right?—which is tricky. Examine it carefully! Our suppliers should always be businesses that guarantee honesty and propose a fair market price for both products and services. And not all of them can guarantee that.

The Pope's Accusation: "Our costs are spiraling out of control"

The financial situation inherited from Ratzinger and Bertone—as described by the auditors and seconded by Francis—was a dead-end, prebankruptcy scenario. On the one hand there was total chaos in the management of resources and spending, which was spiraling out of control, with inflated costs, deceptive contracts, and dishonest suppliers dumping obsolete and overpriced products on the Vatican. On the other, cronyism and shady financial dealings prevented change and undermined the policies already adopted by Benedict. This might have been the unspoken reason for Ratzinger's decision to step down. By giving the helm of Peter's Bark to someone else, he hoped to break their grip on power and prevent a storm that might ultimately compromise the financial and the evangelical future of the Church. Francis delivered his indictment in the same room used in the dramatic days leading up to the Conclave, when there had been talk about irregularities and concerns at the meetings on the eve of the voting for the new pope—concerns that may have led Bergoglio to choose the name of Francis, the first pope in history to do so—after the saint who dedicated his life to poverty.

The Pope was not done. While condemning the items that fell under "expenses," the Holy Father reserved his greatest wrath for the handling of revenue—the donations and inheritances left by the faithful. There was a complete lack of "oversight of investments." As we shall see in the next chapter, the question is very simple: does the money left by the faithful end up in good works or is it swallowed up by the black holes in the Holy See's wasteful administration? This question demands an investigation.

So concerned was Francis that he pressed on with another disturbing example. The situation illustrated by the auditors reminded him of Argentina in the dark days of the military junta, of the *desaparecidos*, when he discovered that the Church in Buenos Aires had made some truly unholy investments:

> When I was a provincial prelate, the general accountant told me about the attitude we should take toward investments.[8] And he told us the story of how the Jesuit province of the country has a good many seminaries and made investments into a serious, honest bank. Then, when they changed accountants, the new man went to the bank to check up on things. He asked how the investments were doing: he came to find out that more than 60 percent had gone to weapons manufacturing!
>
> Oversight of investments, ethics, and even risks, because sometimes [you are tempted by interesting proposals and people say]: since this yields high interests, then . . . Don't be so trusting, we need to have technical assessors for this. Clear guidelines are needed on how and into what investments should be made, and they must always be made with scrupulous care and the utmost attention to risks. One of you reminded me of a problem that led to our losing more than ten million with Switzerland, through a bad investment, and the money

> was gone. There is also a rumor that there are satellite administrations [whose investments are not reported in their financial statements]. Some dicasteries have their own money and they administer it privately.
>
> Our books are not in order, we have to clean them up.
>
> I don't want to add more examples that will make us even more concerned, but we are here to solve everything, my brothers, for the good of the Church. I am reminded of an elderly parish priest in Buenos Aires, a wise man who was very careful with money. He said, "If we don't know how to look after money, which you can see, how can we look after the souls of the faithful, which you can't see?"

A Scathing Critique

The Pope delivers a scathing critique of how the Church finances are managed. He does not cite anyone by first and last name but he clearly shares the international auditors' concerns. He has also been informed of the disastrous results of the investments that had been entrusted to UBS, BlackRock, and Goldman Sachs: an initial investment of 95 million euros lost half its value under their watch.

The levels of alarm rise even higher when the Pontiff—the monarch and thus the supreme religious and civic authority of the Vatican State—says that he wants to get to the bottom of the situation, going through each and every office, donation, and expense. For this purpose he will soon create a new commission to comb through the books in search of "wounds," and reorganize the Vatican State.[9]

> I'm sure that we all want to move forward together to continue the work you have been doing for so long. To help you, I have decided to set up a special commission to build on the work you have done and to find solutions to the problems. This commission will have the same profile as the one established for the IOR . . . One of you will be the

> coordinator or general secretary or chairman of this commission to help in a process that I am happy to see moving forward. But we must make an effort to bring it to a conclusion and say so clearly.
>
> We are all good people, but even the Lord demands from us a management for the good of the Church and of our apostolic work . . . I suggest that at least once during these meetings [of the cardinals], to invite the auditors board, for maybe half a day, to have an exchange of information, concerns, and work . . . If you have any suggestions, I am ready to hear them. This much I can offer you, and I thank you most warmly. Are there any questions, comments?

After the Pope's words, the silence is broken, once again, by Cardinal Vallini, who is still trying to alleviate the tension. To disassociate himself from any responsibility, he makes a point of stating that he himself holds no financial posts. His outlook is optimistic: "We're moving toward reforms that were already planned," he begins, "the administrative chiefs are working hard to adapt their departments to a proper management of assets." Vallini tried to downplay the assertions in the auditors' documents and promulgated by the Pope. So who is right? Vallini continues:

> The international auditors, to my way of thinking, have the right perspective for their part but only in terms of finances. They are providing suggestions and provocations that are useful, important, and we are grateful. But it is also true that the question or the dysfunctions stem from one fact—and I don't think, well at times someone might be acting in bad faith, but not ordinarily—from our lack of administrative culture . . . Then, it's true, there are parallel administrations and they have to be fought, too. Where we need to dedicate our efforts is into instilling a new management culture. But I have to say that the work being done these days, and over the past few years, is moving in this direction, and I hope that we can continue to provide even more relief to the Pope.

In other words, Cardinal Vallini believes that the prelates are suffering merely from a lack of management culture. This is the source of their mistakes and of the financial losses. And yes, there is a chance that some people might take advantage.

The Pope is quick to reply. "What Vallini says is true, the culture . . . We improvise. It's the same in Argentina, we make it up as we go, without that culture of clarity, of protocols, of method . . ."

For the moment he avoids entering into the individual problem areas. Francis doesn't want to alarm the cardinals too much. It will be up to the new commission to venture into the bottomless pit of the budgets and balance sheets, knowing that the auditors' warnings are just the tip of the iceberg.

The Auditors' Report

The board of auditors has always had the delicate task of inspecting the books and balance sheets of all the dicasteries that manage the Vatican finances. It consists of five laypeople from different European countries.[10] It meets once every six months at the Vatican together with eight members of the Prefecture, representing the full hierarchy of the dicastery: from the President, Cardinal Giuseppe Versaldi, to the Secretary, Monsignor Lucio Ángel Vallejo Balda, to the Office Manager, Monsignor Alfredo Abbondi.

The meetings are confidential. In addition to the members, two interpreters and a stenographer attend to translate and transcribe the proceedings. Their minutes from 2010 to today read like a constant denunciation by the auditors of the waste, mismanagement, irregularities, and inefficiency that plague the Vatican, with many specific suggestions to improve the situation. For years their warnings had been ignored, and no tangible changes had been made, to the growing discomfort and frustration of the professionals who saw their every constructive criticism ignored.

On December 22, 2010, no longer knowing how to get anyone to heed their warnings, the board of auditors had sent a detailed letter to Benedict XVI, highlighting the most critical areas where action was needed—to no avail, like all the earlier proposals that had never made it past the drawing board. The significance of the fact that the auditors had now resorted once again to writing to the Pope should not be underestimated. The accounting experts felt that the new Pope could move with greater decision and speed.

Francis had not requested the damning document. It was the auditors themselves, only a few weeks earlier, who had realized that they could no longer hesitate and that they had to give the Pope a detailed account of the financial situation. And this report would differ sharply from the optimistic, sanitized, and simplistic indications that Francis had received from the managers who had operated under Ratzinger, some of whom had every interest in painting a rosy picture, in an apparent effort to minimize their own responsibility.

On June 18, fifteen days before the secret meeting, the auditors who work with the Prefecture—laypeople motivated by a deep and sincere love of the Church, as they wrote in their private letter to the Pontiff—attended the early morning mass with the Holy Father at Casa Santa Marta. At nine o'clock that day they all met for one of the two annual meetings dedicated to examining the books of the Holy See and the Governorate.

The meeting was coordinated, as always, by Cardinal Versaldi. According to the minutes—which I was able to consult—the group had an animated discussion. The prevailing tones were pessimistic. While the auditors had expressed their concerns on previous occasions in the past, this time the broadsides were relentless, and they were all from the laypeople on the board (ten of the thirteen members), a squad of solid pragmatic professionals who had reached the conclusion that their every effort to improve things over the years had been ignored. In particular, from the documentation in my possession, the most outspoken members were Joseph Zahra from Malta, an economist; Jochen Messemer from Germany, formerly of the consulting group

McKinsey & Company; Josep M. Cullell from Barcelona; Maurizio Prato from Italy, an accountant; and John F. Kyle from Canada.

The most concise, bitter assessment was from Kyle. "The efforts that have been made over the past twenty-five years have come to practically nothing." He thought it would be "advisable to have a group close to the Pope that can act more decisively and firmly and take measures against those who fail to follow instructions." In his sermon that morning Francis had reminded them—men of numbers but also of faith—that, "To be believable the Church has to be poor," and that "the Prefecture—as the supervisory body—has to address the budgetary problems more courageously." It was an explicit exhortation to act—to come out of the dark.

In the opinion of the General Accountant of the Prefecture, Stefano Fralleoni, the crisis was caused by the fact that some administrations are, "completely uninformed of the criteria for compiling financial statements, which often do not reflect reality, with estimates that come out of nowhere."[11] The absurd dimensions of the problem became apparent when it was learned that the Prefecture itself—which is supposed to oversee the finances of the other departments—didn't even know all the departments it was supposed to supervise. "It would be necessary—the accountant underlines—to complete and update regularly the list of all the entities that constitute the Holy See: only in this manner, in fact, could the Prefecture carry out a complete inspection of all the different realities and their operations."

During the auditors' inspection, they realized that the transparency and efficiency regulations introduced by Benedict XVI and Francis were being disregarded, from the smallest to the largest cases. Salvatore Colitta, the auditor from RB Audit Italia, gives the example of the price list for items being sold at the Vatican. "It hasn't budged in two years," he asserts, "a pen costs 50 cents although its value today should be 1.20 euros. More than 70 percent of APSA's purchases do not follow required procedures but rather emergency procedures. The phenomenon is difficult to control."

"Noncompliance with existing regulations"—Fralleoni goes back on the attack—"is another critical point, because of a practice that has never changed through a kind of inertia. Bookkeeping at the Holy See offices is not standardized, despite the existence of regulations for accounting principles approved by the Holy Father." Another example? Recently a new accounting regulation was introduced for everyone but it was discovered that, "some offices keep their own private stash that they can manage on their own, and thus they don't declare all their revenue." This is one of the points that the Pope will present to the cardinals as "satellite management," because there are offices "that often operate independently although they belong to the same institution."

When the Prefecture conducts an audit, there is always the risk that "it will be perceived as a form of interference." But audits are fundamental. "A great deal of inefficiency could be ended," Messemer concluded, "simply through more regular inspections." Instead the situation was spiraling out of control. Just look at what is happening in the real estate sector. In addition to "outrageous delays in payment"—Colitta continues—"there are self-reductions in rent: the Conciliation Auditorium cuts its own rent by approximately 50,000 euros a month, while the Vatican is still paying taxes based on the old lease." Or take the case of "strategic investments" that had actually led to major losses, such as the Governorate's purchase of stocks in an Italian bank, the Banca Popolare di Sondrio, which resulted in losses of 1,929,000 euros in a very short time.[12]

We Cannot Turn a Blind Eye

Josep Cullell from Barcelona delivered the harshest analysis:

> It's true, the Prefecture can no longer afford to be so gullible, so naïve, but must set priorities and make sure the rules are followed . . . Our finances are unsustainable and completely chaotic. The Vatican has always been characterized by a kind of ambiguity, like the Kingdom

> of Taifa,[13] in choosing a specific institution that would hold all the power, govern and establish priorities, and not only in terms of finances . . .
>
> Both in Barcelona and on the outskirts of Rome there is widespread poverty, also afflicting children, and this is a troubling sign of recession. We cannot turn a blind eye to this and keep restoring monuments. I can't believe the data that has been given to me. The real economy could never allow a situation like this. There are even doubts about earnings from our financial investments.
>
> There are various realities at the Vatican that are unsound: the Governorate, which didn't even bother to present an annual financial report last year; *L'Osservatore Romano*; the Vatican Radio, with losses that were temporarily concealed through "financial wizardry"; the IOR, which could easily be closed and replaced by APSA. The IOR has little to offer and could be replaced by another institution. Closing it would solve many problems for the Pope and for the Church of Rome.

Zahra, the economist from Malta, realized that Francis had to be warned. So he tried to speed up the clock:

> After a long period of status quo, the time has come to change. We're at a crossroads: we need to make a decision. The tone we should take is the one suggested by the Pope, namely firmness and courage, and the goal is to achieve greater transparency, integrity and seriousness. We have to take advantage of the fact that the Pope himself is issuing these guidelines. We can't change attitudes overnight, but we can translate what the Pope is saying into concrete actions in order to gradually achieve the goals we have set.

At the end of the meeting, Zahra, Messemer, Cullell, Kyle, and Prato came to an agreement: it was essential to warn the Pope immediately. They were the ones who signed the shocking letter to the Holy Father.

Five days later, on June 23, the Spanish Cardinal Santos Abril y Castelló entered the scene. A close friend of Francis and one of his few confidants, he was the archpriest of Santa Maria Maggiore, the majestic basilica where Jorge Bergoglio used to pray during his visits to Rome as a cardinal. Abril y Castelló was a reserved, serious, and honest cardinal, far from the scheming characters of the Curia. He had slowly won the Pope's trust by reporting deficits, irregularities and power games, starting with alleged irregularities in the restoration of the basilica where he is an archpriest.[14] It was Abril y Castelló who forwarded to the Pope the concerns of the auditors. They didn't want the Holy Father to misunderstand them or put them in a bind, as had happened so many times in the past.

But not this time. This time, the fuse was lit.

2

The Saints' Factory

An Unprecedented Change

Pope Francis was not unaware of the Curia's attempts to scuttle his reforms, and he knew he would have to fight to prevent his hopes from being crushed by the interests of the few and the inertia of the many at the Vatican. These hopes were also shared by nuns, brothers, priests, and all the humble servants of the Church, who on March 13, 2013, after the appearance of the white smoke, had waited with joy—but also apprehension—to hear the name of the new Pontiff. When Jorge Mario Bergoglio first stepped on to the balcony overlooking St. Peter's Square, he wore no frills or ornaments. He uttered a simple sentence that warmed the hearts of the millions of faithful: "Good evening . . . pray for me," he exhorted them.

On July 18, 2013—only a couple of weeks after his dramatic meeting with the cardinals in the Sala Bologna—the Pope appointed a new commission of inquiry into the Vatican finances: the Commission for Reference on the Organization of the Economic-Administrative Structure of the Holy See (COSEA). Its job was to collect all of the information on the financial management of the Curia, and the Commission would report directly to Francis. It was a brand-new body that would not diminish the authority of the Special Council of fifteen cardinals, chaired by Secretary of State Bertone, but would still present an open challenge to the powers that be. The day of reckoning was near. Francis's move was an implicit reprimand to the men who had managed the Holy See during the pontificate of Benedict XVI and, prior to him, of John Paul II.

The members of the Commission selected by the Pope were vetted and briefed by the Substitute of the Secretary of State, Peter Wells.[1] The chairmanship of the new Commission was assigned to Joseph Zahra of Malta, one of the international auditors who in late June had signed the letter to the Pope alerting him to the impending financial crisis at the Holy See.[2] He was the right man at the right time. In addition to his close relations with the leaders of multinational corporations and international finance, he was trustworthy, a paramount concern for Francis. The selection of Zahra marked the start of a new era and sent a warning signal to the Curia: the Pope prized and was ready to reward those who had the courage to denounce the wrongdoing and opaque interests inimical to the pastoral mission of the Holy Roman Church.

Francis's attitude represented a radical shift from the papacy of his predecessor. Under Benedict XVI, Monsignor Carlo Maria Viganò, Secretary of the Governorate, reported to the Pontiff outrageous expenditures such as a Christmas tree in St. Peter's Square that cost 500,000 euros. As his reward, he was discredited at the Vatican and exiled to the United States as the Apostolic Nunzio (a permanent diplomatic representative of the Holy See) to Washington, a lower-level position. The dramatic expulsion of Viganò was one of the reasons why Benedict XVI's butler, Paolo Gabriele, contacted me and decided to trust me with the thick file of correspondence between Viganò, Bertone, and the Holy Father. (These letters documented waste, corruption, and injustice at the Vatican and were the basis of my previous book, *His Holiness.*)

Zahra was not expecting this assignment but he shifted into high gear immediately. The first item of business was a trip back to his beautiful home in Balzan, a small town of four thousand people in the heart of Malta, where he closed his pending case files. From the office of his financial consultancy on the first floor of the Fino Building, on Notabile Road in Mriehel, Malta, his assistant, Marthese Spiteri-Gonzi, was handling all the details of his move to Casa Santa Marta. To prepare for his new assignment, Zahra set about rereading the minutes of the biannual meetings of the international auditors. After all the warnings that had gone unheeded under Benedict XVI, now it appeared that Francis was willing to hear the truth about financial irregularities and appreciated the individuals who had the courage to report them. In addition to Zahra's appointment as Chair, another auditor, the German Jochen Messemer, also entered the pontifical commission.[3]

The papal decree establishing the Commission, known formally as a chirograph, was signed on July 18. The functions of the new structure were summarized in the seven points of the chirograph. In point 3 the Pontiff was clear: "the administrative bodies concerned . . . are required to collaborate readily with the Commission. The official secret and any other restrictions established by judicial norms do not impede or limit the Commission's access to documents, data and information necessary for the execution of the tasks assigned to it." In other words, the commission would have complete autonomy and access in its investigation. Its every question had to be answered, and confidentiality could not be used as an excuse.

Zahra would work with seven other members: the coordinator and six advisors, "all appointed by the Supreme Pontiff"—according to the chirograph—"experts in the juridical, economic, financial, and organizational matters dealt with by the Commission." Coordination and relations with the ecclesiastical world would be handled by the

Secretary of the Prefecture, Monsignor Lucio Ángel Vallejo Balda, an Opus Dei member who had earned the trust of Francis.[4] The Pontiff knew that he was playing a dangerous game in attacking the entrenched centers of power. "The situation is of an unimaginable gravity," he would say to his closest collaborators. Many anomalies within the Church structures "are rooted in solipsism, a kind of theological narcissism." The basic problem is that a solipsistic Church "falls ill."[5]

All the Commission's Men

The members of the Commission were almost all European, with the exception of George Yeo, an expert in economics and finance who for years had held ministerial positions in his native Singapore.[6] Well-known and respected in the East, he had also been Chief of the General Staff of the Air Force. At the Vatican, Yeo had an important admirer: the Australian cardinal George Pell, who was carefully following the Pope's every move in order to earn a position for himself in the renewal of the Curia.[7]

The youngest member of the Commission, and the only Italian, was a woman: Francesca Chaouqui, thirty years old, born in a small town in the province of Cosenza to an Italian mother and a French father of Moroccan origin. She had worked previously at Ernst & Young, in the field of public relations and communications, prior to which she had learned the ropes at the influential law firm Orrick, Herrington & Sutcliffe Italia. She was married to an IT specialist who had worked with the Vatican for many years. It would be her job to create the new department in charge of Vatican communications, from the press room to the daily newspaper *Osservatore Romano*.

Another member of the Commission was Jean-Baptiste de Franssu, a French manager from the field of strategic consultancy. Cardinal Bertone had brought him to the Vatican and appointed him to various posts: in his first year at the Vatican, he had quickly risen through the ranks.[8]

A Spanish member of the Commission, Enrique Llanos, formerly of KPMG, was a personal friend of John Scott, vice president of KPMG Worldwide, a leading accounting and management consultancy firm.

The most senior advisor was from France. Jean Videlain-Sevestre was also an expert in consultancy and investments, a businessman with significant experience at Citroën and Michelin. He immediately established the approach that his colleagues should take to the investigation: "Our Committee has to be beyond reproach, independent, and competent," he wrote on the eve of the much-awaited first meeting of the group. Its job was to help the Holy Father achieve the objective he had first indicated as the Archbishop of Buenos Aires: "The new Pope must be able to clean up the Roman Curia," he had told a religious group from the Schoenstatt movement.[9]

As their working quarters, the team chose a modest first-floor location in Casa Santa Marta: Room 127, just a staircase and a corridor away from the papal suite. The office would be dubbed "Area 10," the sum total of its numbers. A more revealing nickname was coined by Nicola Maio, the Secretary of the Commission: "St. Michael's Room," after Michael the Archangel, the guardian angel of delicate tasks. (The winged Archangel Michael, with armor and a sword, is always celebrated as the defender of faith in God against the satanic hordes of Lucifer.)

The most popular saying among the members during their meetings was in Spanish, the language of Bergoglio: "*Aquì la gracias de dios es mucha pero el demonio está en persona*"—Here the grace of God is great but the devil is here in person.

The utmost attention and discretion was required to protect the sensitive information that was being gathered. A revolution was about to begin and the Pope's men knew the risks involved. To prevent wiretaps, Zahra immediately signed an agreement with Vodafone (a multinational mobile phone company): every advisor would receive a special Maltese phone number and an iPhone 5. The members called it the "white telephone," after the color of the cover. A private line would be used to send all the passwords for access to encrypted documents, which would be sent by email. At the cost of 100,000 euros, an exclusive server was also provided that would be accessible only to the computers of the COSEA members. Don Alfredo Abbondi, the office chief of the Prefecture, requested from the procurement office of the Governorate a safe in which to keep the most highly classified dossiers. The members of the Commission felt protected by these measures. Little did they realize that every precaution would prove to be useless.

Objective Number One

Four days after the formal act of establishing the Commission, COSEA was already operative. The members were excited and highly motivated. The work promised to be both delicate and massive. "The Holy Father has identified seven key elements to be evaluated in the Holy See," according to the preliminary document.[10] The most important ranged from the "over-expansion in employees" and the "lack of transparency in expenditures and procedures," to "insufficient control over suppliers and their contracts." They needed to find out the "number, physical condition and rents of real estate whose status was unclear," as well as the revenue, to counter the "inadequate oversight of investments in terms of risk and ethical standards." There would also be a careful examination of the so-called "satellite administrations" and the cash-flow and financial transactions in certain dicasteries.

On July 22, the Coordinating Secretary, Monsignor Vallejo Balda—who handled communications between the Commission and the various representatives of the Curia—asked Cardinal Versaldi, the President of the Prefecture and his direct superior, to circulate a letter prepared by COSEA addressed to every administrative body within the Vatican walls. Versaldi did so a few hours later. In the letter, the Commission requested the following documentation: financial statements from the past five years, lists of employees, lists of outside collaborators and their résumés, all wages and compensation, and, finally, contracts for the supply of goods and services that had been signed since January 1, 2013.

The next to the last paragraph of the long letter containing COSEA's requests set off the loudest alarms within the Curia. It was a specific, targeted request on a very sensitive issue in the Church that touched the hearts of millions of the faithful: saints, who through their actions set an example of universal goodness and love. For many Catholics, saints were objects of worship. The Commission wanted to receive immediately the financial statements, movements, and banking documents "of the economic entities relative to postulators of beatification and canonization causes."

The first battle front had been opened. The Congregation for the Causes of Saints was being summoned for questioning. This structure manages the complex process for conferring sainthood or beatitude on individuals who have distinguished themselves by their good deeds. Every cause is handled and proposed by a postulator, who opens the cause, prepares the investigation, documents it, and, over the years, bolsters the file with acts and findings that will hopefully lead to the beatification or canonization of the candidate. Currently there are 2,500 pending causes filed by 450 postulators.

The Congregation was headed by a staunch ally of Bertone, Cardinal Angelo Amato, who was also a close associate of the previous Pope. Amato had taken Bertone's place at the Congregation for the Doctrine of the Faith as the deputy of Joseph Ratzinger, who after his election to the throne of St. Peter made Amato the Prefect of the Congregation for the Causes of Saints.

This powerful cardinal grasped the exact meaning of the message forwarded by Versaldi: the Pope knew where to strike. He was well informed and he acted quickly. COSEA gave the departments only a few days to collect the information: "While taking into consideration the period in which the present request is made, we expect to receive the documentation by July 31." Eight days, for a Curia accustomed to peaceful summer months with little work and a Pope at Castel Gandolfo taking refuge from the summer heat, was an unprecedented timeline.

There were various explanations for this tight deadline. First, the Commission wanted to prevent any alteration and manipulation of information: the less time for the ill-intentioned, the better. And there was an important date on the calendar. On August 3, the members of the Commission would meet for their inaugural session. They would assemble in the small conference room opposite the sacristy of the chapel, in the same place where only a few weeks earlier Francis had urged Zahra and the auditors of the Prefecture to be brave, and report wrongdoing for the sake of change.

The Saints' Factory

The first meeting of the Commission was convened at noon. It was also attended by the Pope, who remained for fifty minutes, taking the floor several times to express his firm will and his encouragement to the participants. I have the minutes of that meeting in my possession. They document the Pope's absolute clarity. (Note below that Francis is speaking—he refers to himself in the third person.)

> We at the Curia need an approach that is different, fresher than our traditional way of doing things. At the root of our problems is a *nouveau riche* attitude that allows money to be spent indiscriminately. In the meantime, we lose sight of the reasons for what we are doing—our goal is that the money go to help the poor and to people living in misery. The current problems are culture and a lack of responsibility. The Pope is confident that the Commission will introduce these reforms, but he realizes that we have to be cautious when we [address questions that might involve] jobs and means of subsistence for the laypeople who work at the Vatican. He insists that the Commission be courageous in making its recommendations and not

> look back. He will always consult the Commission before making changes, but it has no collegial authority. If the Pope disagrees with our proposals, he will discuss them with us and he will make the decision.[11]

Without reforms, the pontificate would fail. So as soon as Francis left the meeting, the members of COSEA established their program of work, with six priorities:

1. APSA: especially the special section—the need for a strategic review and a microanalysis of its operations, including Real Estate;
2. The management of the accounts of the postulants who work for the Congregation for the Causes of Saints;
3. Commercial activities (supermarket, pharmacy, etc.) within the Vatican walls;
4. Management of the hospitals;
5. The assessment of artworks;
6. Pensions.

To help achieve their objectives, the Commission also turned to external advisors from the world of business consultation: giants like KPMG, McKinsey & Company, Ernst & Young, and Promontory Financial Group. A task force of seventy experts from outside companies who would work with the Vatican was set up.

At the request for documentation, many offices replied immediately, sending their papers and offering every possible collaboration. But not everyone complied. The most disappointing response came from the Congregation for the Causes of Saints: "The Congregation"—so read the seraphic response of the department led by Cardinal Amato—"has nothing to do with the management of postulators and is not in possession of the requested documentation."

No documents. No justification and bookkeeping for an activity involving tens of millions of euros, at least not in the possession of the Congregation. Yet these are huge sums of money for which Vatican regulations demand proper bookkeeping. To simply open a cause for beatification costs 50,000 euros, supplemented by the 15,000 euros in actual operating costs. This amount covers the rights of the Holy See and the hefty compensation of the expert theologians, physicians, and bishops who examine the cause. After adding the costs of the researchers' time, the drafting of the candidate's *positio*—a kind of résumé of all his or her works—and finally, the work of the postulator, the amount skyrockets. The average price tag comes to about 500,000 euros. We then have to consider the costs of all the thank-you gifts required for the prelates who are invited to festivities and celebrations held at crucial moments in the process, to say a few words about the acts and miracles of the future saint or blessed. Record spending on these causes has reached as high as 750,000 euros, such as the process that led to the beatification in 2007 of Antonio Rosmini.

Under John Paul II the "saints' factory" anointed 1,338 blesseds in 147 rites of beatification and 482 saints in 51 celebrations—astronomical figures that far surpass any previous levels in Church history. Numbers that had led Pope John Paul II, as far back as 1983, to order that the funds for these causes be managed by the postulators, who were assigned the "duty to keep regularly-updated ledgers on the capital, value, interests, and money in the coffers for every single cause."[12] The postulators conduct a delegated activity that requires oversight. Apparently no one had ever bothered to check on them.

The Commission Freezes the Bank Accounts

Amato's response from the Congregation for the Causes of Saints was baffling. He was implicitly acknowledging that the financial activities involved in these causes were unregulated. The Commission's reaction was swift and severe. On August 3, at the very first meeting, Zahra, after obtaining the Pope's assent, made an unprecedented decision—he asked Versaldi to freeze all the bank accounts linked to the postulators and their cases at APSA and the IOR.

> It is clear that the activity of the postulators is not autonomous but rather "delegated" by a superior authority, to which they must report and be accountable. Since once "a cause has been transmitted to the Holy See the task of oversight is up to the holy Congregation," and since the task of oversight is equivalent to that of a bishop in the diocesan phase of the cause, it is deemed necessary to evaluate in concert with this Prefecture the taking of possible precautionary measures, in order to enable the competent Congregation to do whatever is necessary to perform the task assigned to it. The following is hereby requested: to order, with immediate effect, the temporary freezing of the accounts of the postulators and of the individual causes at the IOR or APSA, whoever the account holder may be.

Zahra also revealed the clue that set off the alarm, which concerns the poor. In fact, Vatican regulations provide that

> for every cause that is brought before the Holy Congregation, the postulators shall deposit a contribution to the Fund for the Causes of the Poor [a fund created to finance beatification causes submitted by the poorest dioceses]. After the beatification of a servant of God, and once all the expenses required for the cause have been settled, 20% of the remaining amounts of the offerings from the faithful collected for that cause [must be] devolved to the Fund for the Causes of the Poor. After canonization, it is up to the Holy See to dispose of the remaining amounts of the offerings collected, one part of which, to be established on a case-by-case basis, will be assigned to the Fund for the Causes of the Poor. From the examination of the

> books relative to the Fund for the Causes of the Poor presented by the Congregation for recent years, it would appear that these obligations have not been fulfilled. In fact, the above-mentioned Fund has grown in a very limited manner.

In other words, the Fund for the Causes of the Poor—indispensable to assuring the processing of applications from dioceses with fewer resources—was not growing. This raised the Commission's suspicions. Zahra requested the freezing of accounts and demanded full documentation for each and every postulator and cause. In the first six months of its investigation, COSEA was shocked to find that considerable sums of cash arrived in the offices of the postulators for which there was no proper accounting, and concluded that there was "insufficient oversight of the cash-flow for canonizations."[13]

Attention was focused in particular on "two lay postulators (Andrea Ambrosi and Silvia Correale) who managed various cases and commanded high rates. Each of them was responsible for 90 causes out of a total of 2,500 divided among 450 postulators."[14] Since each postulator manages an average of five to six cases, this means that two people together control a disproportionate number: 180, constituting a kind of monopoly. Among the most significant examples emerging from COSEA's investigation:

- From 2008 to 2013, 43,000 euros were spent on a canonization that seems to show no progress and no proper budget or financial statements on how the funds were used;
- One lay postulator offered to conduct an investigation even before opening a canonization process, on the condition that he receive an initial payment of 40,000 euros;
- The printing press associated with one of the postulators listed above [Andrea Ambrosi] appears as one of the three print shops that the Congregation recommends to postulators.[15]

Another one of COSEA's files concerns "expenses for a Spanish canonization managed by a professional postulator between 2008 and 2013."[16] The compensation for the postulator was "28,000 euros, another 16,000 for his collaborator, one thousand euros for printing the material and the same amount for various expenses that bloated the costs to 46,000 euros," as indicated in February 2014 to the cardinals on the Council and the Pope.[17]

On Monday, August 5, 2013, at the explicit request of Zahra, and after the Congregation for the Causes of Saints had failed to provide any documentation, Cardinal Versaldi sent four letters containing instructions to freeze accounts at the IOR and APSA. The recipients of the letters were Cardinal Domenico Calcagno, President of APSA, and the lawyer Ernst von Freyberg, the head of the IOR. Versaldi also copied Cardinal Raffaele Farina, the Chair of the Pontifical Commission for Reference on the IOR, established by Francis in June, and its coordinator, Monsignor Juan Ignacio Arrieta.

Over at the IOR, at 10:11 A.M. on the same day, the unusual freezing order issued by von Freyberg became operative, to the consternation of various employees. It would take the whole day to block the huge number of accounts: there were more than four hundred bank accounts in all. This was an operation whose dimensions were unprecedented in recent bank history. By six o'clock that day, not a single euro could be withdrawn from any account linked to canonization or beatification procedures. At the IOR, a total of almost 40 million euros was blocked.[18]

Panic at the IOR

The next day, Tuesday, August 6, the situation became even more tense. At VISA-POS, the IOR office that handles ATM and credit card transactions, one bank official had hesitations. Stefano De Felici wanted written confirmation that the credit cards of a series of high-level clients had been blocked. He gave nine names to the Deputy

General Director of the Institute, Rolando Marranci, highlighting the two most prominent names in bold:

> Good morning.
>
> On the basis of various communications that this office has received, the following credit cards linked to the accounts of physical persons are to be blocked. Here is the list:

Client	*Name*
19878	Ambrosi, Andrea
15395	Batelja, Rev. Juraj
29913	**Gänswein, H.E. Mons. Georg**
24002	Kasteel, Mons. Karel
10673	Marrazzo, P. Antonio
27831	Murphy, Mons. Joseph
29343	Nemeth, Mons. Laszlo Imre
18635	**Paglia, H.E. Mons. Vicenzo**
18625	Tisler, Rev. Piotr

> I hereby request confirmation that I should proceed to block these accounts.

The measures had also affected the bank account of Monsignor Georg Gänswein, the former personal secretary of Benedict XVI, and now the prefect of the Pontifical House. Also blocked were the accounts of Antonio Marrazzo, postulator for the beatification of Paul VI, Giovanni Battista Montini; and of Monsignor Vincenzo Paglia, President of the Pontifical Council for the Family. With the first moves of the Commission, there was already a risk of a diplomatic incident. To prevent matters from escalating, the general accountant of the Prefecture, Stefano Fralleoni, who had attended many of the international auditors' meetings and was now helping COSEA with its investigations, wrote directly to von Freyberg:

> The provision for the temporary blocking of the accounts of postulators and single causes [for canonization] opened at the IOR and APSA should not be applied to the personal accounts of religious postulators and/or employees of the Holy See who meet the proper requirements to hold an account there.

The postulators were almost all religious, with the exception of two laypeople, the already mentioned Andrea Ambrosi and Silvia Correale. The only safe accounts were those held by religious people or employees who had the right and met the requirements for an account at the Vatican financial institutions. Unfortunately from the documentation examined I am unable to establish which of the four hundred accounts was immediately unblocked. In all probability, they included Monsignor Gänswein's.

Deputy General Director Marranci received the order directly from Fralleoni.[19]

> The accounts of Andrea Ambrosi and Silvia Correale do not seem to meet the normal requirements that exist for religious personnel or employees of the institutions of the Holy See. It is thus requested as a precautionary measure, and while awaiting the institution's clarifications of the modalities and origins of the amounts present in these accounts, that the temporary blocking of activities be extended also to the accounts held by the persons highlighted above, according to the same modalities as the accounts held by Causes.

Ambrosi had approximately one million euros in his three bank accounts at the IOR blocked. The Prefecture and COSEA demanded an explanation from him. Ambrosi defended himself in a letter he wrote to Marranci on August 20:

> After being introduced by Cardinal Salvatore Pappalardo in around 1985, having engaged in the activities of a postulator, he [Ambrosi,

> referring to himself in the third person] was allowed to open a personal account, with the exact numbers 19878001/2/3. In the past thirty years there has been a flow into these accounts first of credit from the stakeholders in the various causes as well as donations from the parents of the undersigned and of his wife. The undersigned states that he has never performed professional activities in Italy, that he is not the holder of a VAT number, and that he has always attached to his Italian tax return a statement by the Congregation for the Causes of Saints attesting that he has always performed his activity exclusively for the above-mentioned dicastery. In all these years—almost 40!—the Italian tax authorities have never had any objections. The undersigned, while awaiting, with confidence but concern, the unblocking of his three personal accounts at the earliest, hereby requests that he be allowed to immediately come into possession of 80,000 euros so as to deal with economic commitments already made.

Ambrosi was perhaps the top postulator in the world. For forty years—together with his daughter Angelica and various other collaborators from the five continents—he had handled hundreds of beatification and canonization processes, from Pope John XXIII (Angelo Roncalli) to the Emperor Charles I of Hapsburg. Another interesting activity of the Ambrosi family is the printing shop it owns, which handles the documentation for most of the causes—Novas Res, located in Piazza di Porta Maggiore in Rome. It holds a kind of monopoly, despite the fact that the Vatican has a modern printing shop that could easily publish the prestigious volumes. Nova Res is also one of the three print shops officially recommended to postulators by the Vatican.

The postulator Silvia Correale also wanted an explanation, and requested an appointment with Fralleoni. The meeting was tense. She asked for the immediate unblocking of her account but in the process she gave away some telling insider details of what was really going on inside the Congregation for the Causes of Saints under the leadership of Cardinal Amato. Fralleoni wrote a summary of her remarks for

Monsignor Vallejo Balda, in a confidential document to which I was given access:

> The account in her name holds about ten thousand euros and she says she has no other bank accounts in Italy; therefore this is her sole source of income. She asks if it would be possible to unblock it, and says that she knows and has worked with the Pope and that he knows and respects her . . . The most interesting item to emerge from our conversation is the fact that the Congregation for Saints HAS STILL NOT NOTIFIED ANYONE AND HAS NOT REQUESTED FROM ANY OF THE POSTULANTS THEIR FINANCIAL STATEMENTS FROM THE PAST FIVE YEARS!!! In practice, they're doing nothing. This is also serious because, while speaking with the postulator Silvia Correale, I realized that the balance sheets don't exist . . . Maybe the Prefect [Amato], who turned 75 in June, is waiting to pass the problem on to someone else . . . Let me know whether you think we should proceed to unblock this single account. The postulator seemed honest and sincere to me. I think we could use her in the future to receive more interesting information about how the causes are handled. In the meantime the various other consultants et alia who should be getting money from the causes are starting to get angry . . . The postulator says that some time ago she had handed in a financial statement but the people at the Congregation did not want to put their seal on it. After that she said she didn't do them anymore and that . . . to do them now would take months.

Monsignor Vallejo Balda was shocked:

> This is all extremely serious, what do you mean there are no balance sheets? This woman is handling more than 100 causes . . . how is it possible? This is one of the problems. We have nothing to say about her personal bank account but how is it possible that she has one at IOR [?] . . . I don't trust her . . . Let's talk about this tomorrow.

Fralleoni backtracked immediately regarding the woman's IOR account:

> The fact of having an account at IOR is a delicate matter. The postulator brought up the question of her rights as a person who had worked continuously for the Holy See and was thus similar to an employee. And for her work she is paid about 4,000 euros a month (more than I get . . .). Therefore I will have to study carefully the rules and regulations of the Congregation to assess the situation.

In December 2013, COSEA gave instructions to unblock 114 of the 409 accounts. Ambrosi's money would remain frozen for a long time. He would receive a monthly sum that was sufficient for him and his loved ones to live on. Meanwhile, suggestions arrived from the consultancy firm on how to lend greater transparency to the financial activities of the Congregation and of the procedures for causes. But there were still pockets of resistance, and even standard accounting practices are still not being applied today. In other words, there seems to have been no improvement in the situation.

The Freemasons Could Infiltrate the Reforms

Oversight of the accounting practices of the Causes was creating irritation and discontent within the Curia. In early September 2013, the Catholic reporter Antonio Socchi was slipped a copy of the fiery letter that Zahra had sent to Cardinal Versaldi on August 3, asking him to freeze the accounts. A copy of the letter ended up being published in the September 6 issue of the newspaper *Libero*, which dedicated two pages to the story.

Who leaked the documents to the press? The goal was to discredit the security and confidentiality of the COSEA members. Francis feared unpleasant surprises, so he asked his personal secretary, Alfred Xuereb, also from Malta, to have a private talk with Zahra. Their conversation was very tense. Zahra realized that the Pontiff was "very worried." Francis cared deeply about the commission's investigation, and he understood all too well that without an in-depth picture of the financial situation he would have to abandon his plans for a complete overhaul of the Vatican.

But the Pope's support was still unwavering. On the morning of Saturday, September 14, he welcomed all the members of the Commission to the Holy Mass that he was celebrating in the Santa Marta chapel. It was the day of the second session of COSEA. The suggestion that they attend the Mass had been made by Don Abbondi, the office head of the Prefecture, who was still not certain the invitation would be approved.

Only four days before the Mass, at the last minute, Monsignor Xuereb gave the go-ahead for the Commission to attend. The religious service that is held at the personal residence of the Pope is always very private and reserved to only a few people. By inviting them, Francis was confirming the esteem he held for the COSEA members as well as his attention to their work. This was a signal that encouraged Zahra, on the following Monday, September 16, to send the Pope two confidential letters. The first was a quick briefing on the investigations under way. The second letter was more delicate. He took up the issue of the leaked documents. The explicit purpose was to reassure Francis by pointing to a possible security flaw:

> Your Holiness,
>
> I refer to the concerns you have expressed over questions relative to the confidentiality and security of documents. I wish to assure you that we are taking all the necessary precautions appropriate to the utmost secrecy and security regarding the circulation of documents, including a dedicated network for cellular telephones, and a dedicated server for the exchange of emails and the use of passwords. The unfortunate incident of having a signed letter . . . being published in *Libero* on September 6 may be due to the fact that these letters were with every good intention attached to a letter forwarded by

> Cardinal Amato to all the postulators for the causes of saints scattered throughout the world. This increased the risk of this document spreading. Begging your forgiveness for having given any cause for concern, we are further tightening our security measures on the letters sent by our Commission, reminding the recipients of their utmost confidentiality.
>
> Your obedient servant, Zahra

The most immediate countermeasure was the decision to establish a communication task force, taken at the meeting of October 12, 2013. The task force had three ambitious goals.[20] The first was to manage COSEA's relations with the media—whose activity they hoped would remain dormant, given the delicacy of the subject matter. The second was to "analyze in depth how the Vatican communications system is currently structured," in order to shake it up radically, given the ongoing leaks to the press and the more critical stance international media was taking to the Holy See in the wake of the Vatileaks scandal (the moniker given to the leaking of confidential documents by me, and the basis for my previous book, *His Holiness*). Finally, the task force had "to be able to provide the Holy Father with the most appropriate recommendations to increase the efficiency and effectiveness of Vatican communications, internally and externally."

The media was one of the most delicate fronts to manage. The "enemies" were flocking in large numbers, at least according to the surprising revelations of another member of COSEA, the Frenchman Jean Videlain-Sevestre, disclosed in a grave email that he had sent to his colleagues and to the Pope's confidants one month earlier:

> Our actions will highlight the financial and administrative shortcomings that the enemies of the Church obviously wish to see. I am speaking of some governments, some politicians and much of the media. For example, we must at all costs prevent the free masons from circumventing or even infiltrating our plans of action.

As Sevestre so clearly indicated, the members of the Commission felt embattled. Not only did he fear internal resistance to the reforms of Francis, which were already emerging forcefully, he also feared the Freemasons. They always tracked the financial activities of the Vatican with close attention and sometimes open hostility: the "brotherhood of the masons" might even "infiltrate"—as the Frenchman put it—the Commission's operative plans, in order to manipulate their execution and impede the achievement of their goals.

Similar fears were emerging during the selection of advisors and experts to help the Commission in the conduct of its investigation. After Sevestre met with the renowned consultant Roland Berger in Paris on September 14, 2013, Berger advanced his own candidature, but added some concerns that were bothering him:

> We wish first of all to reconfirm our deep attachment to the Catholic Church . . . You can be certain of the utmost discretion of the signatories of this letter, of their Catholic faith, of their not belonging to organizations that are adverse to the Catholic Church, whether Masonic or of another nature.

These were the first signs of resistance and acts of sabotage that would increasingly hinder the investigation by COSEA. The investigation into the saints' factory would last for months, but the effect of Francis's reform on that Congregation is still unclear today.

3

The Secrets of the Peter's Pence

The Perks of Being a Cardinal

There is a black hole in the heart of the Church that took great efforts for Francis to uncover: a black hole created by mismanagement of the Vatican's finances and compounded by swindling and accounting fraud. Through the Commission that he established in an unprecedented blitz, the pope was able to ascertain that the expenses of the Curia were paid for by money that was supposed to go to the poor. Offerings for charity that Catholics from throughout the world sent to the Vatican were being used to plug up deficits created by a handful of Church officials who maneuvered the bureaucratic levers of the Holy See.

Jorge Mario Bergoglio had chosen the name Francis because his mission for the Church was to help the poor, in service of the teachings of St. Francis of Assisi. From the moment he stepped out on the balcony overlooking St. Peter's Square in March 2013 to salute the crowd, he rejected all frills. He often wore simple, shabby tunics. He invited the homeless to the Sistine Chapel and asked the heads of the Church's religious orders and administrative bodies to shelter the needy in their unused buildings, in the halls, hostels, and dormitories of the great seminaries that had been deserted because of the crisis in vocations.

In addition to rigor and transparency, poverty and charity were the key words of his pastoral language and pontificate. He tried to foster this sense among nuns and priests in particular, starting with the smallest, simplest things, such as the use of motor vehicles. He discussed this at length during an audience with seminarians and novices on July 6, 2013:

> "I tell you, it truly grieves me to see a priest or a sister with the latest model of a car," he declared, "but this can't be! It can't be . . . cars are necessary because there is so much work to be done, and also in order to get about . . . but choose a more humble car! And if you like the beautiful one, only think of all the children who are dying of hunger . . . You are all disgusted when you find among us priests who are not authentic, or sisters who are not authentic!"

He was the first to set the example. When he went to the Italian island of Lampedusa to embrace the refugees arriving from Africa, he used a Fiat jeep provided by a parishioner who lived on the island. On a visit to Assisi, the land of St. Francis, he used a small car, a Fiat Panda. "When a priest from Verona gave him a Renault 4, the Pope accepted it but transferred it to the graveyard of papal vehicles."[1]

Confronted by these words and deeds, unusual for a pope, there were many cardinals in the Curia who, after their initial surprise, tried to manifest their allegiance to the new era, but only in words and smiles. Their real attitude is better expressed by a joke that was making the rounds among their drivers: "They have left their limousines and sedans in the garage, and now they're driving around in economy cars, a Fiat 500 or Panda, but they're still living in the same luxury apartments."

The truth behind these words is apparent in the living quarters of the cardinals who occupy the highest positions in the Church hierarchy. Many live in luxurious homes in the heart of Rome—unimaginable realities for most.

The story of Cardinal Tarcisio Bertone's home made headlines. By combining two apartments, he created an immense residence for himself on the top floor of the Palazzo San Carlo at the Vatican. This is not the exception, but the rule. The cardinals of the Curia reside in princely dwellings of 400, 500, even 600 square meters.* They live alone or with a missionary nun—usually from a developing country—as their assistant, cleaning lady, or housekeeper. The apartments have rooms for every whim and fancy: waiting rooms, television rooms, bathrooms, reception rooms, tea rooms, libraries, rooms for the personal assistant, the secretary, the files, and rooms for praying. And these dwellings are often in stunning buildings, like the splendid Palace of the Holy Office, immediately behind the colonnade of St. Peter's Square: it dates back to the sixteenth century and had once been the headquarters of the tribunal of the Inquisition.

The largest apartment in the Palace of the Holy Office—a full 445 square meters—was given to Cardinal Velasio de Paolis, born in 1935, a hard-core ally of Ratzinger and President Emeritus of the Prefecture for Economic Affairs of the Holy See. Slightly smaller is the 409-square-meter apartment of the eighty-one-year-old Slovenian cardinal, Frank Rodé. The former archbishop of Lubljana, he had been a personal friend of Marcial Maciel, the disgraced founder of the Legionnaires of Christ, who had been suspended from the ministry for pedophilia.[2] Rodé is also a member of the Pontifical Council on

* The data on the leased apartments of senior cardinals are based on the 2013–2014 audits ordered by Francis.

Culture. Cardinal Kurt Koch, President of the Pontifical Council for the Promotion of Christian Unity, had to settle for a house of 356 square meters.[3]

Another group of cardinals lives not far away, on the opposite side of St. Peter's Square, in a beautiful building, in the heart of the Eternal City. This is the residence of the Canadian Marc Ouellet, born in 1944, Prefect of the Congregation for Bishops and President of the Pontifical Commission for Latin America. His apartment is almost 500 square meters. Cardinal Sergio Sebastiani, eighty-four, also a member of the Congregation for Bishops and of the Congregation for the Causes of Saints, lives in a 424-square-meter apartment. (Let us not forget that all cardinals older than eighty have a role that is primarily symbolic, and do not have the right to vote in the Conclave.)

Raymond Burke, an American cardinal born in 1948 and a patron of the Sovereign Military Order of Malta, is quite comfortable in his 417 square meters, as is the Polish cardinal, Zenon Grocholewski, born in 1939, who had been the Prefect Emeritus of the Congregation for Catholic Education until March 2015. His residence is 405 square meters. A stone's throw away, in the Borgo Pio neighborhood, is the 524-square-meter princely residence of the American Cardinal William Joseph Levada, born in Long Beach, California, in 1939, a loyalist of Ratzinger, who appointed him as his successor at the Congregation for the Doctrine of the Faith. In 2006, Levada was summoned to testify, in San Francisco, about the sexual abuse of minors by priests in the archdiocese of Portland, Oregon, where he had been Archbishop from 1986 to 1995. The priests were later found guilty of abuse. By comparison to these sumptuous quarters, Room 201 of the Casa Santa Marta, the home of the Pope, was almost a closet, barely 50 square meters.

The cardinals' privileges do not end there. The cardinals did not have to pay any rent, only the utilities, for as long as they hold an official post in the Curia, after which they are charged a monthly rental fee of 7–10 euros per square meter. In reality, however, even after the mandatory retirement age of eighty, some cardinals hold onto a dicastery assignment that allows them to continue to benefit from the no-rent policy. The typical response to criticisms of the sizes of these apartments is that various rooms are needed to accommodate the two, three, and even four nuns who live with the cardinal to administer to his domestic needs.

The cardinals of the Curia administer the most important departments of the Holy See, however: they control the heart of the universal Church. And it was from here that Francis felt that the evangelical and charitable work of the Church should begin and emanate throughout the world. But I have to use the conditional "should," because the reality is a different matter completely.

Where Does the Money for the Poor End Up?

According to the Vatican website, the Peter's Pence is

> the financial support offered by the faithful to the Holy Father as a sign of their sharing in the concern of the Successor of Peter for the many different needs of the Universal Church and for the relief of those most in need . . . The faithful's offerings to the Holy Father are destined for Church needs, to humanitarian initiatives and social promotion projects, as well as for the support of the Holy See. The Pope, being Pastor of the whole Church, is attentive to the material needs of poor dioceses, religious institutes and of faithful in grave difficulties (the poor, children, the elderly, those marginalized and the victims of war or natural disasters; concrete aid to Bishops or dioceses in need, Catholic education, assistance to refugees and immigrants, etc.).

The pontiffs have always valued the charitable aims of the Peter's Pence, and have urged the faithful to give generously. "'Peter's Pence' is the most characteristic expression"—Benedict XVI emphasized—"of the participation of all the faithful in the Bishop of Rome's charitable initiatives."[4] He describes the central importance of charity in his encyclical *Deus caritas est* (2006), noting that, "The Church can never be exempted from practicing charity as an organized activity of believers, and on the other hand, there will never be a situation where the charity of each individual Christian is unnecessary, because in addition to justice man needs, and will always need, love."[5]

Yet according to the financial statements and balance sheets—which I was able to consult directly—the management of the Peter's Pence is an enigma cloaked in the most impenetrable secrecy. Every year the amount of the collection is publicized but there is no explanation of how it is administered. In other words, we know how much money has been collected from the faithful but not how it is spent. Absolute secrecy is maintained around this detail.

This paucity of information raised the suspicions of the COSEA members, who wanted a clearer picture of the situation. They had also sensed that their success depended on getting the Peter's Pence managers to comply with the audit. It was clear that something was amiss when the charity did not reply to Versaldi's July 2013 request for financial reports, data, and documents. They did not reply, not by the deadline indicated by the Cardinal, nor by the end of autumn. They did give a few informal, evasive answers, but nothing written. Not a single clear, formal, and thorough document emerged from these queries.

Was this just the classic example of buying time until attention shifted away from the problem? If so, rather than respond negatively, evaders usually prefer to send partial signals, involve other persons, and pretend they don't understand the request, maybe by claiming that the documents have gone missing. This seemingly casual strategy ended up raising the suspicions of the COSEA members and of the financial consultants of McKinsey, KPMG, and Promontory Financial Group who had been hired by the papal Commission. The issue almost provoked a diplomatic incident in the Curia. The story helps to illustrate the hostile climate in which Francis has to operate. Through the documents that have come into my possession, I am able to reconstruct every step of the conflict.

The problems started in December 2013 when the Secretariat of State and APSA proved to be less than forthcoming in their answers to the Commission's requests for documentation. On December 2, in a letter to Reverend Alfred Xuereb, Francis's personal secretary, the Commission requested the Pontiff's direct intervention:

> Most Reverend Monsignor,
>
> Among the tasks awaiting us in the short term there is also an inspection of the activity and the role that the Secretariat of State plays at the economic and administrative level. This was already mentioned to the Secretary of State at a recent meeting. [The former Secretary of State, Tarcisio Bertone, had retired after reaching the age limit. In his place Francis had appointed Cardinal Pietro Parolin, who took office on October 15, 2013.] Based on what came out at the meeting, we believe that an ad hoc action—formal, explicit and unequivocal—could help confirm the desires of the superior Authority.

The Commission feared that its investigation would continue to be paralyzed by inertia and resistance. Indeed, the letter did not produce the desired effect: the stalemate continued. On December 18, Filippo Sciorilli Borelli of McKinsey of Zurich, one of the Commission's outside consultants, made another attempt to gain clarity. He managed to schedule an appointment for the next day with Monsignor Alberto Perlasca, the man inside the Secretariat of State in charge of the Peter's Pence. To prevent yet another postponement, Borelli sent an advance email detailing point-by-point the information and documents he would be requesting on the bank accounts and the expense items for the fund. The email was sent from his computer at 2:09 P.M. on December 18. At 2:16 P.M. the prelate's response arrived in his inbox. It ran to a total of seventeen words:

> Very good. Better at 9:30. With regard to your questions, we'll see if and how to respond. Regards.

The next day, December 19, the team of consultants—Ulrich Schlickewei of McKinsey, Claudia Ciocca of KPMG, and Carlo Comporti of Promontory—met with Monsignor Perlasca at the Vatican. They were expecting answers—finally—about where the offerings of the faithful had ended up. The meeting was cordial, and the three laypersons asked numerous questions, but the answers they received were unsatisfactory. When they left the room, the three of them looked at one another, shocked and aggrieved. They perceived a seemingly impenetrable brick wall. When they got back to the office, they decided to notify chairman Zahra.

> Today we had a meeting with Monsignor Perlasca to obtain a better understanding of the use of the St. Peter's Pence. The meeting was cordial but we did not learn anything new. We were told that part of the money is used to pay the deficit of the Curia, while the other part is for the commitments of the Holy Father, but not for the setting up of reserves. When we requested more details, they refused to reveal anything more.

What was the reason behind all the mystery? Without the requested information the investigation into the Vatican finances was at risk of running aground—an investigation that had started at the express request of the Holy Father. The concerns mounted. Other complaints were made to chairman Zahra, always by the consultants:

> One of the biggest gaps is the Peter's Pence, where they did not give us access to a complete vision of the collection and management of the funds (we're talking about at least 30–40 million euros, which is the net of the total revenue minus the financing of the Secretariat of State and APSA). A second gap is, to put it bluntly, "what they are

not telling us." We don't know whether other funds or assets, in addition to the Peter's Pence, are being kept off the books of the Secretariat of State.

What They Don't Want to Say

Five months had already gone by since its first letter to the Vatican's administrative bodies and the Commission was still at the starting point. There was still no way of knowing whether there were off-the-books funds that were not included in the consolidated financial reports. So the members decided to go straight to the top. On January 3, 2014, Monsignor Vallejo Balda, the coordinator of the Commission and the liaison with the Curia, wrote a firm letter to the new Secretary of State, Monsignor Pietro Parolin, with a request for clarification. In the letter he refers explicitly to the Pope's wishes twice in six lines:

> Most Reverend Excellency,
>
> For some time now, in fulfillment of the tasks assigned by the Holy Father to this Pontifical Commission, a large-scale audit *in loco* has been under way at the main Entities of the Holy See that conduct activities that are significant at the economic and administrative level. We were pleased to find, almost everywhere, a cordial reception and concrete collaboration, a sign of the profound awareness of and loyal adherence to the *desiderata* of His Holiness. This activity also involves necessarily the Entity that you direct. Pursuant to the dictates of the Pontifical Chirograph by which this Commission was established, I would therefore like to cordially request that you provide instructions for our operators to be provided with all the documentation, on paper and in digital format, pertaining to the attached list. As you well know, we are working on a very tight schedule; we therefore request that this documentation be made available by January 10. While remaining available for any needs you may have,

and thanking you already for the cordial collaboration that we know will be forthcoming, I avail myself of these circumstances to confirm my utmost devotion to your most reverend Excellency.

Monsignor Vallejo Balda

Attached to the letter Parolin found a long list of twenty-five entities on which documentation was requested.[6] The Pope's task force was particularly interested in the last two points:

> We have not yet received: the list of bank accounts, stocks and the like, held or managed by the Secretariat of State (or any other activity) and a full vision of the management of funds collected (expenditures, investments, etc.) of the Peter's Pence and other sources of revenue.

The Chairman of the Commission, Zahra, was well aware that the information provided was still insufficient. He waited impatiently for a reply from the Secretariat of State. Without that information it would be impossible to have a clear picture of the situation and propose a credible reform. After waiting in vain yet one more time, on January 16 he drafted an alarming letter to Francis:

> Your Holiness,
>
> I regret to inform you that your Commission is unable to complete the consolidated financial position of the Holy See due to the lack of fundamental information. We have requested from Monsignor Parolin a list of bank accounts held by the Secretariat of State, and of the investments made into bonds, funds and stock, as well as information on other accounts such as the Peter's Pence, but they never arrived. We realize that the Secretariat might wish to maintain confidentiality on some of these accounts, but it is not willing to make available financial information about any of them.
>
> Without a complete picture of the financial situation of the Holy

> See, your Commission will not be able to evaluate the various risks present in the economic administration of the Vatican. This is a vital part of the work of the Commission and the members cannot complete their assignments if the evaluation of the risks for the Vatican is not taken into consideration. We would be most grateful if you could instruct us on this matter, since we do not wish to disappoint Your Holiness by not providing [analyses] of this important sector of our mission. We ask for your blessing.

On January 30, an answer finally arrived, either thanks to the direct intercession of Francis or the pressures of Xuereb on Parolin. The Secretariat of State delivered a twenty-nine page dossier bearing the grandiloquent title: "The Venerated Financial Report." In the first confidential document that I was able to read, it emphasized that

> the Peter's Pence consists of the traditional gathering of offerings collected on the feast day of Saints Peter and Paul at all the dioceses of the world and of all the offerings delivered during the celebrations to the direct collaborators of the Holy Father or his envoys. It is entrusted to a special office of the general affairs division of the Secretariat of State that is in charge of managing the collection of offerings for the charitable works of the Holy Father and for the Holy See.

The Secretariat of State then went on to specify that this information was protected by the utmost secrecy:

> While on the one hand an analytical report on the revenue relative to the Peter's Pence is published annually, on the other absolute confidentiality has been maintained to date, in compliance with Superior instructions, on how the report is used, since it is excluded from the consolidated financial report of the Holy See.

In practice, to date, the offerings for the poor are still a black hole: absolute secrecy on how the money is spent and only an "itemizing" of how much is taken in, thereby sidestepping the requirement of accounting in the official financial reports. A decision dictated by "superior instructions," in other words, by the Secretary of State or the previous Pope. Why all the secrecy? What was done with the money? Here is the response, vague but illuminating:

> The collection is used for charitable initiatives and/or specific projects indicated by the Holy Father (14.1 million), for the transmission of offerings with specific targets (6.9 million) and for the maintenance of the Roman Curia (28.9 million). Plus the setting aside of 6.3 million from the Peter's Pence fund.[7]

This means that more than half of the offerings that arrive from the faithful throughout the world and that should go to the needy ends up instead in the coffers of the Curia: to be exact, 58 percent, not counting the sum that was set aside. If we do an item-by-item check of the "donations of the Holy Father," what clearly emerges from the Secretariat's unpublished document, is that the Curia largely used that 14.1 million to balance the shaky finances of the Holy See rather than for charitable works: 5.5 million euros went to the printers, 1 million to the library, and 309,000 euros to the foundations. In other words, of the 53.2 million taken in through the Peter's Pence (2012)—to which we should add the three million in interest payments—a good 35.7 million (67 percent) was spent on the Curia and another 6.3 million (12.4 percent) was not used, set aside as reserves of the Peter's Pence fund.

In the Red

For every euro that finds its way to the Holy Father, barely 20 cents end up in actual projects to help the poor. This situation is enabled by a lack of financial oversight in the Apostolic Palaces. Almost every department in which former Secretary of State Bertone convinced Benedict XVI to appoint his Italian loyalists is showing a deficit or other problems, as the confidential file shows:

> From the summary outlines of the financial situation, it appears that 2012 ended with a financial deficit of 28.9 million euros, based on the difference between the 92.8 million in revenue and 121.7 in expenditures. The expenditures consist of the 66 million deficit of APSA [real estate management], the 25 million deficit of Vatican Radio, 25.4 million for the operation of the pontifical nunciatures and 5.3 million for the operation and direct expenses of the Secretariat of State. Given the above-mentioned revenue, the Secretariat of State recalculates in advance the deficit of APSA and, in a broader sense, of the Roman Curia, which is unable to achieve the desired balanced budget through its own resources.

Therefore, every year the Secretariat of State is forced to come up with huge sums of money that it withdraws directly from the offerings of the faithful to the Holy Father.

> The Secretariat of State is thus forced every year to dip into the resources of the Peter's Pence, removing a sizeable amount for the maintenance of the Roman Curia, especially to cover the costs of personnel employed there, which is the largest single budget item . . . Over the years the Secretariat of State has de facto and by necessity taken on the role of a financing agency through the "improper" use of the Pence, collecting other resources through the pontifical nunciatures that are the liaison between the Holy See and the bishops' conferences and dioceses of the world.

This was the worst possible news for a Pope who had humbly chosen the name of the saint of the poor.

If these sums of money were not being spent, then why weren't they invested in order to make them more profitable? I was able to ascertain that the 377.9 million total of the Peter's Pence reserves is divided up into bank accounts in twelve different banks: the largest sums are deposited in the IOR (89.5 million) and Fineco of Unicredit (78.5 million). Fifty-eight million euros are sitting in the vaults of the Merrill Lynch commercial bank. At Credit Suisse 46.5 million is held. Between 2011 and 2012, all this money has guaranteed truly modest interests: only 2,979,015 euros, not even one percent, a ridiculously low rate. Why? And above all, why are the set-aside euros not used?

Thirteen Unanswered Questions

Francis's men were left speechless by the financial report. By carefully examining the information they had received, the financial consultants working for the Commission found numerous irregularities, rather obvious mistakes, and various discrepancies. After reviewing it for a few days, in the late afternoon of February 10, 2014, Filippo Sciorilli Borrelli of McKinsey decided to make his move. He sent Zahra thirteen questions about the finances of the Secretariat of State. Precise questions regarding deposits, expenses, and the actual management of the Pence. The first question concerned the interest rates, which were too low. How was this possible? His findings left no uncertainties:

> In the document it is stated that the average annual interest rate recognized by the IOR for the Peter's Pence Fund [generated] three million euros in 2012. In 2012 89.5 million euros were deposited at the IOR. Does this mean that the interest rate was three percent? Is this statement true or false?

If true—and there was no reason to doubt that it was—then it is not clear, "what to make of the interests on the other known deposits (for example, the 58 million at Merrill Lynch). If the above statement is false, then how do you explain that the overall interest rate is barely one percent of the total funds invested (in 2012, three million in interest on a base of 377.9 million euros)?"

Sciorelli Borelli wanted to know why the annual deposit made by the Holy Father to the *Osservatore Romano* (5.3 million in 2011, and 5.6 in 2012) does "not appear under the item 'to cover the deficit,' although it falls under the deficits of the Curia?" And, "To what does the item Peter's Pence c/allocations of 7.3 million in 2012 and 2.1 in 2011 correspond?" Finally, when you look at the actual deposits in the various banks of the 371.6 million indicated as the Peter's Pence reserve fund (2011), only 353.4 is accounted for, "a discrepancy of 18.2 million euros. How do you explain this negative difference?"[8]

The answers were not forthcoming. The thirteen questions never became official. They never even left "Area 10," which holds the most important secrets of the Commission's work. So COSEA had to make do with partial and often misleading reports. It's difficult to say the exact reason why. Some in the Apostolic Palaces believe that both in the leadership of the Commission and within the Secretariat of State, the usual practice was to nip in the bud any question whose results might be unpredictable.

The same dilemma had beset Ettore Gotti Tedeschi, the former President of IOR, when he wanted to avail himself of the top consultants on the issue of money laundering, originating from the Banca d'Italia, to get the Vatican on the "white list" of the countries in compliance with the rules of financial propriety. On this project, Benedict XVI was subject to the influence of Bertone's men, who discredited Gotti Tedeschi and altered his proposals claiming that he would expose the Vatican to dangerous interference by the central bank of a foreign state. Tradition dictates that in the Curia the influence, weight, and power of a layperson is always inferior to that of a cleric, regardless of whether he is a cardinal or a simple priest, and regardless of whether he knows how to manage bookkeeping and financial reports or is completely inadequate to the task.

The Secret Bank Accounts of the Pope

The financial situation of the Secretariat of State was a web of confusion and major losses. The tangle of accounts opened at different banks was evidence enough. Fifteen years after the fact, four accounts for the 2000 Jubilee were still open. Of these, two were at APSA, where the Secretariat of State manages eight accounts altogether. One of them is listed as "Vatican Radio, Slovak newsroom," with an ending balance of $134,000.

Does the Pontiff have his own bank account? Decades have gone by without ever finding the truth. Various improbable theories have circulated, followed by halfhearted denials or even more imaginative reconstructions. It was not until the confidential papers photocopied by Paolo Gabriele, the butler of Benedict XVI, and published in my book *His Holiness*, that it emerged that Ratzinger, on October 10, 2007, had ordered the opening of account number 39887 at the IOR to receive from a company fifty percent of his royalties from more than 130 publications.[9] Large sums of money poured in the account, like the 2.4 million euros deposited in March 2010 by the Joseph Ratzinger Benedict XVI Fund.

From the unpublished documents sent in early 2014 by the Secretariat of State for the bookkeeping audits, a truth emerged that no one had ever been able to verify. Each pope has his own personal bank account. In many cases, it has remained open for years after his death. The most mysterious accounts are in fact held by deceased pontiffs, with currency converted into euros, of course. In particular, the account of Pope John Paul I (Albino Luciani), who died in 1978, is still open. The account number is 26400-018, and it is held by "His Holiness John Paul I." It has a balance of 110,864 euros. Who manages it?

Thirty-seven years after his death, there are still two accounts in the name of Pope Luciani's predecessor, Paul VI (Giovanni Battista Montini), who was recently beatified. From the documents that we were able to read, there is one account, number 26400-042, titled

"Personal Account of Paul VI," with a balance of 125,310 euros, and another account, 26400-035, with a balance of 298,151 dollars. Evidently, Montini preferred to diversify his accounts into different currencies, to avoid the need for damage control in the event of devaluations or financial crises.

There is still no answer today to the delicate questions raised by the existence of these and many other similar bank accounts. If they are really held by deceased persons, the accounts should be closed. Yet they remain open, and in some cases quite a few years have gone by. How is this possible? Is someone moving money through them? An heir, perhaps? If so, what right did he or she have to keep an account at the IOR, where laypeople are not allowed to bank. These are all questions that for unclear reasons would not be conveyed to Monsignor Peter Wells, the Assessor for General Affairs of the Secretariat of State, or even to his superior, Monsignor Angelo Becciu, Substitute for General Affairs of the Secretariat of State, the last bastion of the old guard.

4

Handcuffs in the Vatican

Cardinal Rambo Embarrasses the Curia

The Peter's Pence was not the only black hole in the Vatican finances. There were others whose measure was difficult to take because of the limited, even patchy data returned to the Commission for Reference on the Administrative-Economic Structure of the Holy See. What little documentation did come in was tainted or hard to interpret. The Commission had hit a wall. Even its most astute and swift moves were immediately obstructed by an equally intelligent and unexpected countermove.

At the secret July 3, 2013, meeting, Cardinal Agostino Vallini had begged for the Holy Father's indulgence, arguing that the irregularities in the Vatican finances were the result of ignorance rather than a deliberate cooking of the books. But there was nothing innocent about the misconduct of the men in charge of the Vatican finances. They suddenly turned into razor-sharp officials when it came to outwitting the Pope's auditors. As a result, after more than six months since its inception the Commission was still unable to give the Pope a full and accurate picture of the Vatican's financial health. There was no way he could know which funds he could earmark for charity, the missions, and all the actions to aid the poor that were the heart and soul of his pontificate. Paradoxical but true: in a theocracy like the Vatican, the Pope could not get his hands on basic information.

The Pontiff is often the last one to know and to be briefed, especially on money matters. It was still hard for him to know with any precision how much money was coming in and how much was going out. This made it almost impossible for Francis to bring the work of renewal that he was promoting tirelessly every day, inspiring Catholics around the world and filling them with hope. Everything was anesthetized, paralyzed. The smoke screen was obviously not accidental. It was meant to conceal superficiality, inertia, personal interests, and more. Without knowing the financial situation of the Vatican in detail, it was impossible to identify the problems and critical areas, and thus to propose solutions. And the idea of imposing the reforms was unthinkable.

But the Commission did not give up. Its investigation expanded from the Peter's Pence and Congregation for Saints to new areas that often harbored surprises. One of its main targets was the Administration of the Patrimony of the Apostolic See, APSA, the administrative body that manages assets, stocks, and real estate, in addition to minting metal coins, headed by an Italian cardinal and Bertone loyalist: Domenico Calcagno.

Calcagno had been appointed President of APSA by Benedict XVI in July 2011. He made headlines after an investigative report for the popular Italian TV show *Le Iene*. The reporter Paolo Trincia found that between 2002 and 2003, Calcagno, as the Bishop of Savona, had ignored repeated instances of sexual violence against minors by a pedophile priest. The diocese of Savona had reportedly been aware of the priest's strange behavior since 1980, when he was removed from a school in Valleggia, in the province of Savona, after fondling a boy. He was sent to Spotorno (only ten kilometers away), but he was still allowed to supervise a Boy Scout troop at the local Catholic youth center. Following new complaints, the new bishop of the diocese, Monsignor Dante Lanfranconi (currently the Bishop of Cremona) moved the priest to another parish. Once again he was sent to a place only a few kilometers away, in the town of Feglino, where he was allowed to open a community center for troubled youths.

Calcagno became the Bishop of Savona in 2002. Before dying, Father Carlo Rebagliati, former treasurer of the diocese, revealed that he had warned Calcagno about the pedophile priest and the danger to the minors with whom he was in daily contact. The Bishop's response, according to Rebagliati, was evasive: "They might just be rumors," he said. The Bishop had also been contacted by one of the victims of abuse, who testified that, "Calcagno . . . told me not to go to court, because the priest was a very fragile person who might commit suicide and then I would have that on my conscience."

The Bishop did not address the problem until the following year. He wrote a letter to Cardinal Joseph Ratzinger, who was then the Prefect to the Congregation for the Doctrine of the Faith, asking for "advice on what approach to take." Calcagno attached a file to the letter. It was an internal document of the Savona diocese, compiled by the Vicar General, Monsignor Andrea Giusto: a chart that summarized the behavior of the priest, going through every instance, from the first episode in 1980 until the most recent complaints twenty-two years later, by social workers from the area. The chart was a blatant admission, in black and white, in which the diocese revealed that it had moved the priest from one parish to another for almost a quarter of a century. But it concluded with a reassuring sentence: "Nothing has come out in the newspapers and no investigations are under way."

Ratzinger's reply has never been found. The only thing we know for certain is that after the letter, the priest was moved to Portio Magnone (twelve kilometers away from Feglino), reappearing magically at another Boy Scout camp in the area. And once again, a youth at the camp reported him for sexual molestation. The man continued to be a priest until 2010, when, thirty years after the first reports of abuse, he wrote in his own hand a letter requesting his dismissal from the priesthood.

The television report, which included the testimony of five boys describing incidents of abuse they had suffered between 1980 and 2005, cast a shadow over Calcagno but did not interrupt his brilliant career. Only four days before becoming Pope, Cardinal Jorge Mario Bergoglio—hounded by journalists about Calcagno's participation in the Conclave—preferred not to take any questions.

Calcagno had also appeared in the news recently because of a rather unique extravagance for a prelate: his passion for firearms. The journalist Mario Molinari of *Savonanews* reported on the cardinal's rich private collection of revolvers, Smith & Wesson .357 caliber magnums, an Escort pump rifle, and many more, all duly registered and declared. There was a small arsenal of collector's items and more modern pieces that the Cardinal used at the firing range, where he had been a member since 2003. When he was asked for an explanation, Calcagno is said to have replied with the comforting tones of a good country priest: "They are all kept safe in a vault under lock and key."

Relations between Calcagno and Francis were only good on a formal level. The Argentine Pope distrusted the old guard and its shadowy management of the Curia's books.

Few people realize that there are actually two active banks at the Vatican. In addition to the IOR, there is APSA, a little-known entity at the heart of the Vatican financial web that is recognized throughout the world as a full-fledged central bank. One of its two sections, the special section, performs a sensitive function: it handles investments in stocks and bonds, and manages bank accounts and deposits. In practice, it manages the cash flow of the Holy See. Until November 2013, the head of the special section of APSA was Paolo Mennini, the son of Luigi Mennini, the historic right-hand man of Monsignor Paul Marcinkus, the most controversial figure in Church history because of his role in the Banco Ambrosiano scandal culminating in the death of "God's banker," Roberto Calvi.[1]

APSA would be yet another source of serious problems for the pontificate of Francis.

The Incredible Case of Monsignor Scarano

In March 2013, before the election of the new Pontiff, the prosecutors' offices in Salerno and in Rome had begun an investigation into the financial activities of Monsignor Nunzio Scarano, the chief accountant of the special section of APSA. According to the indictment, the evidence gathered, and various wiretaps—even during the tense, frenzied days of Benedict's resignation and the preparations for the Conclave—instances emerged of money laundering and attempts to import large amounts of capital from abroad through illegal channels. In practice, according to the indictment, Scarano provided a simple system of laundering money through his account at the IOR: he offered cashier's checks for hundreds of thousands of euros in exchange for suitcases stuffed with 500-euro bills, which earned him the nickname, "Monsieur 500."

Scarano, originally from Salerno, had worked in a bank before becoming a priest at the age of twenty-six. A lover of luxury, he had always enjoyed rubbing shoulders with celebrities, and could count among his friends jet setters from the world of cinema and television. He befriended some of Italy's most popular showgirls, like Michelle Hunziker. But his true passions had always been real estate and money. In Salerno he bought and remodeled a 700-square-meter house and started up various real estate companies. In Rome he lived in an apartment owned by APSA: 110 square meters, on Via Sant' Agostino, a few blocks away from Piazza Navona and the Italian Senate. Unlike other illustrious cardinals over the age of eighty living in princely residences, Scarano had to pay the rent: 740 euros a month. Similar apartments in the same neighborhood were commanding rents as much as three times greater.

Immediately after Francis's election, disturbing rumors were circulating at the Curia and in Casa Santa Marta about a criminal investigation into the Monsignor. The newly elected Pope realized that he had to move with extreme caution. The situation did not materialize until May 29, after the deposition of Father Luigi Noli, an old friend of Scarano. As an employee of a central office of the Holy See, the APSA accountant enjoyed a kind of diplomatic immunity guaranteed by the Lateran Pacts signed in 1929 by the Vatican Secretary of State, Pietro Gasparri, and Italian Prime Minister Benito Mussolini. The investigators had to pursue their leads with the utmost discretion, through the proper diplomatic channels, but they were able to formalize the arrest warrant.

The Pope was at a crossroads reminiscent of the dilemma faced by John Paul II in 1987, when the Italian Supreme Court rejected the arrest warrant that the Milanese prosecutors had issued against the President of the IOR, Paul Casimir Marcinkus, on the charge of fraudulent bankruptcy, and against Luigi Mennini and Pellegrino de Strobel. The Supreme Court's ruling confirmed that the Italian court system had no jurisdiction over the actions of persons who report to the Vatican. The three men were found to be employees of a central office of a foreign state and therefore immune from prosecution without the authorization of senior Vatican officials, which would never be granted. After long discussions and negotiations, Marcinkus, Mennini, and de Strobel did not serve a single day in prison.

In the first weeks of Francis's pontificate, the old nightmares resurfaced, starting with the Banco Ambrosiano scandal and the murder of its president, Roberto Calvi, whose body had been found hanging under the Blackfriars' Bridge of London in 1982.

The Pope had to decide on the freedom of a man, of a priest, so he consulted his colleagues. Opinions were divided within the Secretariat of State and between cardinals strolling in conversation through the splendid gardens of the Vatican. Some felt that the warrant should be rejected, as had always been the case in the past. Allowing the arrest would set a disturbing precedent in the history of relations between

Italy and the Vatican City, and future decisions would be held hostage to it. Francis listened in silence. Only later would everyone realize that his mind was already made up. The policy of a soft but decisive revolution prevailed: a tangible sign of his break with the past.

At dawn on June 28, 2013, Monsignor Scarano was placed in handcuffs and is currently facing two trials, one in Rome for corruption, and one in Salerno for money laundering. The Pope was not at the Vatican. He was on his way back from a trip to Brazil. When he was asked for a comment on the plane, his answer was unsparing: "Do you think Scarano ended up in jail because he was similar to the Blessed Imelda?" The Holy Father was citing, ironically, the fourteenth-century child from Bologna who had died in ecstasy after receiving Holy Communion. His reply signaled the growing unbridgeable distance between the allies of Francis and his adversaries in the world of intrigue that characterized the finances of the Curia.

Money Laundering at the IOR

The Scarano investigation and the ensuing scandal ended up in the headlines of newspapers and television news programs throughout the world. Until now we have had no idea about what really happened after the arrest behind closed doors in the Vatican. Tensions ran high between the old and the new guard. On July 3—only five days after Scarano's arrest—at the meeting where Francis announced the establishment of the COSEA commission, Ernst von Freyberg, the new President of the IOR, explained to the cardinals and the Pope the irregularities he had found in certain accounts at the bank, and the risk that there might be more:

> What kind of problem do we have? It is mainly a problem of physical persons who use their accounts for illegal transactions, money laundering in every sense. They can be members of the clergy, they can be lay persons, there is no rule as to where the risk is greatest.

This may have been the first time that the President of IOR admitted that money laundering occurred at the bank. Or rather, the first time that we have the means of knowing for certain that inside the Vatican they were perfectly aware of certain illegal activities. It was a clamorous statement that confirmed the many suspicions that had festered since the scandals of the 1980s—suspicions that were always denied in official press releases. For decades the Vatican would not even confirm that the IOR was a bank.

Von Freyberg was convinced that his words would never leave the room, as if the cardinals and senior executives in attendance were under the seal of the confessional. Instead his shocking words were leaked and I am making them public for the first time in this book. Von Freyberg went even further by intimating that it was not easy to hunt down the money launderers, who could be religious or lay account holders. Practically every account was suspicious.

> I think there are not so many cases. I myself checked on the computer the ones reported in the press on the first day, and they weren't there . . . What is true is that Scarano's account was present, an account that, to look at it today, had not been right for ten years, but he's a real professional in money laundering . . . this was not good . . . Our problem is this: we are living in a triangle of true facts, like the Ambrosiano, like Scarano; of false rumors, like Osama Bin Laden and all the others; and of total silence on our part.

These were strong and shocking assertions, considering that until a few weeks earlier the Monsignor had played a major role at the Vatican. They raise the question of how Scarano had been able to act with such impunity for so many years, and who his enablers had been. For ten years Scarano had cultivated his personal business interests, apparently without attracting any notice. His individual culpability would be ascertained at the trial, but at the same time someone must have been protecting him.

Mennini Father & Son

At APSA, the freewheeling monsignor's superior was not just any banker. He was Paolo Mennini, the son of Luigi Mennini, the right-hand man of Marcinkus, who had narrowly avoided arrest in 1987. The sins of the father are not necessarily visited on the sons. Mennini was not even questioned during the investigation, but the coincidence that both he and his father should be linked to financial wrongdoing at the Vatican was still quite striking. This became particularly noticeable after Scarano's arrest, and it caught the eye of the new cardinals who had been chosen by Francis, who were still relatively innocent of the dynamics and the most recent financial shenanigans in the holy circles.

Since 2002, Mennini had been the head of the special section of APSA, which manages the cash flow of the Holy See. He was a powerful man. He lived in a 174-square-meter apartment, in a beautiful building on Via di Porta Angelica, a stone's throw from Saint Anne's Gate, one of the main entrances to the Vatican City. He, too, had a very affordable below-market rent, paying only 843 euros a month for his spacious apartment. He played a crucial role at the heart of the Holy See's financial web, coordinating the bank accounts and all the foreign real estate agencies—which manage a total of 591 million euros in assets.

The Commission wanted to get a clear idea of what was going on in Mennini's department, where 102 positions were operative. After an audit by Moneyval—the European Council body that assesses compliance with money-laundering regulations—APSA had closed 31 savings accounts held by persons, entities, or companies that were hard to identify or that were not entitled to bank privileges at the Vatican. This reduced the number of positions to 71, all of whose holders had been identified. Six of them were entities: the Saints Peter and Paul Association, the Circle of St. Peter, the Equestrian Order of the Holy Sepulcher, the Baby Jesus Hospital, the Féderation

Internazionale des Associations de Médecins Catholiques, and the International Association of Catholic Hospitals. Two were affiliated companies that deal with buildings in France and Switzerland: the realtor Sopridex SA of Paris and the Profima SA Societé Immobilière et de Participations of Geneva. Finally, there was personal account of Cardinal Giovanni Lajolo, former President of the Governorate, and other accounts that remained secret.

But there were more surprises to come. On November 18, 2013, at the COSEA meeting in Paris, Jean-Baptiste de Franssu described what he had found in his analysis of APSA accounts:

> Eighty-nine accounts have been identified, for in addition to the 74 initial accounts another 15 accounts have been identified because APSA was involved in their imminent closing. Of these, 43 are institutional because their consolidated funds are at the Holy See, while 46 are non-institutional (the remaining accounts). There is also an account held by the S.O. [APSA's ordinary section], which has to be analyzed to understand its nature.

Relations were tense between Francis, his collaborators, and Mennini Jr. and matters weren't helped by rumors about the investigation that had been leaked. On July 8, 2013, Monsignor Scarano was questioned by the Italian prosecutors. His explosive revelations on that occasion were reported four months later in an article by Maria Antonietta Calabrò for *Corriere della Sera*:

> In the transcript, which was classified in October, Scarano spoke at length about Mennini and the way Finnat Banking Group stocks were always handled, according to him. So much that the prosecutors questioning him asked if he realized that he might be implicating Mennini in the manipulation of stocks of an Italian bank. The son of Paolo Mennini, Luigi (after his grandfather) is the managing director of Finnat. Scarano's statements also concerned Cardinal

Attilio Nicora, his successor Domenico Calcagno, and the office chief of APSA.[2]

Mennini did not seem daunted by the suspicions surrounding him. Late in the evening of October 24, 2013, for example, he expressed his satisfaction with his superior, Cardinal Calcagno, at having found the right channel for purchasing 20–25 million dollars in foreign currency, a circumstance that stand in this never-before-published letter:

> Most Reverend Eminence,
>
> I am pleased to confirm that it was possible to arrange with our Swiss correspondent the provision of banknotes in foreign currency, also for significant amounts (20–25 million USD). The first price quoted was 0.05% of the amount requested, all inclusive (transportation, delivery to our offices and insurance coverage). I have succeeded, for the moment, in lowering the rate to 0.04%, and in the negotiations I will try to get it even lower. Considering that the costs of transportation will take a sizeable cut, it would be advisable to execute operations only for very large amounts. I remain at your disposal and send my kind and most devoted regards.

Paolo Mennini would leave his post on November 11, 2013, when his second five-year term expired. But Zahra interpreted his actions during his final days as a declaration of war. It all started with a note that Mennini left on Cardinal Calcagno's desk on November 13, after a telephone conversation with Timothy Fogarty, "senior vice president—CBIAS—of Federal Reserve, New York," as Mennini indicated in the document. In the one-and-a-half page note, Mennini emphasized that, to supply the cash, Fogarty would prefer to deal directly with APSA and not have to go through the Promontory consultants, who were working with the Vatican central bank in that period:

> Mr. Fogarty was happy to be able to speak with me. He confirmed receipt of the Swift message sent to him by APSA on November 5, 2013. With regard to the provision of hard foreign currency, he confirmed that the Federal Reserve usually provides banknotes to central banks, but prefers to guarantee this service only when it is difficult to find availability through commercial banks and financial institutions. He would like to be considered as a last resort. He told me that he would prefer to speak about this subject directly with APSA and, in addition, that he does not understand the exact role and need of Promontory's mediation in this specific instance. This is because he considers APSA a central bank with a clear consolidated relationship with them . . . Going back to the issue of banknotes, Mr. Fogarty . . . told me that he will inform Ms. McCaul [Elizabeth McCaul of Promontory] by telephone that he would prefer to deal directly with APSA to arrange this type of service. He also specified that the banknotes would be delivered physically in their vault, so it will be up to APSA to arrange for transportation to the Vatican City. [He is] definitely able to provide APSA with the right contact required for this need. At the end of the conversation Mr. Fogarty mentioned with pleasure his visit to Rome a few years ago and in particular his visit to the Vatican museum and gardens.
>
> Paolo Mennini

From the documentation in my possession, I am able to reconstruct that Zahra interpreted this note as a clear attempt to jeopardize the reform of APSA, and to discredit both the COSEA Commission and the activities of Promontory. He wrote to the coordinator of the Commission, Monsignor Vallejo Balda:

> Dear Father Lucio,
>
> Mennini is waging war . . . let's speak about this later today. But he has to be replaced immediately.
>
> Joe

The same policy was taken by another member of the Commission, Jean-Baptiste de Franssu, who wrote to the analyst Elizabeth McCaul and to Zahra:

> This is not a very satisfactory situation and I imagine that we should expect more and more of this type of "Scud missile" from Mennini as long as he is around. The sooner we are dealing with his replacement, the better. What should we do over there, Joe, to speed up the process [of change]? Of the two questions raised, I imagine we should not change in the least the strategy we have developed vis-à-vis the Fed, you, and Promontory.

All the while Mennini continued to report to the office. On November 20 the McKinsey consultants, including Ulrich Schlickewei, remarked on his presence to Zahra:

> In the past few days, Mennini has continued to come to the office regularly for the transfer of his duties to Monsignor Mistò. For the moment no official successor has been appointed, but a date should be set for the final exit of Mr. Mennini.

On November 22 the relations with the Federal Reserve were suspended. Calcagno wrote to Vice President Fogarty to indicate that Mennini was no longer an APSA official. In his immediate reply, the American banker tried to put this case and the embarrassment behind them:

> For more than seventy years the Federal Reserve Bank of New York has enjoyed a productive relationship with APSA, and in particular I have had the pleasure of working with Mr. Giorgio Stoppa as well as with Mr. Mennini on questions related to your account with us. I can't wait to maintain and improve the relations between our two institutions, and I can't wait to develop effective working relations

with the deputies during this transitional period for APSA . . . I hope that my conversation with him during this transitional period will not be a cause of difficulty for you, Cardinal, or for APSA. I am preparing a note with APSA on the provision of banknotes in US dollars, and I would be happy to know to whom you would prefer that I address it at APSA.

In the next few months Mennini's activities would continue to be monitored discreetly. He still had important posts with the APSA real estate agents in Europe, which led de Franssu, in a letter of January 22, 2014, to ask Cardinal Calcagno to quickly have Mennini removed from the various boards of the companies associated with APSA, "considering the risks to our reputation we believe that this matter has to be addressed with a certain sense of urgency."[3]

Sample Audits: 94 Million in Off-the-Books Accounts

The Commission continued to comb through the books of the administrative bodies of the Holy See. The international banking community and the institutional oversight bodies, starting with Moneyval (the Council of Europe's Committee of Experts on Anti-Money Laundering Measures), had always viewed Vatican banking with a certain skepticism. In its first mutual evaluation report of the Holy See in July 2012, Moneyval had already identified various gaps in the financial statements. The Vatican had long resisted the anti-money-laundering regulations adopted in modern countries. The proponents of greater transparency at the Vatican tended to be punished rather than rewarded, like Monsignor Viganò, who was banished to Washington, and former IOR President Ettore Gotti Tedeschi, who was ousted from the bank on May 24, 2012 after being subjected to a smear campaign.

During the first year of Francis's papacy, Vatican bookkeeping was found noncompliant with common modern and transparent accounting standards. When COSEA started to sift through the accounts, the situation the examiners found was even worse than they had expected. According to a document in my possession submitted to the cardinals in February 2014, "There are significant amounts of money, properties and other assets that are not recorded in the annual financial reports of the Holy See."[4] In other words, "there is an unidentified amount of money in the bank accounts that is not recorded."

This was a denunciation of a system that had been in place since the times of Marcinkus and the IOR scandals. During critical moments it was kept quiet. To prevent reforms, it came out again forcefully as soon as the crisis was over. Large sums of money were being held in bank accounts listed to nonexistent charitable foundations. Hidden assets were kept off the books. Securities were not included in the normal bookkeeping so that they could be used for obscure purposes. The international auditors had repeatedly expressed their alarm, reporting the existence of "slush funds," enabled by a kind of double-entry bookkeeping practiced by some departments. But the Pope did not ignore the reports, and he requested further exploration and verification. The size and the extent of the problem becomes even more disturbing when we read the confidential internal documents:

> An analysis of the four sample entities reveals an amount of at least 94 million that is not recorded in the annual financial statements of the Holy See as of December 31, 2012. With 43 million to the Congregation for Asian Churches, 37 to the Nunciatures, 13 to Propaganda Fide and 1 to the Congregation for Saints.[5] This is caused by the lack of preventive oversight whereby the various congregations and councils . . . have no information about how much they are allowed to spend or the type of expenditures they are allowed to make. It is estimated that considerable assets are managed by the Secretariat of State that do not appear in any financial statements, and that have not been examined by outside auditors. [By the same token] no

transparency exists on the management of the residuals of the Peter's Pence.

The Risks of Those Ten Billion in Investments

Francis wanted to know more about the management of the immense sums of money held in the vaults, derived from revenue, offerings, and the Peter's Pence. Were these assets being used to generate income? Where and according to what criteria? Investments represent one of the largest sources of earnings for Vatican accounts: they guarantee interests that can help pay the high expenses of the Curia and facilitate the evangelical action. But the investments were also exposed to extremely high risks that were being uncovered in many departments. Starting with APSA:

> Various Vatican institutions manage assets that belong to institutions of the Holy See, for a value of four billion euros, and assets held by third parties, for another six billion, for a total of ten billion euros. Of these, nine are invested in stocks and one in real estate. Major gaps have been identified in governance, in the process of investment and distribution of the same. One example is from the diversification of the financial portfolio of APSA for 1.1 billion euros starting in September 2013. The investments of 60% of the APSA clients are concentrated on four or fewer stocks. Of 60 APSA clients, with a current portfolio of 1.1 billion, 35 are exposed to an extremely high risk in their portfolios, a risk of loss of value due to the lack of diversification.
>
> Another specific example is the concentration of APSA Certificates of Deposit (CDs) at issuing banks. Of 255 million invested, 80% is invested at [a single credit institute], Banca Prossima, creating high exposure to financial risk. APSA is a hybrid entity that conducts too many functions: from the management of holdings to pay service similar to those of a commercial bank, to the emergency cash

procurement, to the providing of support services (human resources, information technology, procurement) to other entities of the Holy See.

In the event of a sharp downturn in the market, it was incredibly risky to concentrate as much as 80 percent of investments in a single credit institution or on just a few stocks. There is no explanation in the documents I have seen as to why the prelates of the Curia chose Banca Prossima, but this choice certainly placed the client—in this case the Vatican—in a high-risk situation. At APSA, the inspection by the Promontory Financial Group also found 92 dysfunctions connected to various "typologies of risk." Here are the most significant:

1. Reputation: some bank accounts identified with suspicious activities [were] handed over to AIF [the internal audit organ];
2. Loss of income: weak procedures for the management of real estate holdings, insufficient performance by the stocks;
3. Holdings management: the Investment Committee is ineffective;
4. Operative level: use of paper orders. Not addressing the risks identified could lead to potential major financial losses for the Holy See, the inability to spot suspicious transactions and to continue to procure liquidity at the Holy See.

Faced with this situation, Francis's revolution stepped up its pace, moving toward precise goals and following specific strategies: to prevent scandals and an uproar, the cardinals of the old guard were not fired but effectively "put into receivership," like Versaldi at the Prefecture, with the monitoring oversight of the COSEA coordinator, Vallejo Balda, or Calcagno at APSA, in a kind of protective quarantine.

In the meantime, Francis was preparing his next revolution. The whole economic structure of the Holy See was being redesigned, cutting the Secretariat of State in half to reduce its enormous power. Cardinal Parolin and his deputy, Giovanni Angelo Becciu, would continue to manage diplomatic activities and internal affairs. But on financial matters, Francis studied the rules and regulations to create a new body that would effectively "void" the power centers that he had not been able to destabilize.

In February 2014, the Pope issued a *motu proprio* (a decree of his own initiative), ordering "a new coordination for economic and administrative affairs," a kind of Vatican superministry for the Economy. The organization would be divided into two parts: a Secretariat for the Economy, led by Cardinal George Pell, and a Council for the Economy, consisting of eight cardinals and seven laypeople, of various nationalities and with financial expertise and recognized professionalism, to which a General Auditor was added, appointed directly by the Holy Father. The new auditor would act as a watchdog over the powers that be. The message was delivered by the Holy Father's spokesman, Federico Lombardi, in the calm and collected tone of official communiqués: "The Prefecture for Economic Affairs, currently led by Cardinal Giuseppe Versaldi, will work closely with the auditor."

The normal functions of APSA would also be downsized: all of the activity pertaining to real estate management and personnel would become the competence of a new body. In the next chapters I will describe this revolutionary reform, which was decided, "pursuant to the recommendations of the COSEA Commission," according to the official press release. The Pope's agenda would continue to be unrelenting and intolerant of delays.

Other problems and critical areas would arrive from a new source, the Governorate, the body that manages all the commercial activities (from the museums to the shops), procurement (from energy to the telephones), construction projects, and contracts. A torrent of money is involved there, too. But Francis would not retreat. With his loyalists he moved inside and outside the walls to seek new allies and break with the past once and for all.

5

The Sins and Vices of the Curia

The Pontifical Commission ran into another problem almost immediately: it had cast its net too wide. There were too many financial transactions to analyze, too many million-euro contracts to inspect. It would be impossible to complete the audit in a few short months and provide Pope Francis with the prompt, specific, and effective indications he would need to initiate his reforms.

The auditors were in a race against the clock and also against the odds, if past experience was any indication: in the last decades of the twentieth century, every previous attempt at reform had failed. The Curia is like a soft belly, absorbing and normalizing any attempt at change. Inertia is its default mode. "Popes may change, but we remain," was a favorite saying of the cardinals who, while feigning an openness to change, would stop at nothing to delay or even derail the reform. But Francis remained firm in his response: "A cardinal enters the Church of Rome, not a royal court. May all of us avoid habits and ways of acting typical of a court: intrigue, gossip, favoritism and partiality."[1]

In late 2013 COSEA found itself being stonewalled by the Governorate. Neither the President of the Governorate, Cardinal Giuseppe Bertello, nor the Secretary General, Monsignor Giuseppe Sacco, had satisfied COSEA's preliminary request for documentation. In a letter of July 31, 2013, this is how they responded to the letter from the head of the Prefecture, Cardinal Versaldi:

> Most Reverend Eminence,
>
> . . . I hasten to inform you that for the exercise of its institutional purposes, the Governorate has for the current year issued 18,850 orders for the procurement of goods and/or services (some in fulfillment of existing contracts). The orders made in previous years and that, to date, have not yet been fully processed, amount to 4,649, for a total of 23,499 documents (60% of which concern the purchase of goods for resale). No documentation has been produced for these operations and indications in this regard are awaited.

Francis was so troubled by what he was hearing that he demanded more detailed information. It is the job of Monsignor Alfred Xuereb, his personal secretary, to shield the Holy Father from attempts at sabotage. Xuereb assessed the situation carefully, seeking the advice of others, in particular Monsignor Paolo Nicolini, the head of the Vatican museums. Nicolini represented the institutional memory of past reform initiatives, and he gave Xuereb a detailed account of the wasteful and faulty renewal processes that had taken place first under John Paul II and then under Benedict. Time and again, good ideas and high hopes had met the same bitter end: frustration and zero results.

At Xuereb's request, Nicolini prepared a three-page document in January 2014 with the title "A Bit of History." His informal report mentioned in particular a project to standardize administrative procedures from 1999, during the papacy of John Paul II. The new system was obsolete and lacking in transparency.* In a three-year period, the Cap Gemini Ernst & Young corporation was paid an astronomical fee: ten billion in old Italian liras (the equivalent of 5.6 million euros) for its consultancy on the Vatican accounting system. Although the initiative was needed, it was far too expensive and it did not solve the problems. In his report Nicolini described both the enthusiasm and the disappointments of that period:

> It was a moment of great expense but also of great reflection for a structure that from an administrative and managerial point of view was approaching the threshold of the twenty-first century unprepared, outdated, and unable to provide responses in terms not only of efficiency but also and especially of justice and transparency.

Other more ambitious modernization projects would soon follow. In April 2008, during the papacy of Benedict XVI, Tarcisio Bertone initiated Project One (P1), which is still active today. The objective was to build a single digital platform for financial and administrative data: a system, in other words, that would provide one standardized accounting and management system for all the Vatican departments. Thanks to Project One, for example, the ticket office of the Vatican museums is completely online today.

But the system was already outdated at the start, and risked turning into a significant but idle investment.[2] It failed to link the various dicasteries of the Holy See, from the Prefecture to APSA, the IOR, and the Secretariat of State. The goal of this exorbitantly expensive computer system was to provide a comprehensive picture of the administration of the Holy See, but not everyone was interested in a comprehensive vision, and there were those who sought to obstruct

---

* The end result of every previous attempt at change had been sky-high professional fees and instances of monsignors being discredited for their efforts to clean up shop, as happened, for example, to Monsignor Carlo Maria Viganò, former Secretary of the Governorate.

it, as the COSEA Commission found when it took up the situation of the Governorate.

The Governorate is the executive authority of the Vatican State. An organization with 1,900 employees, "it oversees general accounting procedures, the keeping of account books, the management of the State treasury and the preparation of budgets and financial statements, as well as audits," according to the Vatican website. The Governorate manages and coordinates all the activities involved in the running of the State, including commercial and cultural activities, building maintenance, contracts, motor vehicles, and procurement of energy and telephones, tobacco and office computers. The structures that provide the largest cash flow to the Vatican—through the revenue from the shops, museums, and other commercial activities—are also controlled by the Governorate. Very few people are aware of this vast commercial network within the Vatican, which also boasts a supermarket, two of the seven Vatican-owned gas stations, a clothing store, a perfume shop, a tobacconist, and a store that sells consumer electronics.[3]

Already in 2009–2010, a confidential analysis by McKinsey into the Governorate's books uncovered a disastrous situation. For various expense items, such as maintenance, the Vatican was paying as much as 200–400% more than the going market rates. The President of the Governorate, Cardinal Giovanni Lojolo, asked the banker Ettore Gotti Tedeschi to help him straighten out the finances. Gotti Tedeschi requested the financial statements of the discastery and received pro bono consultancy from McKinsey. The data he found was alarming—the Governorate was hemorrhaging money—and it was brought to the attention of Monsignor Viganò, whom Benedict XVI had appointed as part of his clean-up effort. Viganò got right down to work, but as soon as his investigation started to delve into the interests of companies and groups that were well-ensconced in the Vatican, he was subjected to a smear campaign in the media that convinced

Ratzinger to transfer him to Washington. And at the Governorate it was back to business as usual for years to come.

The Governorate manages substantial sums of money, and the auditors were hard pressed to examine its many transactions, contracts, and inventory in the short time available. For the sake of swift and effective action, they brought in strategic analysts of Ernst & Young Spain—they were the only firm with the requisite expertise in this area—despite previous problems with the Italian branch of the corporation. On November 12 and 13, 2013, a team of twelve strategic analysts held a marathon meeting in Madrid. A few days later they moved to Rome to get started with their audit of all the financial reports, accounts, and affairs at the financial heart of the Vatican State.[4] A fourth task force was thus formed to audit the Governorate, joining the commissions already established to examine the Vatican bank, the Peter's Pence, and the Congregation for the Causes of Saints.

The auditors began to comb through the accounting books, department by department and office by office. They started with stock counts, to try to understand whether the warehouses actually had the merchandise indicated in the balance sheets. The results of their inquest were unbelievable. According to the confidential report to the cardinals, "No items were found during the stocktaking."[5] There was no trace of many goods that appeared, instead, in the balance sheets. This alarming situation applied to almost all of the Vatican's commercial activities. The report went on to say that, "During the past two years, there have been 1.6 million euros in losses, on the basis of warehouse discrepancies."

What had happened to the merchandise? Had it been simply miscounted during the inventory? Or had someone removed items from the warehouses? If so, this might mean that there was a black market where the stolen goods were sold. An even more troubling theory was circulating at the Vatican. Some people wondered whether the goods had ever been in the warehouses in the first place. The possibility of a simple counting error was immediately excluded. The inventory was checked and double-checked, and the results always matched the findings of the initial analysis. In particular, among the "losses due to inventory differences," according to the COSEA report to which I had access, there was a gap of 700,000 euros at the supermarket, a 500,000 euros at the clothing warehouses, 300,000 at the pharmacy, and 100,000 at the tobacconist. Discrepancies were found at all the various commercial activities. A total of 1.6 million euros had mysteriously vanished into thin air. Either that or a fake inventory had been drawn up for goods that were never actually purchased.

The task force then widened its net to include the items sold at the many museum shops, such as gadgets, souvenirs, and books. Once again they found many, many discrepancies. According to their count, some ten thousand illustrated volumes were missing, and couldn't be found in the shops, the warehouse, or the offices. The books were for the most part guidebooks to the art on display at the Vatican museums and in St. Peter's basilica. The experts on the Commission wondered whether the books had been stolen by a dishonest employee or if their absence pointed to even more serious crimes—in particular, to massive financial fraud.

A Tax Haven

The concerns of the experts stemmed from unique features of the Holy See. To make purchases outside the Vatican, the Governorate issues a little-known "personal exemption from sales tax." This document allows Vatican citizens and employees to buy "goods and services" at steep discounts because they do not have to pay a Value Added Tax, the sales tax that exists in 63 countries of the world. But to make these duty-free purchases, the goods or services must be used "within the Vatican state or by Vatican residents."

This tax exemption can also lend itself to fraud. Some people might claim to be buying goods at wholesale prices for the Vatican (tax free) in order to sell them at retail prices outside the Vatican, thereby pocketing sums that normally go to the tax authorities. This might explain the missing ten thousand books, but it might also represent a much more widespread practice, as a simple example illustrates. A gentleman with a "personal exemption" buys twenty computers wholesale that he claims will be used in Vatican offices, and so he doesn't have to pay sales tax. Once he has purchased the items, rather than deliver them to the Vatican he turns around and sells them at full price in Italy or another European Union country, pocketing the 20 percent sales tax for himself, an act of fraud. There are suspicions that some individuals at the Vatican take further advantage, making these purchases only on paper.

The Pontifical Commission of Inquiry saw more than one danger here. "An individual could purchase the products"—according to the report to the cardinals—"and either use them outside the Vatican or even sell them in Italy without supervision, posing a significant risk to the reputation of the Holy See."[6] If the public were to discover this tax evasion one day, it would be extremely damaging to the Vatican's image, but not "financially" damaging, of course, as the consultants working for the Commission wrote.

The fact that the report did not point to specific cases was no cause for optimism. On the contrary, this manner of buying and selling was taking place at the Vatican "without oversight," as the Commission rightly noted. If there was no oversight, then it would be impossible to detect the illegal trafficking. And there were other suspicious dealings involving currency exchanges between Italy and the Vatican. In 2012, the Vatican registered 598 declarations of currency coming in and 1,782 declarations of currency going out, to Italy. During the same period, at the RomaUno customs office the parties involved presented only 13 declarations of incoming currency at the Vatican and 4 declarations for outgoing currency. These numbers warned of a massive tax evasion.

To continue down the road of no oversight could cause irreparable harm to the Vatican. The Commission indicated forcefully that the only "road to pursue"—according to the document in my possession—"is to improve the tax policies in order to minimize the risk related to the Vatican's tax haven status quo."[7] In other words, as long as the Vatican City remains duty-free, it will always be seen as a possible tax haven. As was observed by the deputy prosecutor of Rome, Nello Rossi—who has run various investigations involving the IOR—there is no Italian customs office and not even the blandest form of control over what is imported into the Vatican. The closest customs office is probably the one at Fiumicino airport.

The introduction of "appropriate oversight measures on the issuing of tax exemptions," was considered an urgent matter. The Commission had to ascertain who the beneficiaries were, what purchases were being made, and where the items were actually consumed or used. There was talk of a historic upheaval. For the first time in the history of the Holy See, the introduction of a system of taxation was contemplated. Reform of the sales tax had become an urgent matter, and it was imperative "to consider introducing a tax on commercial sales," a watershed development.

The Curia responded to the proposal with little enthusiasm, if not outright contempt. To initiate systematic controls over the tax-free status and introduce a sales tax at the Vatican shops would of course negatively impact the beneficiaries of these questionable earnings. Francis was now making new enemies inside the Apostolic Palaces who were working behind the scenes to impede the Commission's work and thwart its goals. For the moment, any thoughts on the matter were relegated to the back burner.

The "road map" indicated to the cardinals by the Commission was not followed. After I saw the documents and reconstructed the Commission's initiatives, I had to ask myself the inevitable question: will the Pope have the strength to create a financial police force in the

Vatican and to introduce a system of taxation on merchandise? Or is the Vatican destined to remain a kind of "offshore" state with no system of taxation?

The irregularities in the Vatican's commercial activities are many and obvious. The Holy See appears to be brimming with shopaholics. Bishops and cardinals seem to have an overweening passion for the latest televisions and electronic gadgets. The anomaly did not escape the notice of the RB Audit Italia experts, who had prepared an informal preliminary report on October 9, 2013. The numbers speak for themselves.

"It is odd," wrote the consultant Salvatore Colitta, "that in the consumer electronics sector there should be a sales volume of more than 4.8 million euros from a single supplier, and a local one, at that." Why was there such a high volume from a single supplier? It would be better to stipulate "agreements directly with the manufacturers," the report goes on to say, "which would allow more convenient purchasing conditions and consequently more competitive sales prices and better profit margins."

To make matters worse, it was also discovered that the Vatican stores, which offer merchandise at cut-rate prices, were filled with customers who were not always entitled to shop there. Customers are supposed to have a special "buyer's card" legally reserved for employees and inhabitants of the small state. The Vatican has 5,000 employees (many of them Italian citizens) and barely 836 inhabitants, which means that there should be about 6,000 buyer's cards altogether. But the number of active buyer's cards was actually much higher: 41,000 cards for as many customers, almost seven times the number of people who were entitled to them.

At the Vatican it was an open secret that almost none of the customers met the requirements, but no one was complaining. The customers purchased items at reduced prices, the shop employees had a steady sales volume, and the Governorate was reaping huge profits. The revenue for 2012 was 44.5 million euros: 15.3 million from the shops, 13.1 from fuel, 7.8 million from the sale of clothing, 4.8 million from electronics, and 3.5 million from the tobacconists. The analysts of Ernst & Young Spain found even more anomalies and petty favoritisms and listed them in a document that I was able to examine:

1. Supermarket: negative margin (revenue up by 9% but costs up by 17%); more than 17,00 products on a 900 m^2 sales floor (reference point is about 10,000 products per 1,000 m^2).
2. Fuel: 27,000 persons bought gas, and 550 of them exceeded the limit of 1,800 liters per year. 18% of sales registered to a "service card" (without specifying the cardholder's name).
3. Clothing and Electronics: more than 16,000 customers; more than 22,700 products.
4. Tobacco: more than 11,000 customers, 278 of whom exceeded the limit of 80 cartons/year; 14% of sales registered to a "service card" (without specifying the cardholder).
5. Pharmacy and Perfume Shop: 17% drop in revenue; 30% of sales stem from fragrances and skin-care products; 1,900 customers a day.

"Close the Vatican Shops"

The auditors questioned whether these commercial activities were truly consistent with the pastoral mission of the Church and, for example, if the sale of fragrances was at odds with the spirit of the Gospel. They submitted these questions for a commercial opinion and strategic guidelines to the analysts of Ernst & Young Spain, whose conclusions can be summarized in a very clear outline. The sale of fragrances, electronics, tobacco, over-the-counter medication, and supermarket items were described as "no fit" transactions that made no real contribution to the evangelical mission and represented, in fact, a risk to the reputation and the image of the Church.

COSEA shared this assessment with Francis, adding its own criticism of all the "commercial activities that are inconsistent with the public image of the Holy See and harm its mission: tobacco, fragrances, clothing, electronics, gas."[8] The Commissioners took a tough and unequivocal position, proposing that radical steps be taken:

> We have to examine the commercial and cultural activities to reduce the financial and reputational risk, and bring them into line with the mission of the Church . . . [and thus] cease all activities that damage the image of the Holy See.

The cigarette, electronics, fragrance, and clothing stores should be closed while the commercial businesses should be converted for the purpose of "improving all the activities that strengthen the mission of the Church: museums, philately [the collection and study of postage stamps], numismatics [the study or collection of coins, paper currency, and medals] and activities for pilgrims." The Pope and his trusted men believed strongly in a change of direction aimed at enhancing the museums, since they represented a huge source of income. Their argument found support in the figures provided by Ernst & Young:

> Vatican Museums: 6% increase in revenue, while costs have grown by 9%; 84% of income is generated from ticket sales, and the other 16% is from food services, souvenir and bookshops, and audio guides to the collections (outsourcing activities). The Museums department is currently the body within the Governorate that employs the most people (approximately 700) and generates the highest economic returns (an estimated total income of 105 million for 2013). In 2006 the museums took in approximately 62 million. Profits from 2006 to 2012 went from 33 to 54 million. In 2012 the museum's total costs were about 24 million (mostly due to personnel costs). There were

an estimated 5.5 million visitors in 2013: the number of visitors can fluctuate from 10,000 to 22–25,000 per day.

Regarding ticket sales:

> Tickets purchased online include a four euro service charge. In 2013 the service charge will generate approximately 10 million euros. In 2013 it is expected that online ticket sales will account for 70% of all tickets sold. Most of the revenue generated by the museums comes from ticket sales (approximately 90% of the total). The rest comes from the six food sales points (from 3.7 million in 2006 to 5.2 million in 2012). The outside company that handles food services gives 25.5% of its proceeds to the Vatican. According to the terms of the current contract, the outside company purchases the raw materials used for food services from the Vatican City.[9]

The first figure to come under consideration was the number of employees, approximately 700. The internal analysis found that a good turnover rate would optimize the output of the available human resources. The most viable idea would be to keep the museums open for the whole weekend, which would increase receipts by 30 percent.

But no one at the Apostolic Palaces seemed very receptive to these possibilities, although Ernst & Young's proposals had reached Francis's inner circle:

> The museums should be considered one of the pillars of the Vatican's economic development. [They could only grow] comparing the key performance indicators with the development of potential growth strategy proposals, including extending the hours every day and to certain days of the week (for example, staying open on Sunday), expanding the exhibition area, raising ticket prices, and exploiting the "brand" to increase the sale of merchandise.[10]

A Secret Unsigned Contract with Philip Morris

According to the statistics of the World Health Organization, tobacco smoke is the second-leading cause of death in the world and the leading cause of preventable death. Given the obvious health risks, COSEA considered the sale of tobacco the most negative commercial activity at the Vatican. To support or even simply tolerate smoking could not be condoned by Francis's pontificate. Selling cigarettes is the activity most alien to the Church's mission and the most threatening to its image and reputation in both theoretical and practical terms. This was made quite clear in the late afternoon of November 18, 2013, at a two-hour presentation on the Holy See's various commercial activities.

The presentation was given by two laymen of the Curia, Sabatino Napolitano of the Governorate's Department of Economic Services and Enrico Bartelucci of the General Accounting Office. The two men assured the auditors that "the Vatican City"—as can be read in the report written immediately after the meeting—"does not engage in promotional activities for tobacco." This meant there was no advertising, no promotion of smoking, and no push to sell cigarettes. Their policy was to safeguard health and to condemn those who profit from tobacco sales. Their actions, unfortunately, told a different story. The Vatican, like any other state, had a strong interest in selling as many packs of cigarettes as it can. There could be no clearer proof than a letter of February 2013, which the Commission would examine a few months later.

The letter was written during the last days of the pontificate of Benedict XVI. On February 11, 2013, the Pope announced his resignation, to the shock and dismay of the faithful throughout the world. In the same period, business proposals arrived in the Curia that were not quite consistent with the message of the Holy Gospel. On February 21, one of the Vatican's cigarette suppliers sent an email to the Governorate management on the subject of the "2013 Agreements."

The text listed all the benefits that would accrue by reaching a certain sales threshold:

> Dear Sirs,
>
> Pursuant to our telephone conversation, I wish to confirm the following:
>
> 1. Bonus target
>   - Annual sales volume of 1.7 million — 12 thousand euros
>   - Annual sales volume of 1.8 million — 14 thousand euros
> 2. Contribution for Introduction
>   We take note of your agreement to the introduction of the 2 Winstons (Winston One and Winston Silver) and confirm our special contribution of 4,000 euros (2,000 euros as a reference)
> 3. Danneman Cigarettes
>   We have no budget available, but since we believe this product could be interesting to you, we are ready to provide you with a contribution of 1,000 euros to introduce it.
>
> At your disposal for any further information you may require,
> Paolucci & C. International, SpA[11]

In their reply the only point that the Governorate managers objected to was the clause regarding Danneman cigarettes, which was immediately rejected. Napolitano wrote, "Not possible. OK only under the same conditions."

I have no way of knowing if and according to what terms the proposal was accepted. But I do know that there were negotiations with the titans of the tobacco industry to receive a bigger cut of the profits a few weeks later, in March, in the midst of the Conclave. The cardinals had arrived from all over the world to elect the new Pontiff. On the evening of March 13, on the fifth ballot, a majority of cardinals voted for Jorge Mario Bergoglio. In the meantime, the Vatican's commercial activities continued unabated. Business is business. On that same date, a document arrived on the letterhead of Philip Morris, the powerful tobacco holding company. It appears to be a commercial contract valid for one year, indicating parties, terms, and fees. The letter's contents are jaw-dropping:

> The Governorate agrees to conduct merchandising activity on behalf of Philip Morris International (PMI) brand cigarettes. For the conduct of these services, Philip Morris International Services Ltd. Rome branch will pay the Governorate a fee in accordance with the terms and conditions of the present agreement. The Governorate will provide the following information on a monthly basis:
>
> - The volume of purchases (COT) for each brand at the Duty Free Shop of the Vatican State.
> - Competitive promotional campaigns under way and/or already conducted, product launches and initiatives relative to the retail sales price.
> - Information received from the Governorate will be kept confidential and reserved solely for internal use, except when Philip Morris Rome has a different need to divulge said information . . .
>
> For the provision of these services, PMIS-Rome will pay the Governorate a fee of 12,500 euros . . . The invoice should be sent to the PMI Service Center Europe Sp Z.o.o at Al.Jana Pawla II 196 Krakow, Poland. The payment will be credited to the bank account in Germany held by the Governorate.

The contract is unsigned and should be considered a draft for an agreement that would become more nuanced. In the accounting analyses being conducted by Francis's men, however, it could have been worse. Unsigned agreements were examined to understand whether approval was pending. Incredible, but true.

There was more. Contracts were also found with sums indicated that were reduced by half in an addendum bearing either the same date or the date of the next day. This meant that if a supervisor asked to review a contract with a friendly company, he would see the official version without the amendments that had magically reduced the amount that was to be paid to the Holy See. This practice of outright deception occurred repeatedly in leases. The contracts would indicate one amount while in the files an addendum would cut the amount in half.

These two documents were not submitted anonymously to the COSEA commissioners. The man who believed that the Pontifical Commission needed to evaluate the email with the sales incentives was Francesco Bassetti, a layman who had worked at the Vatican since 1999 as an account auditor. He had the courage to bring these seemingly inexplicable papers to his superiors.

"Do not obstruct the mission of Francis"

Under the pontificate of Francis, the atmosphere had definitely changed: the draft contracts with the powerful multinational tobacco corporations were carefully evaluated, where in the past they had looked the other way. As we have seen, however, the Pope's will would not always prevail in the Apostolic Palaces. Indeed, that would rarely be the case. As discussed earlier, John Paul I, the so-called Pope of Change, had wanted to reform a Curia that had been infiltrated by a group of senior prelates with ties to the Freemasons. He died mysteriously after only thirty-three days of his pontificate. While Pope John Paul II was deeply committed to fighting Communist regimes, he didn't seem to realize that the IOR was involved in money laundering. When Benedict XVI was confronted by the strife within the Curia, corruption, and the evangelical problems of the Church in the world, he made the historic decision to hand over the helm of St. Peter's Bark to a new leader.

Today, almost three years since the beginning of Francis's pontificate, his reform of the Governorate has still not taken effect. The shops alien to the Church's mission are still open, churning out profits and serving thousands of customers who can make purchases there by exhibiting a buyer's card to which they are not entitled. The museums have not extended their hours, ignoring the proposals of Ernst & Young. They remain closed on Sundays, except for the last Sunday of the month, when admission is free from 9 to 12:30, and the doors close at 2:00 P.M.[12]

At the November 17, 2013, meeting in the Palace of the Governorate, clear guidelines had been given for the reform, based on the instructions of the Holy Father. On one side of the table were the analysts of Ernst & Young with Andrées Gomes, senior manager of EY Spain; on the other, the commissioners, from the coordinator, Monsignor Vallejo Balda, to Enrique Llano and Filippo Sciorilli. Vallejo Balda was very clear that the reform of the Governorate had to follow four cardinal points:

1. Independence of the Pope (in the sense of freedom of action and a means for performing his work, not as an end in itself).
2. Integrate the activity of the Governorate into the mission of His Holiness and make it consistent with the mission of the Universal Church.
3. Structure and associated risks (economic and reputational).
4. Sustainability / economic contribution.

As my reconstruction of the events illustrates, there has still not been any movement on these four strategic principles requested by Francis and outlined by Ernst & Young.

The situation is complicated, even Kafkaesque. One man who knew a thing or two about it was a member of the new guard, Cardinal George Pell, who would soon be chosen by Francis as the Prefect of the

Secretariat of the Economy. Pell started to comb through the account books. He demanded transparency and shared Francis's policy for a Church without privileges and on the side of the poor and needy.

On March 26, 2014, the new Secretary of the Governorate, Father Fernando Vergez Alzaga, decided to address to Pell his heartfelt congratulation on his becoming the Minister Plenipotentiary of the Pontiff's finances. He wrote a letter that deserves to be read in its entirety, from the first to the last illuminating word:

> My reverend Eminence:
>
> I ask first of all you please accept my warmest congratulations on your appointment as Prefect of the Secretariat of the Economy. At the same time, I am pleased to inform your Eminence that the following arrangements have been made on behalf of the most Eminent Cardinals:
>
> - The purchase of food, in amounts compatible with family needs, at the Annona commissary or the Community Warehouse at a 15% discount.
> - A 20% discount off the list price limited to a total of 200 packs of cigarettes per month.
> - A 20% discount off the list price for clothing.
> - A 400 liter a month supply of fuel at special prices subdivided as follows:
>   a) Voucher for 100 liters.
>   b) Special price vouchers (15% discount off the going price) for 300 liters.
>   - To be requested with cardinal vouchers (white) to be used at the internal facilities of the Holy See.
>   - and/or vouchers for use outside of Rome at gas stations that do not belong to the AGIP-Eni group, exclusively for motor vehicles with Vatican City and Diplomatic license

> plates. To get these arrangements under way, it would be useful for a member of your staff to contact the fuel office of the Economic Services Department of the Governorate.

While remaining at your disposal for any further clarification you may require, I avail myself willingly of this opportunity to renew the assurances of my humble regard for Your Most Reverend Eminence.

Your devoted servant, Fernando Vergez Alzaga

Perks and preferential treatment were still being offered under Francis and promised to the Curia nomenclature and even the new Pope's trusted men. The letter left a bitter taste with Cardinal Pell, who filed it away. The following October someone from inside the Apostolic Palaces leaked it to a reporter who covers the Vatican for the newspaper *la Repubblica*, Marco Ansaldo. The journalist remarks that he has almost never seen a cardinal smoking. So who are all those cigarette cartons going to? In his article Ansaldo does not exclude the possibility that they are resold by someone who is pocketing the difference between the discount and the resale price: "There are even nasty rumors that the person who receives the cartons turns around and sells them on eBay."

6

The Immense Real Estate Holdings of the Vatican

The Roman Catholic Church has immense real estate holdings, ones that are internationally unique. No one knows their true extent and value, however—not even the Curia. Some data is registered in its financial statements, but the COSEA Commission soon discovered that those statements were unreliable. APSA's holdings—ranging from commercial and residential properties to institutional buildings—turned out to be worth seven times the amount recorded in the account books. The market value of APSA is 2.7 billion euros, a figure that the Commission was able to document accurately the first time that they investigated the holdings.

The rentals in question were managed with both carelessness and cunning. This practice applied not only to apartments granted to Vatican higher-ups—the princely residences provided free of charge to some cardinals, described in Chapter 3—but also to homes leased to many outside collaborators or friends. I had exclusive access to all of APSA's rental records. Of about five thousand properties, mostly in the center of Rome and in the Vatican City, the monthly rent is less than 1,000 euros. Hundreds of documents were classified as A0 (*Affitto* 0), which stands for "zero rent." Other tenants pay less than 100 euros per year: that's right, per year. One particularly lucky tenant—whose apartment is located in the heart of Rome—pays 20 euros a year. In the Curia, the home is a status symbol, the proof of how much its inhabitant counts.

Favoritism and opportunism are the order of business for APSA. The Commission discovered that one of Italy's largest banks, Banca Intesa, had paid a security deposit of only 1,864 euros for an office it was renting from the Vatican. These vulgar, paradoxical circumstances are particularly intolerable by comparison to the situations of ordinary citizens. I was able to document this through my access to the papers reserved for Francis's trusted men.

A little background will help the reader to understand the climate and the characters that Francis and his men were confronting. One example of a grasp for power is illustrated in this story focusing on Monsignor Giuseppe Sciacca. Born in 1955 in Aci Catena, Sicily, a small municipality in the Province of Catania, His Eminence apparently had a weakness for comfortable and—above all—spacious living. He loved to throw cocktail parties and dinners for friends, but he apparently considered his beautiful apartment in the Palazzo San Carlo too modest (for which he paid no rent, of course).

On September 3, 2011, Sciacca was appointed Secretary General of the Governorate. Benedict XVI's loyal friend, Tarcisio Bertone, had convinced him to entrust the Monsignor with the delicate role of number two man at the Governorate, taking the place of Monsignor Carlo Maria Viganò. As I related in *His Holiness*, Viganò had attempted to straighten out the finances of the Governorate, denouncing the inflated contracts, excessive spending, and even episodes of outright theft. Rather than be rewarded for his efforts, he was exiled to Washington as Apostolic Nuncio, after a vigorous mano a mano with Bertone. He had encroached on too many interests, making enemies along the way, and the Curia doesn't forgive.[1]

Viganò had lost his position after a vigorous standoff with Secretary of State Bertone. Sciacca, on the other hand, posed no threat to the status quo. He would serve under the President of the Governorate, Cardinal Giuseppe Bertello, another Italian and a Bertone loyalist, like most of the heads of the various dicasteries that control the Church's finances. Bertone's influence in the Curia was at its peak in the fall of 2011. He had managed to create a power block by putting Italian cardinals and bishops that he trusted into the most strategic positions: a block that Francis inherited from Ratzinger, and with which he engaged immediately in a pitched war.

Less than one year into his prestigious appointment, Monsignor Sciacca was itching to do something about his "modest" home. He wanted another apartment, more spacious and accommodating, but he didn't know how to go about getting it. The only solution was to wait for the right opportunity, and the right opportunity came knocking one fateful morning. All he needed was a little cynicism and cunning and the deal would be done. With the speed of a jackal, the Monsignor devised a plan that was so brazen that it seems unbelievable even today.

Sciacca's target was his neighbor, an elderly mild-mannered priest in declining health who lived with a nun and who had stopped going out some time ago. He was no longer seen taking walks around the Vatican. The Monsignor inquired after him and learned that in recent months the poor priest had been under constant care and medical supervision. At the moment, he was in the hospital receiving emergency specialized care. Rumors about his health started to spread: many wrote him off as dying while others doubted he would ever return to his apartment.

The time had come to act. Sciacca called in his trusted construction company, pointed to the dividing wall between the two apartments, and asked them to knock it down to connect the two units. He needed more valuable square footage to make his abode more comfortable. Although the workers were surprised at the request, in a few hours the job was done and a passage had been built into the neighboring apartment. A new room, to be used as a parlor, appeared magically in the Monsignor's residence, while the apartment of the ailing priest, unbeknownst to him, was downsized.

Sciacca did not stop there. He also "incorporated" the furniture of the appropriated room, which had come from the "Floreria," the Governorate office that also handles the furniture of senior prelates. The priest's personal belongings were placed in cardboard boxes and left in the hallway, as if he were preparing to move. Finally, the door from the newly conquered room to the rest of the priest's apartment was walled up.

The story was greeted by shock, hilarity, and discontent within the Curia—especially when the elderly priest, who had no intention of moving on to greener pastures, returned home. Imagine his astonishment! As soon as he opened the door he realized something was wrong: his apartment had been modified, and was missing one room, but he was too old to fight back and seek justice.

Not so his brave and trustworthy housemate, the nun, who conferred with some other nuns, asking their advice. While they invited her to use caution, she found the injustice intolerable and decided to go all the way to the top and address the Pope himself. She wrote a passionate letter to Benedict XVI telling him the story and pleading for justice and mercy. But these were the last months of his papacy, and a few weeks later the situation changed irreversibly: the elderly priest died, Ratzinger resigned, and Francis became the new Pontiff. The tide was turning.

Only five months into Francis's papacy, he demoted Monsignor Sciacca, sending him notice of his transfer to a new assignment. In a matter of a few days he was to leave his office at the Governorate and assume a new post. Rather than wait for a coveted spot to open up on the Holy See's roster of senior positions, a new position was tailor-made for Sciacca. On August 24, 2013, he was appointed as the Adjunct Secretary of the Supreme Tribunal of the Apostolic Signatura. This was the Tribunal that handles legal and administrative cases, and its Prefect was American Cardinal Raymond Leo Burke, who was not exactly in Francis's good graces. Burke and Bergoglio had sharp theological differences. The Wisconsin prelate, born in 1948, continued to celebrate the Tridentine Mass despite the liturgical reforms almost sixty years earlier through the Second Vatican Council. His days were also numbered: in November he, too, was removed from office as part of the ongoing "soft revolution" of Francis, which would continue throughout 2014.

Getting back to the matter of the enlarged apartment, the Monsignor was called upon to quickly evacuate the premises after losing his post at the Governorate, and the apartment was assigned to another prelate. Stories such as these went public for the first time, traveling all the way to Casa Santa Marta and Francis, who was left speechless. The incidents also revived old stories about misdeeds that had never been addressed with the necessary firmness. Cardinal Santo Abril y Castelló related to Francis and the priests and monsignors closest to him problems he had discovered upon his appointment as archpriest of the Santa Maria Maggiore. The treasurer of the Basilica, the Polish Monsignor Bronisław Morawiec, was convicted of embezzlement and misappropriation of Church funds and sentenced to three years imprisonment for withdrawing large sums from the rich Basilica's account at the IOR. To understand what and how much had been misappropriated, the new archpriest wrote up an inventory of sorts.

One of the missing items was a set of keys to an apartment in the adjacent building, one which houses priests and ecclesiastics. The front door of the apartment was locked and the entrance was clean and neat. Officially, the home did not appear to be rented, and it was ready for a new tenant when necessary. At least, this was the situation on paper—but as soon as the inspectors gained access, they were shocked to find that the apartment had been inhabited for quite some time. The priest in the apartment downstairs had cut a hole in the ceiling to connect the two units with a spiral staircase, which he bought at his own expense. This allowed him to double the square footage of his living space, convinced that no one would ever notice. Once the illegal expansion was discovered, his superiors were immediately notified.

Cut-Rate Deals on Real Estate

These two cases are not isolated. The immense real estate holdings of the Vatican are a challenge to Francis's program and another thorn in the side of his Pontificate. The recent history of the Vatican's management of its real estate has not exactly been happy. Under both John Paul II and Benedict XVI, the convents, buildings, and churches were administered without a common strategy, and management was characterized by waste, nepotism, and outright scandals. But these problems were never addressed, and passed along from pope to pope for decades. The status quo prevailed, enabling the more powerful or more astute to take advantage of the general state of neglect.

Fundamental information was missing from the records, starting with the most important: the value of the real estate holdings, which no one knew. There was no comprehensive assessment of properties of all of the Vatican's administrative bodies or of the Church's entities and religious orders in the world, such as a general land registry that would provide a standardized list of all of the properties. The dicasteries' data banks did have assessments, but their listings and descriptions were incomplete. Not all of the properties were listed, and the units that were listed did not always include the basic financials. This created the potential for many more stories like that of Monsignor Sciacca.

I am not speaking of religious orders with properties in remote corners of Africa but rather about entities within the Holy See. I was able to see the internal database of APSA, which administers 5,050 assets in apartments, offices, stores, and land in the City of Rome. It's a highly confidential database that I managed to access and make public. Until

2014 APSA's financial statements were not even published. In combing through the data, a number of peculiarities crop up. First, no one within the Vatican walls has apparently updated photos of the assets, nor are they organized in any way. Even the square footage is often missing: for over 50 percent of the units—2,685 to be exact—there is no indication of the size of the apartment, shop, or office, making it impossible to assess the appropriateness of the rent. In many other cases the exact location within a building is missing or there is no indication of the rental fees. Taken as a whole, these factors prevent income optimization and the adoption of effective strategies when properties are being bought or sold.

The fact that the Vatican's real estate holdings outside the Holy See are subject to taxation, thereby greatly reducing its rental income, should not be underestimated. APSA President Cardinal Domenico Calcagno, a Bertone loyalist, addressed this uncomfortable issue in his July 30, 2013, letter to Zahra:

> It appears that a number of assets have not been recorded in the APSA patrimony, despite their belonging to various entities in the Roman Curia (as a by no means exhaustive example, there is real estate held by the Apostolic Camera, the College of Cardinals . . .), while, on the opposite side, there are properties [that appear] to be formally owned by the Holy See but have for some time been fully possessed and used, often without any form of contractual agreement, by parishes and religious institutions . . . As things currently stand, delicate issues relating to both the financial profile and more in general to the responsibilities stemming from ownership of these assets remain unsettled. . . . Although these assets are considered tax exempt because they are "formally" declared to be related to "needs of worship," they are instead used for other purposes (even commercial) without any possible inspection or assessment by the current administration, which remains ignorant of the way the asset is actually used. The tax issue is a very serious one because exemption is strictly limited to use of

these properties "for needs of worship," while no exemption is granted for other uses, exposing APSA to the risk of a tax audit.

Another troublesome issue: the assets inevitably age and thus require renovations that can significantly drive up the costs of upkeep. In the 2014 fiscal year, APSA set aside 4.5 million euros for planned extraordinary maintenance and another 4.7 million for work on properties used for institutional purposes, such as the Palace of the Holy Office. In other words, a single administrative body earmarked at least 9.2 million euros for maintenance.

When the Governorate decides to do work on a building, it does not always hold the competitive bidding processes required in most European Union countries. The companies are often chosen by "direct call," through which a private bid is tendered, leaving ample room for discretion. This means there is no effort to obtain the best estimate, and no way to keep costs under control.

Francis criticized this very practice in his remarks to the cardinals at the famous July 2013 meeting. The problem reappeared a few months later, during COSEA's audit of the rental income. One issue was extraordinary maintenance of APSA property, outfitted for institutional use and included in the 2014 budget. There was no price tag on much of the planned work, especially jobs listed under "miscellaneous building, installing, outfitting and refurbishing work required to meet fire safety standards."

Two cases were scrutinized: the historic San Calisto Palace and the Palace of the Chancellery, a glorious Renaissance building that houses the Holy See's three tribunals: the Apostolic Penitentiary, the Apostolic Segnatura, and the Roman Rota. "Without a final project"—according to the internal documentation—"a provisional sum of 254,257 euros was earmarked for each job."

Cardinals, bishops, and bureaucrats do care very much about the decorum of their apartments. They want everything to work perfectly; for the doors, windows, faucets, and radiators to be efficient, and the walls to receive a fresh coat of paint on a regular basis. APSA never forgets to earmark funds "for the appointment of quarters reserved for the Superiors of the Roman Curia," not unlike other absolute monarchies in the world. As much as 700,000 euros in cash is kept ready, so that when a cardinal decides he needs to redo his home, there will be no delays and the work can be done promptly. Sometimes the tenants have renovations done at their own expense, for which they are reimbursed by the Holy See. To cover these out-of-pocket expenses, the Vatican administration earmarks 500,000 euros "to reimburse tenants for expenses incurred in the restructuring of their apartments."

APSA was not the only administrative body guilty of such practices. The inspection by RB Audit turned up other instances of peculiar restructuring expenses. The ordinary and extraordinary maintenance expenses of the Congregation for the Evangelization of Peoples, formerly known as Propaganda Fide, raised more than a few questions:[2]

> The Congregation does not have an actual roster of suppliers, i.e., a list of companies based on their meeting economical, organizational and technical requirements, which can be invited to participate in competitive bidding. The creation of a roster would be a valid tool for consulting the market divided up by service category. As matters currently stand, rather than have competitive bidding in the strict sense, the Congregation, on the basis of a specific project and specific technical requirements, approaches companies that meet the requirements, asking them to present their bid for a supply or service contract . . . It would be advisable for the Congregation to supervise more closely the assignment of contracts, by proposing, for example, a new method of awarding contracts with high price tags and for particularly complex projects.

One Hundred Square Meters for 20.67 Euros a Year

The sales and rental market was another delicate issue. In the past twenty years the Curia and religious entities have been periodically embroiled in scandals involving the sale to friends or friends of friends of property whose value had been drastically understated. Headlines were made by real estate property sold at cut-rate prices: from Propaganda Fide to the assets of the IOR, whose former President, Angelo Caloia, was accused by the Vatican judicial authorities of embezzlement; the homes purchased by Monsignor Scarano; and the former monasteries converted into clinics and luxury hotels. Caloia's trial is ongoing. The Promontory officials also sifted through APSA's sales records from the past fifteen years. Relatively few properties had been sold, only 6 percent of the total assets: "228 units were sold"—according to the special confidential—"and 79 were donated. These included 20 apartments, 23 churches, refectories and residences were gifted, while 119 homes were sold."

The rental market was equally troubling. Church-owned apartments were almost never rented at market prices. The price reductions were astonishing—ranging from 30 to 100 percent less than average market rates. This meant a loss of tens of millions of euros in income, and in extreme cases the properties came to represent a liability, considering the huge gap between rental income and extraordinary maintenance expenses.

The Promontory and RB Audit consultants inspected APSA, Propaganda Fide, and the IOR to get a clear picture of the catastrophic general situation. They gave their report to the COSEA commissioners, who in turn forwarded it to Francis and his closest collaborators. The documents to which I had exclusive access for this book show numerous discrepancies and irregularities, as the Commission's report highlights:

> Various Vatican institutions manage assets belonging to the institutions of the Holy See (valued at approximately 4 billion) and assets on behalf of third parties (approximately 6 billion) for a total of 10 billion euros, of which 9 is in securities and 1 is in real estate . . . Many Vatican institutions thus own real estate assets for a comprehensive

> value of about 1 billion euros. This estimate, based on about 70% of the portfolio, has a higher market value, however.[3] With regard to the APSA assets (commercial, residential, and institutional units), the market value is estimated to be 7 times higher than that the amount entered into the balance sheets, for a total of 2.7 billion euros. With regard to Propaganda Fide, instead, the estimated market value is at least 5 times higher than the amount in the balance sheets, for a total of half a billion euros.
>
> The rental income of Propaganda Fide's property could be 50% higher if rents were raised to market rates for all external lessees. This fact regards only 219 commercial and residential units out of the 470 total. No information is available on the surface area of the remaining units. Moreover, former employees continue to receive an employee discount (about 60–70% below market rates) for as many as 8 years after they have stopped working for the Vatican. If we compare the actual rent per square meter of Propaganda Fide properties to market potential, the former would be 21 euros per square meter while the latter would be 31 euros per square meter, with an annual loss of 3.4 million euros. [According to the audit] of management [there is] a lack of oversight, efficiency and an adequate strategy for the use [of the properties].

APSA's rental properties in Rome are divided into three categories: by type of contract (new or renewed); contracting party (employee, retiree, or external); and zone. Depending on the zone, prices can range from 5 euros per square meter in Castel Gandolfo and Ladispoli to 9.88 euros for a penthouse in the center of Rome.[4] This means that a beautiful rooftop apartment in a historic palazzo facing Saint Peter's Square can cost as little as 1,000 euros a month—truly super-discounted prices. Not to mention that retirees receive an additional discount of 15 percent off the rent.

The discounts were inexplicable, however, with the so-called "external" tenants—private individuals or companies that are not employed by the Holy See. For each building, APSA has a chart indicating the rental fees to be charged. The maximum fee is 26 euros a square meter per month for a beautiful home on Via dei Coronari, in the city center, with breathtaking views of Rome. Here, too, prices are below market. In addition to being discounted, the amounts listed for rentals to external tenants rarely correspond to the actual payments made by the tenants. In 50 percent of cases, the rent collected was far lower than even the minimum amounts indicated in the charts, leading the task force consultants to ask a number of questions:

> Discrepancies between the rental fees paid and the fixed rates in the charts, a failure to adjust rents to changes in the "status" of the tenant, too many late payments and too much information missing from the documents. The systematic analysis of the data shows a frequent discrepancy between actual rent and the fixed rates both at the properties in the same price zone and within the same building.
>
> What appears particularly odd is that the rent indicated on the contracts for apartments leased to external applicants was lower than the minimum fee of reference in at least 259 cases out of 515 . . . Special mention should be made of the security deposit system to protect the solvency of the lessees. While there is virtually no risk for Vatican employees or retirees, the risks become concrete with the externals. In some cases the deposit was not commensurate to the value of the lease. I am referring in particular to the customer Banca Intesa, which for an annual lease of 163,369 euros, paid a security deposit of only 1,894 euros, the equivalent of 1.16% of a year's rent. The bank also seems to have a vague history of outstanding debts [as of October 9, 2013, the date of the RB report].

It is remarkable that the Vatican's external clients would include a bank, and that the bank's lease agreement was actually "facilitated," allowing it to pay a ridiculously low security deposit, hardly necessary considering the bank's size and influence. There was also a paradoxical note referring to the "vague outstanding debt situation" of one of Italy's largest banks.

The late payments piled up exponentially. The Propaganda Fide Congregation was owed some 3.9 million euros in overdue rent, more than one third of which (1.6 million) was from the first nine months of the year.[5] APSA, instead, had accumulated rental arrears of 2.9 million euros, a full 9 percent of total rental income.[6] To make matters worse, an odd new practice was added to the mix. Some tenants, without consulting the landlord, had taken the initiative to lower their own rent, sometimes by as much as 50 percent.

> Equally strange is the fact that approximately 18% of arrears consists of credits owed on expired leases . . . Credits owed by tenants with expired leases amounts to approximately 770,000 euros . . . Another issue is the self-applied discount, as a result of economic hardship, which was not formalized through a rider to the contract, and consequently the entering into the books of rental income that would never be collected and on which taxes had been paid . . . Emblematic of the practice is Borghi S.r.l., which for months had unilaterally reduced its rent, paying a monthly sum of 50,000 euros rather than the more than 93,000 established in the contract [with] arrears reaching 400,000 euros.

The investigation turned up even more outrageous stories, such as prestige addresses offered at zero rent for no apparent reason. The A0 (*Affitto 0*) or "zero-rent" properties were given not only to cardinals but also to laymen, bureaucrats, and private individuals. Properties were often given rent free as a form of compensation for individuals who deserved a higher salary than allowed by the Vatican pay scale because of their professionalism or educational background. But that was not always the case.

The hundreds of rent-free apartments were a coterie of preferential treatment, an expression of privilege at odds with the principles cherished by Francis. It was not clear why an asset that may have been purchased using the donations of the faithful should be granted free of charge, with an open-ended lease.

Many surprises were being uncovered in the contracts for the 5,050 properties that APSA leased in the city of Rome. The annual rent for 715 of the units (homes, offices, and stores)—almost 15 percent—was listed as "zero" in the income column. The apartments were often in luxury buildings in the heart of Rome, a few blocks away from St. Peter's, either in the Prati neighborhood or the historic center. Another 115 properties had ridiculously low rent, between 1.72 and 100 euros per month. One employee, whose initials are given as F.A., pays a monthly rent that is the equivalent of lunch at a pizzeria: for his 97-square-meter apartment on Via di Porta Cavalleggeri, he signed a lease on November 1, 2011, for a yearly rent of 20 euros and 67 cents. The contract does not indicate whether the utilities are included. This is almost half of what one of his neighbors pays: J.L. has a yearly rent that is almost twice as much, 51.65 euros a year, but for an apartment of 142.99 square meters.

Promontory reported these incidents of mismanagement in a confidential file that was delivered to the Holy See. The overall surface area of the APSA patrimony is 347,532 square meters, providing revenue of 23.4 million euros, but with the much higher market potential of 82.8 million. Increasing the rents to market level would raise the earnings rate from the current 1.14 to 4.02 percent. In other words, APSA derives very little income from its real estate holdings, also because 44 percent of its units, according to Promontory, appear to be unrented. If market rates were applied, the homes given to employees would generate income of 19.4 million euros rather than the current 6.2 million. The "institutional" buildings, which generate no revenue today, would guarantee another 30.4 million euros. The margin for the commercial units is smaller: it would increase from 14.6 to 17.5 million euros.

Backstabbing in the Curia Against the Friends of Francis

The story that will follow shines an important light on the infighting and envy that rules life in the Curia. The unwitting protagonist was Benedict XVI. Guzmán Carriquiry Lecour began his career at the Vatican under Wojtyła and Ratzinger and was later appointed to important posts by Bergoglio. Born in Montevideo, Uruguay, in 1944, he was a director of the Catholic Youth and University Student Movement, first in his native country and then for all of Latin America. A lawyer, he began his service to the Holy See in the 1970s. In 1991 Pope John Paul II appointed him Undersecretary of the Pontifical Council for the Laity, a post to which he was confirmed by Pope Benedict XVI, who in 2011 appointed him also as the Secretary of the Pontifical Commission for Latin America. Today he is considered perhaps the most influential and powerful layperson at the Vatican. He plays a strategic role that has only grown after the elevation of Francis to the throne of St. Peter. In fact, Guzmán is a personal friend of the Pope. The two men have known each other for years and have sincere affection and respect for each other. Married with four children, Guzmán lives in a rent-free home on Via delle Grazie in Rome, a 138-square-meter apartment. His home is not far from St. Peter's Square and St. Anne's Gate, the Vatican gateway closest to the Tower of Nicholas V, which houses the offices of the IOR.

This no-rent apartment was reported to the COSEA Commission by the President of APSA, Cardinal Calcagno, the scheming prelate and wily connoisseur of the Curia's secrets. On September 30, 2013, Calcagno forwarded to the chairman of the Commission his thoughts on the matter in the file Zahra.doc. The document was unsigned and written on plain paper. The first part appeared to be a report on APSA's difficulties in managing the properties of the Holy See. The document describes a chaotic situation bordering on anarchy, and throws in an occasional cutting remark:

> The administrative situation of the Holy See, at least from the point of view of the Administration of the Patrimony of the Apostolic Seat (APSA) is characterized by more than a few gray areas that, in recent decades, have grown steadily darker rather than dissipating.
>
> Notice must unfortunately be taken of the administrative presumption of certain Vatican realities that consider themselves somehow preempted from the need for managerial oversight and possible observations on the criteria for expenditures and expected compliance with the annual budget. The first situations to come to mind are those of the Prefecture of the Pontifical House and the Office of Liturgical Celebrations of the Supreme Pontiff: in both cases it is not uncommon to be told, however elegantly, that observations cannot be expressed on them since they are realities that must take care of the person of the Holy Father. Various Vatican offices do not look kindly upon any corrections or criticisms that APSA might present in the face of requests, or expenditures already undertaken, made in the spirit of luxury and with a lack of moderation.
>
> In addition to the increase in Entities and Foundations there has also been an expansion of the administrative office of the Secretariat of State, which rather than limit itself to the possibly delicate affairs that the Holy Father wishes to reserve for it, manages and administers a considerable sum of money, whose provenance and management criteria no one knows or can say, not even the Prefecture for the Economic Affairs of the Holy See.[7]

Near the end of Calcagno's report, an interjection appears—a few words laced with venom—referring to a single case: the only specific case mentioned in the whole report. It is the story of a home that was supposedly granted in accordance with the express wishes of Ratzinger:

> Along these lines, there is no lack of exceptional personal cases that nevertheless place a burden on the finances of APSA, arranged for *pro Gratia* by the Supreme Authorities: just to mention one, there is

> the case of Professor Guzmán Carriquiry, to whom the Holy Father Benedict XVI granted, for himself and his spouse, the arrangement free-of-charge of an apartment for the duration of his natural life.

Calcagno is one of the cardinals of the old guard, and he seemed to be out of step with the new era. His relations with Francis were formal from the start. These lines from his report could be interpreted, without malice, as the classical curial knife between the ribs. The men who had led the Curia for years, exercising uncontested power, were feeling the pressure of Francis and his minute inspection of the books of their dicasteries. There had been plenty of infighting during the pontificate of Benedict XVI, but either he was not informed of it or he refused to intervene. A scholar, lover of classical music, and subtle expert on Church doctrine, rather than call for investigations he limited himself to condemning "the human ambition to power" so frequently cited in his sermons.

With the arrival of Francis, the cardinals were in culture shock. The international auditors championed his message in their meetings. And the growing reaction of the Curia, as this book documents, is potentially explosive. Calcagno, for example, was now reporting to the Commission preferential treatment that had been granted to a friend of the Pope, the lawyer Guzmán Carriquiry, as if to say, "if you want skeletons in the closet, I'll show you where to look."

For his part, Guzmán had no trouble explaining the apartment to anyone who might ask. It was a benefit granted to him to round off his salary. In the past years he had entertained various job offers with much higher pay than he received from the Holy See. Faced by the possibility that he might leave, the Vatican evidently gave him the apartment as compensation for his lower earnings.

Calcagno was feeling the pressure, and he realized that the investigation into the real estate holdings could also cast suspicion on perfectly legitimate interests and property dear to his heart, starting with a twenty-hectare farm on Via Laurentina, just outside the Gates of Rome. Here, at the expense of the Holy See, someone had created a farm with a promising future.

The Ranch

A few hundred meters away from the Laurentino cemetery, consecrated on March 9, 2002, is the San Giuseppe Agricultural Company. We are in Roma Sud, the area of the capital city where there is perhaps the biggest building boom. Here the craving for cement has been translated into the Fonte Laurentina neighborhood, with thousands of low-rent apartments in the vicinity of the Great Ring Road, the expressway that circles the city, popularly known as the GRA.

For now, however, fields and farmland still dominate the landscape, and the area is relatively peaceful, an oasis of rest and relaxation from the chaos of the metropolis, were it not for the macabre discovery, on March 8, 2011, of the mutilated torso of a woman bound in wire, with all of her organs removed; a crime that is still shrouded in mystery.

The San Giuseppe Agricultural Company, on Via Laurentina 1351, registered as a sole proprietorship on June 8, 2011. Twenty-two hectares cultivated primarily with wheat (for animal feed), medicinal herbs, and olive trees. There were originally eight hundred trees, whose fruit produced olive oil through a cold press. The name of the company is announced by a simple sign at the entrance to the farm, showing in block letters the names of the farmers, a family of Romanians—father, mother, and two children—who cultivate the land. They live there in a house owned by APSA, with a no-rent lease. Their surveillance became indispensable after this promising agricultural realty became the logistical base of a gang of thieves. Cardinal Calcagno explained this circumstance in a letter to Versaldi on May 29, 2013, in response to urgent requests for clarification from the Commission:

> The fence had been cut at various points and an out-of-the-way area of the farm had been used by a gang of thieves as a deposit for stolen

> electric material (copper wire). This was reported to the Carabinieri at the Via Ardeatina station, who conducted a stakeout to surprise the thieves when they were recovering the loot. During a violent storm that hit the area during the night, while the Carabinieri unit was away, the thieves made off with the loot.

Once past the gate, the visitor is immersed in nature. On the right is a dirt road, lined by rows of olive trees, with twenty-two plants on each side, leading to a farmhouse that seems to be uninhabited but is well cared for. On either side of the second floor, the stucco has been redone and the casings are new, as if only one part of the house had been recently restructured. The path toward the house, a couple of hundred meters long, is quite pleasant: the visitor is welcomed by turkeys, hens, geese, and a couple of peacocks (a male and a female) that have the bad habit of singing at night, keeping the neighbors awake. In the barn there are three horses and two donkeys. The garden has everything—tomatoes, garlic, onions, peppers, melons, eggplant, potatoes, watermelon, cauliflower. And strawberries, planted for the children and for other guests of the farmer's wife.

According to the neighbors, other characters often appear at the farm. Important figures: eminences and excellencies. "I was taking my grandson to play in the fields this summer when he suddenly disappeared from sight and it scared the living daylights out of me," a woman who has been living there since the 1960s told me. "I saw him again a few seconds later near an elderly man carrying a cane and wearing a long, threadbare black coat. I thought he was a shepherd, and even said to the boy, 'leave the shepherd alone and come here!' At that the man smiled at me kindly and said, 'Signora, I am not an ordinary shepherd. I am a shepherd, but not of sheep. I am a shepherd of souls.' At the beginning I didn't understand, so I asked him to explain himself, and he told me he was a cardinal, but to call him 'Don Alberto,' so I did."

The few neighbors of the San Giuseppe Agricultural Company

mention other names, well-known personalities who spend a good deal of time around here. Two in particular: "Cardinals Nicora and Calcagno." Attilio Nicora, Calcagno's predecessor at APSA, was from January 19, 2011, to January 20, 2014, the first president of the Vatican Financial Information Authority, a body that Ratzinger had created to oversee all the financial operations of the Holy See and bring them into line with the new anti-money-laundering regulations introduced by the European Union. According to the neighbors, Cardinals Nicora and Calcagno were familiar visitors to the area, which they may have been using as a country home to relax, "in the two renovated apartments inside the farmhouse." The nephew of one cardinal, who was doing his university studies, also stayed there for a while.

Nicora had "accompanied the project and the establishment"—according to Calcagno—"of the San Giuseppe Agricultural Company, with the collaboration of Paride Marini Elisei, trusted notary of APSA and of the administrative office of the Secretariat of State. On September 13, 2011, a modal contract was drawn up between APSA and the Agricultural Firm for the leasing of the Laurentina and the Acquafredda estates." This operation brought another forty-one hectares of land under the property of the Vatican.

But who did this land belong to? This is the beginning of another story with many question marks and few certainties. What is clear is that these twenty-two hectares once belonged to the Mollari siblings—Letizia, Giuseppina, Domitilla, and Luigi. Devout Catholics, all childless, they agreed to leave their property to the Church. This episode dates back to March 22, 1975, when Letizia, Giuseppina, Domitilla, and Commendatore Luigi—who was already an employee of APSA—decided to donate the land to the Holy See in a document signed before the notary Alessandro Marini. The donation was accepted by the Secretary of State, the same Cardinal Jean Villot whom Pope John Paul I had wanted to dismiss.[8]

The San Giuseppe Agricultural Company currently operates on this land. Its partners include another person whose surname is

Calcagno: not Domenico, but Giuseppe. Was he perhaps a relative of the Cardinal? Verifications and investigations were attempted into this potential conflict of interest. The Prefecture requested an explanation from the Cardinal, who was so irritated that to disprove any possible connection, he even searched the gravestones in the family cemetery. Upon the return to the Vatican of the men whom we might refer to improperly as "cemetery inspectors," Calcagno wrote, "From the information gleaned from the gravestones at the Tramontana cemetery, it is not possible to arrive at the genealogical contact point with a possible common ancestor."

The men sent by Calcagno indicated the whole family tree, name by name, starting with his great grandfather Pietro. "When I was a seminarian I had asked the pastor"—the prelate concludes—"if I might see the parish's baptism registers. I remember that the research proved to be laborious immediately because since the late 1500s the overwhelming majority of Tramontana inhabitants were registered as 'Calcaneus de Calcaneis.' To avoid blood relationships the men of the Calcagno family would marry women with a different surname." Attached to his letter was a diagram from which it appeared, however, that between him and Mariangela, the wife of Giuseppe Calcagno, there was a relationship, but a very distant one: she was a fourth cousin.

The ties between the Agricultural Company and the Vatican is still strong, if it is true—as some of the farmers' relatives averred—that the Romanian family, "works for the Vatican, and it is the Vatican that brings in day laborers every now and then, when the need arises."

The APSA database that I have seen confirms that five parcels of land at Via Laurentina 1351 do indeed belong to APSA, as do four buildings, three apartments, a "residential complex," eleven warehouses, and three storage facilities. None of these properties appear to be rented, with the exception of the 75-square-meter house (inhabited by the farmer and his family). So who is living in the other houses? This is a mystery shrouded in the deepest secrecy. At the Holy See rumors circulated of risibly low rents—150 euros a month—offered to prelates so that they might enjoy one of these country homes, an ideal refuge outside the gates of the city. The possibility cannot be ruled out with any certainty, but according to the official figures in the database, if this were true they would have to be phantom leases: from the data in my possession those houses appear to be unrented. There is no question, however, that significant attention and interests were converging on the farm. On April 13, 2013, Francis penned a chirograph on the matter, giving Calcagno "a mandate to handle every legal action, including the right to act in a judicial forum" with regard to the farm adjacent to Acquafredda. The Pope thus gave Calcagno the possibility to divest the asset or transfer it to a third party.

Various ideas and proposals had been advanced over the years. In 2008, for example, there were plans to build a solar panel facility, an ambitious project to bring in 203,000 euros a year that unfortunately collapsed. The future of the property is still unclear. While on the one hand the company "has taken measures to deposit a reimbursement of 7,800 euros (meaning 650 euros a month)," on the other, it was receiving substantial assistance. Also, in the lease it is expressly stated that the agricultural company "has the right to request reimbursement for expenditures made or, in the event that the expenses exceed 20,000 euros for each project, to proceed to the advance sale as provided for by the lessor [the Holy See], but only after prior authorization."

A careful audit was done of the farm's account books and of transactions in the APSA bank account number 19560, held by the "Fondo lavori Laurentina" [Laurentina Works Fund]. The inspection came to focus on a bank transfer of 57,982 euros on January 2, 2013, whose provenance was unclear. It turns out the money came from a 1.5 percent commission applied by APSA to a financial transaction payable to the Bergamo diocese, but which had never been paid to the diocese. According to the Commission's reconstruction of the facts, on that same day a deposit of 3,865,499 euros was made into an APSA account opened at the BSI bank of Lugano, with the memo "Bergamo diocese, Zogno parish, payable to Casa Santa Maria of Laxolo." According to APSA's internal accounting, the money ended up in IOR account number 19412002 of the Bergamo diocese, but only after the 57,982 euro transfer for farm expenses had been cancelled. I was unfortunately unable to find out who had deposited that immense sum of money and why the commission had been withheld, rather than sending a bank transfer for the full amount to the Bergamo diocese.

In addition to the agricultural company at Via Laurentina 1351, there was also a warehouse registered to Edil Ars. S.r.l., a company that specialized in the restoration of historic buildings and—by a strange coincidence highlighted on the homepage of its website—"a subcontractor of works at the State of the Vatican City for the Administration of the Patrimony of the Apostolic See and for the Governorate."

"We had a storage facility there, nothing more. Our headquarters is located elsewhere, on Via di Porta Cavalleggeri 53," is what I was told on the telephone. The company pays an annual rent of 30,000 euros for a huge commercial space. Today Edil Ars. no longer exists, and has been incorporated by another company, Ap Costruzioni Generali, which does the same kind of work, with the same people and from the same location, on Via di Porta Cavalleggeri, a few hundred meters from St. Peter's Square.

Edil Ars. was the same company that had infuriated the former President of APSA, according to a letter that Cardinal Nicora had written to Cardinal Bertone in 2008. The company was considered too "unreliable":

> On April 17, 2002, Monsignor Carlo Liberati, a representative of the ordinary section of APSA, drew up a leasing contract with the Edil Ars. company of Signor Angelo Proietti, granting free of charge occupancy of the barns, warehouses and a house and the use of water from the pre-existing artesian well. In reality, Edil Ars. went well beyond the allowances of the lease in its occupancy, modifying de facto the purposes of the locations and making increasingly difficult

> the collaboration with the pontifical villas [which were managing the asset at the time] . . . Considering the deterioration of the locations as the result of the storage of enormous quantities of materials, including the presence of polluting substances, and of various pieces of construction equipment, on December 22, 2006, APSA formally cancelled the leasing contract with Edil Ars., since the counterpart had proven to be unreliable.

Edil Ars did, however, enjoy the full confidence of Marco Milanese, who had been on the staff of former Italian Finance Minister Giulio Tremonti. Edil Ars presented a 400,000 euro project to restructure a house Milanese owned on Via di Campo Marzio, inhabited by Tremonti. Edil Ars had also been awarded contracts between 2002 and 2006 from the publicly traded company Sogei. These stories made headlines in the Italian newspapers in 2011, with pictures showing the dome of St. Peter's in the background.

The Vatican Colonies in Europe

Another aspect of the Vatican's real estate patrimony are the "colonies," prudent real estate investments abroad into marquee buildings in various parts of Europe—downtown Paris, London townhouses on the Thames, dreamy apartments in Lausanne and other parts of Switzerland. The market value of these properties amounts to approximately 591 million euros.

This information is in the public domain today thanks to an investigative report by Emiliano Fittipaldi for the weekly magazine *l'Espresso*. Now the public knows all about the Sopridex holding company—valued at 46.8 million euros—which manages some of the most prestigious buildings in the center of Paris.[9] "The staff includes a manager, three employees, cleaning personnel"—according to the article—"and 16 concierges." The Promontory analysts documented the income of the staff and the members of the board: 56,000 euros is paid to the chairman of the board, and 6,825 to the three board members, one of whom is Paolo Mennini. The director of Sopridex, Baudouin de Romblay, received a gross salary of 12,956 euros per month, also for his thirteenth-month bonus. Fittipaldi combed through the wages of the sixteen concierges who work at the various properties: their salaries range from 7,000 to 29,000 euros. The 38,563 euros paid to their replacements during vacation was also verified and entered into the books. Seventy-five percent of the expenses for concierge services were billed to the tenants, while the remainder was covered by Sopridex.

In the French capital the Vatican owns "500 properties grouped into various buildings," with a market value quite different from what appears in the financial statements. The confidential documents report that the income amounts to ten times more than what is declared, 469 million. The reason for this discrepancy is quite simple. The more the value of the property is understated, the lower the property tax owed to countries where there are real estate taxes.

The Swiss properties were administered by another holding company, Profima SA, founded in Lausanne in 1926, which in the past had been used as Pope Pius XI's strong box for part of the so-called "damages" the Vatican had received from Italy after the signing of the Lateran Pacts.

Profima SA belongs to a financial archipelago consisting of nine other companies. These include Rieu Soleil and Diversa SA, which handle "savings management"—according to the analysts' report—"holding securities, including stocks, in Roche."[10] Four other holding companies have almost exactly the same name, except for the last letter (S.I. Florimont B., S.I. Florimont C, S.I. Florimont E, S.I. Florimont F) and they are in good company with the other three "Siamese twins" (S.I. Sur Collanges A, S.I. Sur Collanges B, S.I. Sur Collanges C). A total of ten companies in Switzerland—a sophisticated network that controls a patrimony worth billions—report to the Vatican. "The ten companies"—according to the analysts—"were established to manage one property each, between Geneva and Lausanne." Altogether they own assets indicated in their financial statement at 18 million, but their actual value is quite different: 49 million.[11]

In London, the properties are managed by British Grolux Investments Ltd., founded in 1933, which administers homes and luxury stores, with a market value of 73 million euros but entered into the books at 38.8 million.[12] British Grolux also manages various properties located outside of the city. Altogether, according to the Promontory analysts, the real estate holdings of APSA—in Italy, Switzerland, France, and Great Britain—are worth a total of 2,000,709,000 euros. But the financial statements report a far lower amount: only 389.6 million euros. This discrepancy represents the deep contradiction within the Vatican today. On the one hand there is a sophisticated archipelago of holding companies led by managers in double-breasted suits who control immense wealth; on the other, a Pope who demands that the Vatican clean up its act and who is fighting for a poor church, following the dictates of the Gospel.

7

Holes in the Pension Fund

A Deficit of Half a Billion Euros

The Afterlife, for believers in the Christian faith, is a place of peace and liberation from the body and from sin. But the attachment of Catholics to worldly evils, to be condemned, seems to be very durable, at least according to the charts of mortality rates in the Curia. Catholics, especially those who reside in Rome, in the Vatican, and in the rich West, live longer, even five to ten years more than the average.

If earthly life is lengthened, we should all be happy, but that is not necessarily the case. Rather than give joy, this statistic is a source of concern at the Holy See. This might sound absurd, but there are reasons for it. The longer a person lives, the longer they receive retirement pay, adding to a deficit that has been growing year after year without anyone paying adequate attention. But if this fact were made public, it could increase tensions among the employees within the

Vatican walls. Can you imagine the demonstrations and picketing that would take place in the Vatican City?

The alarm was raised by the head of the Prefecture, Giuseppe Versaldi, who, with regard to the financial situation and expenditures—especially the management of social security funds—had even feared for the survival of the small state's administrative bodies and, consequently, of the Vatican itself.

When a lay manager sounds the alarm on a troubling financial situation—in this case, the pension fund—few people take notice and even fewer pay any attention at all. There are two reasons for this: the ecclesiastical nomenclature of which Francis is so critical has very little sense of responsibility, and the long togas tend to minimize everything laypeople say, no matter how well supported it is by data and careful audits. "The Church does not consist of numbers but of souls": this is the generic response of the cardinals when a lay official allows himself to make a criticism.

This is what happened in 2012, when the cracks in the pension system started to appear. On June 12, the consultant to the Prefecture, Jochen Messemer, spoke at the meeting of the international auditors. Many of his colleagues were literally astounded by the gravity of the situation that he described and the harshness of his words. His statement centered on the uncertain future of the pensions for the current 1,139 retirees and the 4,699 employees of the small state, when they themselves would retire, slowly but surely.[1] "The bankruptcy of the diocese of Berlin," Messemer thundered, "was caused by the inability to understand what was really going on, to grasp the risk that was being run. [2] To underestimate the pension potential could lead to a disaster of this kind."[3]

His alarm sparked no reaction. Six months later, on December 19, once again before his colleagues on the board of auditors, Messemer tried to be more explicit and incisive, as the minutes of the meeting make clear:

Mr. Messemer wishes to address the problems of the pension fund. Consideration should be given to three main liabilities that have accrued:

1. For employees who have already retired (current average value of pension contributions): 266 million euros;
2. For active employees (current average value of pending contributions—presently active): 782 million euros;
3. For employees who will be employed in the future (current average value of pending contributions—active in the future): 395 million euros.

This adds up to a total of an approximately 1.47 billion euro liability on the pension fund. The current endowment is the equivalent 369 million euros and, by comparison to the total liability of about 1 billion, can only guarantee 26 percent coverage. The value is too low by comparison to other pension funds. Even the poorest dioceses try to assure 60–70 percent coverage.[4]

Messemer then raised the question that was fundamental to sketching out a credible operating plan for the future: since retirement pay lasts for the duration of a person's life, how could anyone project the average number of years that a pension will be paid to employees who go into retirement? The only data available, to which he was referring, came from the mortality chart:

As for the mortality chart, when was it last updated? According to some statistics, Catholics tend to live longer. This statistic, if true, could represent a serious problem since, by living 5–10 years longer, the whole chart would become unreliable because, with the accrual of liability, the deposits made until that moment would not be sufficient to cover them . . . There has never been any

> discussion of investment policies for this fund. In economic terms a pension fund cannot disregard the behavior of the market. We have to effect stress tests, and insert clauses on what to do in cases of loss.
>
> These are technical but necessary aspects. When you manage a fund of this type you need a good dose of responsibility. The employees work for 40 years on 80 percent of their wages (excluding the 20 percent withheld for the pension fund). There's nothing worse than saying that the fund is not solvent . . . We cannot err on the side of superficiality. The basic framework of the pension fund is outdated. We need to establish a working group to address these issues confidentially.

Apart from the collective dismay, his criticism would never go beyond the perimeter of the room in the Prefecture where the experts were assembled. The summary of that meeting, nine pages written by the trusted note taker Paola Monaco, was too disruptive to be addressed, so the document remained in the ironclad safes of the Prefecture. It was only six days away from Christmas: the last Christmas for Ratzinger as Pontiff and for Bertone as Secretary of State.

With the election of Bergoglio to the papacy in March 2013, the wall of silence started to crumble. Messemer's appeal was welcomed in May by the cardinals chosen by Francis to help the Pontiff in his leadership of the universal Church.[5] So the minutes made it out of the locked box and ended up discreetly in the black leather [carpette] of the senior prelates who had the full trust of the Pontiff. From the Secretariat of State, Cardinal Wells proposed that Messemer become a member of the COSEA Commission because of his expertise in the field of social security.

In August 2013 the troubled issue of the pension fund was taken up as one of the official subjects of inquiry of COSEA. This was all done with the utmost secrecy, to avoid disturbing the peaceful sleep of the precious hardworking community that every day labors away at the Vatican and knows nothing of the pension system, which is so severe that it could compromise the future of many employees.

In the end, Messemer's proposal that a task force be formed did not fall on deaf ears, and action to that effect was quickly taken. The mission was assigned to a giant in the field of management consultancy: Oliver Wyman, a multinational company headquartered in New York with offices in more than fifty countries. Wyman was delegated to conduct an actuarial study to estimate the financial health of the pension fund and assess whether the paychecks withholdings were sufficient to guarantee a safe future for everyone. COSEA also asked Wyman to "develop a proposal to cover the deficit," as the internal documents indicate, and to restore the health of the fund, assuring a serene old age to all the Vatican employees, from the cardinals to the Swiss guards.

Here, too—as was often the case on the various critical fronts opened by the teams deployed by Francis—well-informed cardinals, bishops, and monsignors were divided into two factions. The optimists, loyal to continuity with the past, proposed the sale of some real estate to balance the budget. And they spread the word that the actual deficit amounted to "only" 40 million euros. This is the number that had been circulating ever since the last audit of the pension fund, in 2011, by a Roman expert, who estimated the deficit at precisely this amount. For them there was no reason to panic, and the situation was under control.

The realists, instead, described the actual situation. They were the loyalists of Francis, including the Spanish Cardinal Santos Abril y Castelló and the Frenchman Jean-Louis Tauran. They knew that the size of the deficit was much greater than the unofficial figures being circulated, and that all the data showed the Vatican social security system on the edge of collapse. The picture they painted was hardly reassuring. The cardinals closest to the Pope proposed another set of urgent and, above all, serious inspections. They were all rightly convinced, as the other financial questions had made crystal clear, that viable countermeasures could only be identified and enacted through solid data.

Francis's collaborators were shrewd enough not to contradict the optimistic reports circulating within the Vatican walls, which downplayed the size of the deficit, saying it only amounted to a few tens of millions. Their strategy was aimed at reassuring the people and preventing the spread of panic or alarm. On the issue of pensions, a very delicate hand was being played: it was essential that the pensions be safeguarded to prevent unpredictable reactions by the employees of the Holy See, which might spark a domino effect with repercussions in the media, and provoke a chain reaction of rampant destabilizing events such as strikes and protests.

In late September Wyman's team was able to offer a preliminary assessment on the basis of data collected from various Vatican dicasteries. A top-secret document was drafted and sent in a sealed envelope on October 11 to Zahra, the Chair of the COSEA Commission, and to Messemer, who had been assigned to follow this specific project. The next day was a relatively peaceful Sunday. The COSEA commissioners met early in the morning for the third time. After a quick coffee and welcoming remarks, Messemer and Zahra did not conceal their desire to share all the information they had received. Wyman's report gave a sharp photograph of the situation that shocked the experts assembled at Casa Santa Marta. Their profound distress emerges clearly in a few lines of the meeting summary:

> The consultancy company that was hired, Oliver Wyman, presented already on October 11 a preliminary report on the data it had acquired on about forty Vatican offices. Now it will focus primarily on the pension fund, which at first glance shows a heavy exposure to risk that is extremely troubling.

In fact, the first indications report a deficit that was far greater than what had been imagined in the spring, comparing the available data with the reports prepared in past years. The unofficial figure that had been rumored in the corridors of the holy palaces shot up to incredible levels: the deficit had increased to half a billion. But even this projection would prove to be too optimistic.

"The Vatican Risks Extinction" According to the Head of the Prefecture, Cardinal Versaldi

Francis's goal was to return the Holy See to the dictates of the Gospel in every sector, from finance to management and administration. Health insurance and pensions also had to be rethought, according to these criteria. The reform of the pension system should thus not be studied in isolation but rather in connection to a new model relationship between the worker and the Holy See. The functions and role of the Labor Office had to be reviewed, correcting and rationalizing three key points: human resources, pensions, and health insurance. This is made clear in a COSEA memorandum of late October 2013, which proposes the creation of a new strategic office to manage everything having to do with workers. The document appears to be the draft of a speech written in the first person and bearing the signature of the Pope.

The title is revealing: *Pontificum cura*.

> The concern of the Pontiffs for all the collaborators has always been a unique characteristic of the government of the Apostolic See. In recent times many measures have been taken to render their service more serene and fruitful. In 1988, through the Apostolic Constitution *Pastor Bonus* (art. 36), the Labor Office of the Apostolic See was established . . . Since 1993 the pension fund has been operative, unifying, for all Vatican employees, the administrative center for the treatment of retirement and the allocation of the pension check.
>
> Over the years the health insurance fund has been kept updated to provide a good level of services, allowing health care that, while it can always be improved if adequate resources exist, can stand

comparison in timeliness and drug coverage with the care afforded citizens of many more economically developed countries.

In recent times . . . a commission has been established at the Secretariat of State to regulate, standardize and make more transparent procedures for the hiring of new lay personnel. Finally, mention should be made of the not infrequent increases in the base salary and special mention should be given to the existing system of automatic pay raises. This system, adopted in the past by various countries, has been deactivated almost everywhere as a result of the economic crisis under way. By the same token, also in state organizations in our vicinity, profound changes have been made to the criteria for calculating the pension check.

The Providence of the Father has always assured the Holy Church the necessary means to perform its duties: spiritual means and material means. This fills us with serenity, but it should also commit everyone to use these means in accordance with the letter and the spirit of the Gospel. In particular, the use of material means, which through the charity of the faithful throughout the world arrive at this Apostolic See, must be directed toward the primary purpose for which they are given. They must therefore not be diverted from their immediate goal, wasted, or used in a way that is inappropriate.

All the gifts received must be accounted for in accordance with what the Gospel indicates to us and urges us to assess. All the more so in the midst of a profound economic crisis like the present, which creates so much distress and poses so many material and spiritual problems for the people involved. I wish to contribute to the serenity of all those who, to any degree, collaborate in the service of the Bishop of Rome for the Universal Church.

Therefore, for the sake of achieving correct use of the material assets and while awaiting the contribution that the Commission of Eight Cardinals will make to the achievement of the broader reform of the Roman Curia, I felt it was advisable to begin gradually to take measures in this direction, so as to assure also for the future the economic resources that enable, for all employees, job stability, a fair salary, adequate health care and an appropriate economic allotment that will allow them to live with dignity after their working life is over.

These are important words because they anticipate the de facto reform of the Curia on the key issue of employee relations. Francis's challenge was to redefine the balance between temporal power and religious power and to translate it into the architecture of a new state.

In particular, the investigation highlighted that there were too many workers and too many personnel offices. According to the latest data available to the commissioners there were actually 21 personnel offices with 35 staff members employed throughout the territory of the Holy See. Each one of them administered its own small share of the 4,699 total of employees.

This situation applied not only to APSA and the Governorate, whose human resources offices have a staff, respectively, of 7 and 14 employees. There were also similar structures at Propaganda Fide (2 units), Vatican Radio (3 units), the IOR, the Printing Shop, and *Osservatore Romano*, and so on, all the way to the St. Peter's Chapter (2), the Fabbrica of St. Peter's (2), the Vicar's Office (2), and even the library, with 2 units, while the cutting of paychecks is handled by APSA.

The guidelines provided in *Pontificum cura* thus set the goal of creating a single personnel office:

> Among the many changes that should be made to achieve proper use of economic resources, having listened to various collaborators, I have decided to proceed with the unification of all the resources destined for the management of the activities relative to the personnel of all the administrative bodies that, to any extent, report to this Apostolic See. Therefore . . . until the new decision is made the regulations indicated below shall be observed, regarding in particular the functioning of the personnel offices of the bodies of the Holy See.[6]
>
> The new Personnel Office will handle in particular the following

> matters . . . It will be a special task to draft and propose suggestions in order to achieve regulations that are more in compliance with the principles of equity and justice. In particular the teachings of the Second Vatican Council will be kept in mind and fully enacted.

In this episode, too, unfortunately, the appeals to be more careful about hiring and assigning jobs went unheeded. The Curia was not sensitive to the Pope's warnings. His every instruction would be ignored: "We have to change our way of thinking"—Versaldi had thundered at the closed-door meeting with the auditors on December 19, 2012—"by trying to look beyond our own limited reality . . . the Vatican can be inspired by the pursuit of common values, which are proclaimed by the Gospel. In any case, rejecting a reduction of expenses would signify risking the extinction of the whole structure."[7] But this appeal also fell on deaf ears. The offices proliferated, duplicating one another's work and increasing expenses in the process. New employees were hired according to criteria that was not always endorsed by the Pope. But he knew nothing of it. The situation was out of control.

An 800 Million Euro Deficit in the Pension Fund

In the meantime, the investigation into the pension system continued. In the next three months, the expert analysts went to the root of the problem—and they were scathing in their reports about what they found. By cross-referencing information, they discovered "a significant deficit in the financing of almost 700–800 million, which was identified in the pension fund." The fund was quickly approaching collapse: the promise of a pension tied up 1.2 to 1.3 billion euros against an endowment not much higher than 450 million, with a deficit of 700–800 million.[8]

This was a structural question that in a few years' time risked jeopardizing the whole pension system for employees who had already retired or were making plans to do so. The risk would only grow because of the incompetence of the persons assigned to administer the fund. The report emphasized, "the lack of knowledge in the fields of insurance and asset management on the part of the fund's oversight bodies."[9]

This was the unvarnished conclusion made by COSEA in the documents it prepared for the February 17 and 18 meetings with the Council of Cardinals of the Economy, which were recently approved by Francis (which will be discussed later). In other words, the pension fund was caught in a bind: on the one hand, there was the rock of the deep deficit, on the other, the hard place of the professional incompetence of the persons called on to manage the accounts.

These assessments seemed to be confirmed by the management of the fund's assets, consisting of real estate and securities with their own significant risks: "The asset management of the fund is not aligned with the debts of the fund and there are major investments into risky positions [such as] Italian government bonds."[10]

There were also some questions about the real estate portfolio, since it was invested entirely in the municipality of Rome and not distributed among various realities, to prevent overexposure to the market fluctuations of a single city. In reality, in a country, pension funds are not structured around reserves and real estate investments, but count on the contributions of employees and new hires, which steadily finance the pensions of persons who go into retirement. The Vatican is a unique case, however, since the mortality rate is so low and births, for obvious reasons, are so few.

These negative evaluations were not offset by the positive data that Cardinal Versaldi, as the President of the Prefecture, found in the 2013 budget and 2014 estimated data received on December 19, 2013, directly from Cardinal Calcagno:

> Most Reverend Eminence,
>
> . . . The YTD budget shows a possible financial surplus of 27.7 million euros, the 2014 estimated budget projects it at 28 million. The results predicted for the 2013 and 2014 fiscal years are thus high enough to foresee pension fund assets at the equivalent of 479.1 million as of

> December 31, 2014. I am grateful for this opportunity to confirm the assurances of my highest esteem for Your Most Reverend Eminence.
>
> Most respectfully, Domenico Calcagno

In financial management, income from bonds amounts to 10.9 million, from active interests to 461,000 euros, while "the outcome of the overall management (YTD surplus as of December 13, 2013) is 27.7 million, 466,000 euros less than projections in the 2013 estimated budget."[11] An examination of the securities portfolio on September 30, 2013, highlights all the Italian government bonds, which the analysts considered risky, such as the 70 million in multiyear Treasury bonds. In practice, the reserves have been parked in the Italian public debt.[12]

This practice may help strengthen the Church's hand when it lobbies Italian politicians. The Vatican's relations with foreign governments—first in Italy but also in Africa and South America—have always relied on various means of persuasion. These include the pressures I documented in my previous book, *His Holiness*, on the Italian President of the Republic to reconsider the laws on the family and on assisted procreation. But they also involve the acquisition of shares of the public debt or other major financial investments, always in government bonds.

On January 22, 2014, Erik Stattin, a Harvard MBA, EMEA partner, and head of the pension and insurance issues of Oliver Wyman Rome, called a meeting of Vatican representatives and other Commission members, including Messemer. Monsignors Vallejo Balda and Luigi Mistò, Chair of the Health Insurance Fund and Secretary of APSA, together with Cardinal Calcagno, listened to the report. The only one to nod his agreement was Messemer. The meeting was decisive:

> All of the participants agree in maintaining that on the basis of the actuarial audit conducted by Oliver Wyman, the Vatican pension fund presents a very significant funding gap. This gap is so large that it has the potential to jeopardize the future pensions of Vatican employees. The same audit shows, however, that in the short term

the fund is able to finance its activities, which makes it possible to proceed with a restructuring to prevent the collapse of the fund. In any event it is necessary to implement with the maximum urgency drastic measures to prevent the deficit from growing larger.

These measures should include:

- A strengthening of the fund's assets through an injection of capital by the Vatican administrations;
- A redefinition of future pensions. A benchmark of the current Italian pension system should assure a treatment of Vatican employees that is equivalent to what is currently used for employees of the Italian public administrations.

The reform of the pension system should also provide for "the Vatican contributing to solidify the capital in the pension fund. [Finally, there is a need] to adjust the existing benefits for employees to a reasonable economic level." While the "asset management for the pension fund will be managed by the Vatican Asset Management center, VAM, and the Vatican will guarantee a specific interest rate on assets."[13]

Vatican Asset Management (VAM) represents a very particular proposal, to create a single structure that, for the first time in Vatican history, will be called on to manage all the movable and unmovable assets of the Holy See, including, therefore, the pension fund.[14]

Not all of Francis's trusted men were in favor of this plan. In fact, a few months later, in the spring and summer of 2014, the VAM would be the cause of a deep split within the COSEA Commission. For too many months the war had been fought behind the scenes, with skirmishes, dirty tricks, and sabotage. On one side were the supporters of Francis. On another were those who tolerated him. And on yet another were those who criticized him and tried to stop him. And from this latter group came a series of intimidations, attacks, and conspiracies to make the Argentine Pope lose his incredible challenge. At stake was the future of the Church, and not just the Vatican. Now, the conflict would pose an even greater challenge.

8

Attack on the Reform

The Theft of COSEA's Secret Files

IT IS SUNDAY, MARCH 30, 2014. DAYBREAK IS JUST A FEW HOURS away and St. Peter's Square is still deserted. In one of the most closely guarded areas of the world, something unpredictable happens in the wee hours of the night. Thieves, against all odds, defy security and break into the pontifical palaces.

The deepest silence reigned over the Palace of the Congregations, in Pius XIII Square, directly opposite the colonnade designed by Gian Lorenzo Bernini. The gatehouse by Colonnade 3 was locked. Gaspare, the trusted Sicilian custodian, had gone home for the weekend, like the other employees and the cleaning personnel. With the exception of a 353-square-meter home, the residence of Nigerian Cardinal Francis Arinze, and a one-bedroom apartment rented to a peaceful retiree, the four-story building was used entirely for store and office space, including the office of the Congregation for the Clergy, the Congregation for Catholic Life, and the Congregation for the Holy Life. The 781 square meters on the fourth and last floor of stairway D were reserved entirely for the Prefecture for Economic Affairs of the Holy See, the reference point for the inspections Francis had initiated into the Roman Curia. Here the auditors worked elbow to elbow with the COSEA members. This was where most of the confidential documents were kept. This was where the Coordinator of the Commission, Secretary of the Prefecture Vallejo Balda, had his office. It was the symbolic center of Francis's revolution.

The thieves entered the building and the offices of the various congregations using a blowtorch. They went from floor to floor, cracking open every safe they found and stealing the money inside. In general they found not more than a few hundred euros per office. The Congregations and the Prefecture only kept enough money on hand for petty cash. These sums were quite modest, disproportionate to the type of action that was under way. The thieves behaved like professionals. They knew where the safes were located, knew how to open them in the least time possible, and knew how to easily force any door they might come across.

It is what the thieves would do immediately after the break-in that the investigators would find unusual and surprising—a deliberate decision that seems to provide the correct key for interpreting this disturbing nocturnal intrusion.

Once the burglars had entered the offices of the Prefecture, they did not limit themselves to identifying the safe, opening it, and taking the money. They also broke into the room that had several armored lockers. They pinpointed one locker in particular and forced it open. While from the outside the lockers looked identical, the criminals knew exactly which one to open. In opening the heavy armored doors they found no money or precious assets but confidential documents, kept in order in just a few dozen files.

This was not just any crime. In an unprecedented action, the burglars made off with part of the secret archives of the COSEA Pontifical Commission. This was a serious act that risked compromising the

Commission's efforts. What did the files of the Pope's inspectors have to do with the few hundred euros in the various safes?

The intrusion was discovered the next day. The Vatican gendarmerie went into action and the Italian police forces were notified. In a fairly unique occurrence in the world, police forces from two countries launched a joint investigation. The building where the burglary had taken place belonged to an extraterritorial property indicated in the Lateran Pacts. Not only did the Palace belong to the Holy See, but—although it was located right outside the Leonine Walls—it was considered for all intents and purposes a part of the Vatican City. The interior of the property is within Vatican territory and thus the investigation was the province of the gendarmerie. Outside, on the adjacent streets, the Italian investigators were in charge. They checked dozens of videos captured by surveillance cameras in the neighborhood. The police tried to reconstruct the chain of events. The burglars—there were two or three of them—may have entered through the main door, but there was another theory that the investigators entertained at first: the intruders might have come in through the basement, having reached the Palace of the Congregations through one of the many tunnels that connect the buildings of the Vatican. While the theory sounded bizarre, it was in fact plausible. From the cellar of this building you could reach various destinations: the offices of the twin building, where other congregations had their headquarters, or the offices of the IOR, or even the Apostolic Palace and, on the other side, Castel Sant'Angelo. It was maze of tunnels, open-air corridors, covered and uncovered passageways, stairways and elevators (mostly dating back to the world wars in the first half of the twentieth century) that, for someone who knew them well, made it easy to move around sight unseen. It was a parallel world that was an apt metaphor for the Apostolic See, divided as it was between what takes place on the surface and is spread through official communiqués, and that which is consummated in secret rooms. It is an underground world that runs underneath the streets of Rome, upon which thousands of unwitting tourists and pilgrims tread every day. And it was no coincidence that the IOR—the impenetrable bank of the popes—had a storage area with confidential archives in the basement of the Palace of the Congregations, a fact known to very few.

When the investigators went down to the basements, however, they found everything in order, starting with the many dark limousines of the various embassies to the Holy See parked in the garage. The storage areas of the Congregations and of the IOR had not been touched. The corridor that leads to the Apostolic Palace was closed. It would have been difficult for the burglars to go through a tunnel to reach the storage area: the place looked impenetrable, and was known to be under surveillance by many security cameras. At this point, the most realistic theory was that the intruders had entered through one of the main doors, on the side that faces Pius XII Square. But the lock on the door was working and showed no signs of tampering. Did this mean that the thieves might have had the keys? There was no other explanation. This doorway was the obvious entry point, since it was near the staircase leading down to the storage room where the confidential files were kept.

At the Vatican, news of the burglary spread quickly and created unrest and dismay. The members of the Commission were of course among the first to be informed. They were surprised, shocked, and frightened. Zahra was in London on a business trip. He was on the phone all day with his trusted men to hear every development of the investigation. By Monday afternoon, among the various theories raised by the police, the most credible seemed to be a targeted burglary. No one thought it was possible that all those safes had been broken into only to steal a few hundred euros. Who would be so clueless and stupid as to commit a burglary in one of the most guarded places in the world for such meager loot? The true objective—some of the investigators thought—was the papers. The other items stolen looked more like a setup to throw the investigators off the scent.

And why would anyone want to steal the documents? Someone

might have been interested in knowing their contents in order to map the works of the Commission—or maybe the objective was to remove some of them to slow down the works of the men closest to the Bishop of Rome? The burglars were certainly well informed. They knew the place perfectly, had the keys to open the doors, and had brought along the right equipment. And of course, they knew exactly which armored locker to force.

There was yet another theory, the worst of those being explored by the investigators, but one which would gradually become more plausible: the burglary might have been a criminal message, a thinly veiled warning to those who were bringing change. As if to say, between the lines, "We know where you keep your archive. We can go there when we want. We know and we can find everything."

From that day on, the psychological pressures on the COSEA commissioners increased. They felt increasingly vulnerable and exposed. The intimidation theory would receive preliminary confirmation a few weeks later by the leaders of the Holy See.

Both Francis and Cardinal George Pell, who a few weeks earlier had become head of the Secretariat of the Economy (the new structure that the Pope wanted and that will be described in the following chapters) received the news of the burglary with the same interpretation: the action should be understood as a warning to those who were carrying out the most delicate inquiries; to those who were offering the Pontiff the tools for revolutionizing the Curia. Jorge—as the eight hundred priests of the Buenos Aires diocese called him when Francis was still the Archbishop of the Argentine capital and as his friends and closest prelates still call him—has a mild and unflappable character, but he had never expected a move like this.

Sindona's Letter to Threaten Francis

This was not an isolated episode. In those same days, troubling information crossed the desk of Father Mark Withoos of Melbourne, the personal secretary of Cardinal Pell, regarding strange movements by people around the Domus Australia, home of the powerful cardinal who now headed the Vatican Economy. It seemed that Pell was being followed, but it was hard to know why. Father Withoos reported the news to his superior, who urged him to be cautious.

A few days later, on April 10, 2014, an unsigned letter arrived in the Prefecture from London: a single sheet of green paper with eleven lines handwritten in cursive. The first sentence quoted the motto of Anonymous, the powerful online hacker community that stages spectacular actions to denounce corruption and financial shenanigans throughout the world. "We do not forgive, we do not forget. Wait for us!" The letter began with the sentence, "The outsiders are coming in from the outside . . . Pass this [message] to the Pope and to all the interested parties: the game is up."

Though the letter was hard to interpret and could have been a prank, after the burglary the Vatican was on high alert. The sentence "The outsiders are coming in from the outside" seemed to refer to the recent break-in at the Palace of the Congregations. The letter was forwarded to the personal secretary of the Pope, Alfred Xuareb, whom Francis had appointed Secretary General of the Secretariat for the Economy and his representative for dealings with COSEA. Xuareb had a talk with Withoos. Nothing like this had arrived in recent years, but the two men, refusing to be intimidated, downplayed the importance of the letter. "We have nothing to hide. We're not going to play the game of someone who wants to frighten us. Our job is to help Francis." Their approach was commendable, but the individuals operating in the shadows had a few more surprises up their sleeves. The war had just begun.

These were festive days at the Vatican. April 26 was the eve of the Sunday of Divine Mercy, with the Holy Mass scheduled to take place at ten A.M. in St. Peter's Square for the beatification of Pope John XXIII and Pope John Paul II. Hundreds of thousands of pilgrims were expected, and significant security measures were taken. Early in the morning, someone had left a sealed parcel in the mailbox of the Prefecture. The package had no address and no return address. When the clerks opened it they found papers that they recognized immediately as some of the documents that had been stolen from the armored locker one month earlier.

The burglars had chosen to return a set of confidential papers dating back to 1970, regarding business relations between the Vatican, Umberto Ortolani (the corrupt middleman for the Freemasons), and the banker Michele Sindona. There were several letters from Sindona to the ecclesiastical hierarchs of the era, names that would be the source of major embarrassment for the Holy See. Sindona, in particular, was closely tied to the most powerful Mafia bosses active in the United States in the 1960s—from Vito Genovese to Joe Adonis to John Gambino. Together with Monsignor Casimir Marcinkus and the banker Roberto Calvi, Sindona had been the protagonist of one of the worst moments in the Vatican finances. Like Calvi, he also died in mysterious circumstances. Calvi was found hanging underneath the Blackfriars Bridge in London. Sindona was found dead in his prison cell after drinking coffee laced with cyanide, a few days after being sentenced to life imprisonment for having ordered the murder of the lawyer Giorgio Ambrosoli, who had been commissioned to liquidate one of Sindona's banks. For years, the investigators had claimed that both deaths were the result of suicide. Not until six years after his death was it discovered that Calvi had been murdered, but his accused murderers were all found not guilty in a series of trials. In the parcel that arrived in the Prefecture there was also an exchange of letters between Monsignor Giovanni Benelli, at the time the Substitute of the Secretary of State, and Cardinal Sergio Guerri, President of the Commission for the State of the Vatican City, who had written to Sindona. The correspondence made clear that Sindona was to feel at home at the Vatican, thanks in part to a network of relations and agreements drafted over the years. Sindona even received mail at the Holy See, with letters addressed to "Mr. Michele Sindona, c/o Pope Paul VI, The

Vatican, Rome (Italy)." Sindona had also conducted business on behalf of the Vatican worth millions of the old lira, involving the transfer of blocks of shares in important companies, such as the shares that APSA held in the Smalterie Genovesi. (There was also the dramatic story of the huge hole in the finances of the Pantanella Company, into which the Holy See had made a no-return investment for the equivalent of 60 million euros in 1968 and 1969 which it continued to recapitalize, in the desperate hopes of saving a company that clearly had no future.)

In the Vatican, questions were raised, but not any alarms, about how to interpret this delivery, who might have made it, and what message it was meant to send.

The situation became more and more complicated. By that point—as Zahra put it in a few choice words spoken in a conversation with friends—"war had been declared." Cardinal Pell tried to send reassuring messages to show that he was not intimidated. The perfect occasion presented itself a few weeks later. In an interview, Pell referred explicitly to the controversial characters who had been resuscitated:

> This change was requested from the cardinals at the Congregations that preceded the Conclave. One year ago the Cardinals said "Enough." Enough with these scandals . . . Proceed with perseverance. *Nunc coepimus.* We have just begun. We will go forward. We still need to improve. But one thing is certain: enough with Calvi and Sindona, enough of surprises that we learn in the newspapers . . . We need financial transparency, professionalism and honesty.[1]

Some observers in the Curia thought Pell's reference to Sindona and Calvi was extemporaneous, maybe because they did not know the story of the mysterious parcel of letters from the Sicilian banker that had just been delivered to the Prefecture. To avoid media attention and possible resulting scandals, the occurrence was not made public, in keeping with most of the controversial events that take place within the holy palaces. The only element of the whole affair that filtered out was the news of the mysterious nighttime burglary in the Palace of the Congregations. The story of the parcel would have to remain top secret: otherwise Sindona's letters might attract the uncontrollable attention of the media.

To understand what actually triggered this no-holds-barred war, we need to take a step back and relate what happened only a few months earlier, just as the Commission's investigations were going full steam ahead and to touch on every corner of the Curia.

These were critical weeks that would determine a definitive split between the senior representatives of the Vatican. In addition to the COSEA investigations, starting in the fall of 2013 there were also concrete initiatives to reform the Vatican state and change its dicasteries, the rules and regulations that govern them, and indicate new roles, responsibilities, and hierarchies. At some point the "evangelical revolution" of the Curia driven by Francis—to repeat the words of his Uruguayan friend Guzmán Carriquiry Lecour—would risk implosion.[2] There was too much tension, and too many situations that inflame that small world—a world that by the will of the Gospel and of Francis should be a world of peace, mercy, and poverty but instead risked growing further and further away from its pastoral and theological dictates.

Bertone Makes a Noisy Exit

Day after day, in the fall of 2013, the extent of the reforms became clearer to everyone. Francis and his men were trying to make the move from analysis to action. Once the most compromised situations came into focus, the culprits were held accountable and dozens of wayward laypersons, bishops, and cardinals were quickly dismissed. The Pope did not act with stealth. He publicized the guidelines of his pontificate, inviting the involvement of everyone, inside and outside the walls.

Francis sought to be inclusive, collecting in the new power centers the souls of every member of the Curia from the Focolare movement to Opus Dei, from ex-Bertone loyalists to diplomats and the representatives of the episcopates of the two Americas, but he did not always succeed. The pilgrims, parishes, and rank-and-file Catholics were enthusiastic. In the Vatican, however, the Pope's moves often provoked the opposite reaction. Every day the ranks of the malcontent grew by a few new members, religious people who were frustrated or trying to delay a change they feared.

Francis's opponents became more numerous and alarmed when, over a ten-day period in late September 2013, the Pope granted two long interviews that stunned the Curia. The first was granted to the Jesuit priest Antonio Spadaro, the respected editor-in-chief of the prestigious magazine *La Civiltà Cattolica*:

> The dicasteries of the Roman Curia are at the service of the Pope and the bishops. They must help both the particular churches and the bishops' conferences. They are instruments of help . . . The Roman congregations are mediators; they are not middlemen or managers. How are we treating the people of God? I dream of a church that is mother and shepherdess . . . God is greater than sin. The structural and organizational reforms are secondary—that is, they come afterward. The first reform must be the attitude. The ministers of the Gospel must be people who can warm the hearts of the people, who walk through the dark night with them, who know how to dialogue and to descend themselves into their people's night, into the darkness, but without getting lost. The people of God want pastors, not clergy acting like bureaucrats or government officials.[3]

A few days later the Bishop of Rome returned to the same subject. This time he chose an Italian intellectual, an atheist, Eugenio Scalfari, founder of the daily newspaper *la Repubblica*. In this interview he was even clearer:

> Heads of the Church have often been narcissists, flattered and thrilled by their courtiers. The court is the leprosy of the papacy. There are sometimes courtiers in the Curia, but the Curia as a whole is another thing . . . The Curia is Vatican-centric. It sees and looks after the interests of the Vatican, which are still, for the most part, temporal interests. I do not share this view and I'll do everything I can to change it . . . I have decided as the first thing to appoint a group of eight cardinals as my advisors. Not courtiers but wise persons who share my same sentiments. This is the beginning of a Church with an organization that is not only vertical but also horizontal.[4]

Francis gave a harsh direct analysis of all those who had abused their power for decades. But passing from words to deeds would not be easy. In the holy palaces the two interviews became the main subject of discussion among the cardinals. Almost no one had expected such sharp words. It was the first time that a pope had expressed such a firm attitude, a clear sign that his revolution was meant to be much more than empty promises. This time the Curia really did have to change. Francis showed himself to be authoritative but not authoritarian. His decisiveness was always tempered by his kind manners.

Bergoglio's attitude and his groundbreaking public statements made his closest collaborators even more enthusiastic about participating in the change. In particular, the men who had pushed for greater transparency, and been ignored for years, were now ready to stake everything on Francis. They included Monsignor Viganò who, from the nunciature in Washington, started to engage in a more intense dialogue with the monsignors and priests at the Secretariat of State as well as with various laypeople who held important roles within the administrative bodies of the Holy See.

And there was also Nigel Baker, the Ambassador of Great Britain to the Holy See, who on October 3, 2013, sent Peter Bryan Wells, the Assessor for General Affairs of the Secretariat of State, a "personal and confidential" missive. Baker attached to the letter a confidential five-page memo, signed by Thomas Stonor, 7th Baron Camoys, an English politician and descendant of King Charles II of England. For thirty-five years Stonor had been a prominent banker on the board of directors of some of Europe's most important credit institutions, including Barclays and Amex. Ltd. Stonor wanted to forward to the upper echelons of the Holy See a document he considered decisive, a proposal articulating a precise, detailed reform of the Vatican economies.

The surprising thing was the date of the proposal: June 22, 2004. This meant that nine years earlier the banker had submitted the memo to Cardinals Nicora and Bertone, and that his ideas had been ignored. Stonor, in addition to being an expert on financial issues, had also been a close collaborator of the Church as an advisor to APSA. By virtue of this role, and after consulting Cardinal Cormac Murphy-O'Connor, he had sent the memorandum to the top dogs of the Holy See. Its contents were still relevant, which is why the British baron was now going back on the attack through the mediation of the British ambassador:

> The historic structure, with regard to the financial management of the resources of the Holy See, is not only inappropriate for the 21st century but also dangerous to the resources of the Holy See and potentially to its reputation . . . It is dangerous because of the risks due to involvement of money laundering (through the IOR) or simply the mismanagement of the financial activities and/or annual budget. After the Calvi affair any event related to the points discussed previously would in all likelihood damage the reputation of the Holy See. During the sporadic meetings with the APSA advisors, I mentioned some of these concerns, but in vain: perhaps I did not explain myself clearly enough . . . At APSA I notice a lack of decision-making power, which is understandable as a consequence of the Calvi affair . . . I ask myself quite seriously whether the Holy See really needs an entity like the IOR. All of its services could be provided by other banks and with greater security . . . in particular, reference is

made to the very serious risk of becoming involved in episodes of money laundering.

The document was read and interpreted by the men closest to Francis as further proof of the fact that many at the Apostolic See knew how critical things were but had no intention of changing their approach—starting, perhaps, with the Secretary of State, Tarcisio Bertone, whose term was set to expire in a few days. The handover ceremony from Bertone to his successor, Archbishop Pietro Parolin, the Apostolic Nuncio to Caracas, was on the calendar for mid-October.

The audience had already been scheduled, but something unexpected arose. Parolin was unable to attend because he had to undergo minor surgery. The appointment could have been postponed, but Francis seemed not to want the Secretary to be in power even one day longer. So rather than a handover ceremony there was a tense farewell meeting, with clichéd expressions of gratitude.[5] Bertone made use of the occasion to try to rehabilitate himself with the new Pope, describing the "crows" and "snakes" in the Holy See, as he would often repeat to the few loyalists he had left and in public settings.[6] But it was too late.

For some time, the powerful secretary chosen by Ratzinger was more isolated and less influential. "In the first six months of the pontificate"—one prelate let slip in a conversation with some clerics at the end of the ceremony—"the Pope has acted as if Bertone didn't exist." In fact, the Pontiff had gone through the first six months of his pontificate without a Secretary of State. Bertone had never won his trust. This was intimated by Óscar Rodríguez Maradiaga, a loyalist of Jorge Bergoglio and a maverick Salesian, the first cardinal in history from Honduras and the coordinator of the so-called C8, the Council of Eight Cardinals chosen by the Holy Father to help him in guiding the Universal Church.

On the Canadian television program "Salt and Light," Maradiaga revealed that he already knew about the appointment of Parolin on

March 17, during a conversation with the Pope only four days after his election.

Bergoglio had broken every record in changing his top collaborator. His predecessor Benedict XVI, by contrast, had waited fourteen months before appointing Bertone to replace then Secretary Angelo Sodano.

Fears of the Revolution: Less Power to the Cardinals in the Curia, More Room for Laypeople

In the holy palaces Francis's enemies were increasingly concerned by the sharply political slant that the two pontifical commissions were taking. COSEA and the Commission on the IOR were in fact working on two different fronts. The findings of COSEA were well known: throughout its analysis of the accounts of the pope's bank and the other administrative bodies of the Holy See, it identified the inertia, incompetence, and abuse described in previous chapters.

Yet there was another battlefield that was less known. The COSEA commissioners had received a specific new request from the eight cardinals of the C8: don't only look for problems and crisis areas, propose clear solutions, give us advice on how to revolutionize the administration and the whole organization of the state. It was absolutely necessary to redefine once and for all the internal power structure of the Vatican.

A meeting of the C8 in Rome was set for December 2013. To prepare for this appointment, the COSEA members drafted and proposed a strategy to change the Church from the ground up. First there needed to be a readjustment of the balance between temporal and religious power. The laypeople had to take on greater importance in the economic and administrative areas: this was a revolutionary suggestion for an absolute monarchy whose king is a religious person.

The powerful lobbies and networks that had always ruled at the Vatican could not accept this new direction; if the project were to take effect—so argued the many "courtiers," to use Francis's expression—it would be the end.

It was October 2013. The four draft pages of the report of that meeting, which I was able to examine, deserve to be read in their entirety. One gets the impression the members of COSEA have reached the point of no return. Francis's loyalists had no intention of easing the pressure. As the minutes from the meeting attest, the first person to take the floor was George Yeo, the only member of the Commission with experience as a politician, having served as Minister of Foreign Affairs of Singapore. Yeo envisioned a sharp separation between economic power and political-religious power:

> The decisions of the Holy See should be independent from the composition of the Colleges of Cardinals. It is difficult for the Holy See's function to combine those of a Minister of Foreign Affairs and a Prime Minister. We need a Minister of Finance that has full powers and that manages the budget. The Prefecture for Economic Affairs could be transformed into the Ministry of Foreign Affairs, in such a way that all the other congregations would have to contribute to the budget and stick to its demands and projections. The Ministry of Finance should have responsibility for the budget. The Church is missionary and therefore trans-border, and the Ministry of Finance has to oversee its finances. Through the establishment of the Ministry of Finance, the role of function of APSA would be redefined.

He then addressed the question of whether APSA would continue to be the central bank:

> The pre-existing agreements that, as the central bank, it currently has with the Fed, the Bank of England, and the German Bundesbank, should be maintained because it would be difficult to renegotiate them.

On the issue of whether the Governorate should be run by different figures than the present, the men on the Commission felt that the Holy Father would have to be directly involved:

> The Governorate [is another question]. These items should be discussed with the Holy Father: the government of the City with its accounts and its budgets; self-sustenance and the sources of financing of the Ministry of Finance; the uselessness of the cardinals and the other members of the clergy. And other obvious questions such as: security, transparency and good governance [also with regard to] the Vatican museums, [which should be] an autonomous entity.

The meeting helped to align the works of the Commission with the indications that the C8 cardinals had provided after discussing them with Francis. The minutes of the meeting place us at the heart of the revolution, and illustrate clearly the chain of command: the Pope, after consulting them, gave the guidelines to the eight cardinals, who in turn forwarded instructions and priorities to the members of COSEA. And they were briefed by their coordinator, Monsignor Vallejo Balda, who had just received indications about the need for a radical reshaping of the central power in its current formation.

The Curia should be governed by a bishop and not a cardinal, with the power not to "exercise authority" over the Congregations but simply to coordinate their work. The title "Secretary of State" should be changed, and in the future referred to as "Papal Secretary." The position would have even less power than it had under Paul VI, considering that it was especially during the pontificates of John Paul II and Benedict XVI that "the fact that the Secretary of State had to give his approval to every question proved to be an obstacle." For Vallejo Balda, "pontifical councils should be abolished, because among the various functions [of the Secretary of State], the only truly valid one is coordination of the various bishops' conferences." In the field of culture, for example, "Rome cannot spread teachings to influence the rest of the world. In this way the Curia will be more agile and manageable."

The central theme of the meeting is captured in another passage regarding the need to reassess the importance of laypeople with respect to cardinals. This was the strategic policy outlined by COSEA and made available to the C8 cardinals:

> There should not only be cardinals at the head of the administrative bodies: purely administrative organizations like APSA do not require a cardinal. The councils of cardinals will continue to exist. The Governorate can return to its former configuration as a governor, comparable to a mayor, with an assembly of councilors.[7]

Jean Videlain-Sevestre was more prudent, seeking a path that did not break too sharply with the past and that might receive the consensus of the cardinals themselves. He knew that it would be difficult for the reform to succeed otherwise:

> We can see in practice what the problems and critical points are . . . [By resolving them] we will uproot the evil. We go to the roots of the dysfunction and we attain the consensus of the cardinals: they are experts in ecclesiastical life, not in economics. We have to recognize that we run the risk of proposing unrealistic solutions.[8]

In contrast to Sevestre, Jochen Messemer recommended a decisive, resolute approach:

> It is useful to isolate the guiding principles of our reorganization proposal. We should advance 1–3 proposals. We should not be afraid. Our job is to propose solutions that we consider improvements. After that the Holy Father and the C8 will assess them and draw their own conclusions.

But it was not as simple as that. Monsignor Vallejo Baldo made this clear with crude realism: "The truth is that we need money to achieve financial freedom." Without financial independence, in other words, the Curia would always be fragile and exposed to scandals.

Zahra would have the last word:

> We must take into consideration the facts and the objectives mentioned by the advisors. The guiding principles, especially with regard to the laity. The priests should not be careerists. For some positions competent professionals rather than prelates would be more fitting.

After this confidential meeting of the Commission, the international advisors put into practice their recommendations and outlined the organizational chart of the new state that would serve the Church in the world, from the United States to Japan. One's role in the ecclesiastical hierarchy would no longer be considered a form of "power" but of "service."

On November 20, 2013, the Americans of Promontory offered the COSEA members an outline of the new state. Different variants of the organizational structure were proposed, depending on whether there was to be a Ministry of Finance, a central bank, or another type of institution. At the Vatican, a radical constitutional reform of the power arrangements was taking place, with some religious people taking on unprecedented temporal responsibilities.

When these prospects reached the ears of the cardinals in the Curia, the shock could not have been more absolute. Signals, warnings, and actions began that in some cases gave rise to illegal behavior. Some people were ready to do anything to stop the revolution that had arrived in St. Peter's Square from a far-flung corner of the world. The reaction of those adverse to change, which until now had been unorganized, reliant on individual resistance, started to escalate into a full-fledged war between two opposing armies.

9

The War, Act I: Blocked Budgets and Bureaucratic Assaults

As If Nothing Had Happened

"MONEY CONTAMINATES OUR THINKING, IT CONTAMINATES OUR faith." When greed wins out, human beings lose their dignity and become "corrupt in mind, and risk treating religion as a source of income." May God "help us not to fall into the trap of the idolatry of money."[1]

Francis repeated these words in his homilies at Santa Marta and St. Peter's while the commissions pored over the accounts demanding explanations of wild expenses, random privileges, and utter superficiality. But the road to change was long and strewn with obstacles. At the holy palaces, everything continued as it had before, as if nothing had happened. While it had seemed as if something might really change at the beginning, the Pope's new direction provoked discomfort within the walls; a clear sign that his decisions had been right on target. Hypocrisy and smugness seemed to gain ground again, however, when the time came to present the 2014 budgets for the Holy See and the Governorate in December 2013. Six months had gone by since the confidential meeting of the auditors that had given rise to the COSEA Commission.

Anyone who had envisioned an endorsement of the Pope's fresh approach in the new budgets was sorely disappointed. The bitter truth came out on the morning of December 18, 2013, the day of the biannual meeting of international auditors to review and approve the 2014 budgets. The auditors had received the financial documents only two days earlier, studied them hurriedly, and were aghast at what they read.

A heavy silence fell over the room when the Prefecture's consultants entered, knowing they were about to face one of the most dramatic sessions in recent years. After the ritual prayer, Cardinal Versaldi opened the proceedings and put on a display of optimism, underlining "the relative acceleration in the timetable and the structural nature of the reform."

In other words, the "COSEA Commission has set into motion a process of renewal that the Prefecture had hoped for many times and that, in the past, had generated a sense of frustration over the failure to enact the reforms." Murmuring could be overheard in the room: the auditors were not of the same opinion. The papers they had just seen spoke clearly: everything in the budgets was just as before, without a trace of the new era invoked by Francis. Cardinal Versaldi understood this better than anyone. He stopped, took a deep breath, and, in a rhetorical flourish, let a few seconds go by to impose greater authority on the words he was about to utter:

> We should also underline the human and Christian aspect of the reform. All the shortcomings should be highlighted in a spirit of fraternal correction, inspired by evangelical rather than diplomatic criteria. First, a discussion should be pursued with the interested parties. In the event they have persisted in the error of their ways, the Supreme Authority should intervene. We should maintain this approach so as not to lose the results achieved so far. Before "punishing"

> we must seek to correct. Let it be noted, furthermore, that the collaboration of the heads of the Administrative bodies has been good and there is no bad will, but rather a problem of mind-set and the structure of the system.

Although his language was in perfect curial style, open to a variety of interpretations, the gist of the Cardinal's "advice" was not lost on the COSEA commissioners. Versaldi was anticipating the obstacles ahead and wanted to limit the discontent and placate the auditors and their requests for stricter measures. The hunt for the culprits—the senior prelate sensed—would hurt everyone. Any punishment of the wrongdoers would have one effect and one effect only: "to lose all the results achieved."

Versaldi wanted to build a protective wall around the miscreants. But he went further: with all due respect to the Pope, the changes had to achieve general agreement, otherwise the obstructionists would win. While the Cardinal was clearly acting in good faith, to respond to inertia with an equal dose of inertia would lead nowhere. The problem—as the new budgets confirmed—was that the Commission had no results to show, attesting to the indifference if not the hostility of the Church's managers toward the papal dispositions. Versaldi was unsparing about the meager results of the first few months of the new pontificate:

> Despite all our efforts, we find ourselves before two budgets that show no progress over last year, with the exception of the cuts APSA has made to its previous draft estimates.

The data was disheartening. Versaldi's critique dampened all enthusiasm. "No progress" had been made, he repeated. So the Commission found itself back at square one, where they had been in June 2013, when Francis first decided to create the COSEA Commission to address the Vatican's catastrophic finances. Then, too, the Cardinal had lamented that, "in the Vatican great progress has not been made. The finances are unsustainable in terms of expenses. We cannot hope for an increase in income [from donations]. The only solution remains to cut costs." This made it all the more regrettable that the 2014 budgets planned for higher expenditures, as noted by the Secretary of the Prefecture, Monsignor Vallejo Balda. "The budget has clearly gotten worse in every area."

Versaldi's version of the facts had more than a few dissenters. As General Accountant Stefano Fralleoni pointed out, at the Vatican it was customary to spend more and more:

> The audit of APSA was long hard work. Every single balance sheet for every single department was checked. The only thing listed in the kinds of balance sheets shown to us was expenses. Although the administrations in question report to APSA, they also have assets, in addition to expenses, which should be recorded.
>
> There is another paradox. The budgets show an increase in estimated costs, which indicates the intention to spend more. There are always huge discrepancies between the budget and the final balance. This is the result of a mentality that is hoping for the approval of many of the proposed expenses, for the sake of setting some money aside.
>
> There have been many cuts, but we need to know more about some items. Despite everything, the final balance of the Holy See is showing losses of 25 million, and the financial earnings are modest. APSA did not include even one comment in this regard, which is hard for the Prefecture to understand. While it may be complicated to predict the behavior and fluctuations of the market, there are experts who do this as a profession.
>
> Personnel expenses have gone up, despite our suggestion of a hiring freeze, but the most serious thing is that this increase was already recorded in the budget. This attitude smacks of an outright affront to the authorities.
>
> I should add that there was no variation in the field of

> consolidation. This approach was determined more by political than technical reasons. The same is true of the need to standardize accounting principles. The Prefecture's functions are clearly identified but it has been impossible to make them operative.[2]

Zahra, the COSEA Chair, was at the meeting as an auditor for the Prefecture. He, too, saw no improvement and criticized the arrogance of those who refused to change:

> The fact that the same situations are repeated every year indicates a constant rather than a temporary crisis. The problem is not with procedures but with the mentality and the way of doing things. Cooperation from the heads of dicasteries is often less than forthcoming. They can be very haughty, thinking they are the only ones who know how to proceed.

An Outrageous Rejection, a Scorching Climate

The day before the meeting the more inflexible advisors had done a straw poll with their colleagues, noting the growing discomfort of the various professionals and consultants from the oversight bodies. Many were demanding a break with tradition. There were long telephone calls deep into the night, discussions and agreements into the wee hours. The auditors mustered their courage. Together they had to come up with a countermeasure that would take everyone by surprise. They didn't want to just sit around and complain as they had in the past. The frustration that had built up over the years had been too demeaning. Now they wanted to see results. The hours sped by and a secret plan took shape, gathering the consensus of most of the auditors.

The day of the fateful meeting arrived. From the moment the first speaker, Fralleoni, took the floor, the prevailing line was already clear. The General Accountant lowered his gaze for a moment to check the liabilities columns and, weighing his words carefully, recalled an event from 1993, when John Paul II's closest collaborator, Secretary of

State Angelo Sodano, had refused to approve the budget for Vatican Radio. It was a major precedent, a warning to everyone. There was no reason not to repeat such an approach. The speakers that came after Fralleoni took up the charge, adding criticisms of their own. When Maurizio Prato's turn came, he still seemed stunned by the data he had seen, and could barely contain his outrage:

> It is disheartening to see that it's still business as usual, with no sign of change or sense of responsibility to manage accurately, efficiently and effectively the patrimony of the Holy See, and with no attempts to contain costs. As for the consolidated budget of the Holy See, in terms of presentation and commentary, it shows patches of improvement but on the whole, the analysis is discombobulated and hard to grasp.

What was most troubling were the expenses and some disappointing investments. Prato continued:

> With reference to institutional activities, given the overall stability of canonical income [the amounts that dioceses throughout the world send to Rome to support the Roman Curia], the big increase [in expenses] by comparison to the historic trend until 2012 is a result of the increase in personnel costs (3 million) but mainly the big increase in general and administrative expenditures (9 million). There has been a huge decrease in financial activity by comparison to 2012 while . . . 2013 was relatively stable in financial market terms, even with the decrease in earnings. To record such significant losses demonstrates yet again the careless and deplorable management of assets, which is anti-economic, and of investment criteria, despite the repeated appeals from the auditors in recent years.[3]

Versaldi tried to interrupt him. "We have no power over that. It's up to the Superior Authority to make sure its instructions are followed. We tried to do something at past meetings, but we need more effective tools."

The Cardinal was referring, in particular, to two conferences held in the Synod Hall during Benedict's pontificate, "in the attempt to have a global vision of the status quo at the Holy See and the Governorate as a basis for all future operations." But it would take more than good intentions from a couple of congresses to revolutionize a Curia that had been impervious to every previous attempt at reform.

At a few minutes before eleven, the proceedings were interrupted for a coffee break. The Spanish auditor, Josep M. Cullell, still hadn't taken the floor. During the break he conferred with Messemer, Fralleoni, Zahra, Prato, Kyle, and Monsignor Vallejo Balda. On hearing his observations some said nothing, and others nodded, but they all came to an agreement: it would be up to Cullell to get the ball rolling. When the meeting resumed, he was the first to take the floor:

> While it is positive that the documents highlight the problems the International Auditors have been discussing for years, I am not in favor of approving the budgets. I propose that we write an explanatory note on the specific reasons for our rejection. The note could at the very least indicate the points emphasized by Mr. Prato.

The secret maneuver, then, was to not sign off on the budgets and return them to their senders. This dramatic choice would throw a wrench in the Curia's games, but at the same time it could boomerang against Francis by slowing the dicasteries' activities. Cullell went further:

> The budget documentation analyzed reflects the irregularities in the whole structure. A great deal of information remains unclear (increase in personnel, contracts with outside companies, etc.). Without transparency we cannot act. For a while it looked as if the Prefecture was moving in the direction of greater authority, but not much has changed. Without a serious budgetary law that applies to all the Vatican dicasteries, no reform is possible.

It will take more than good will: it will take rules that oblige all the Dicasteries to write up a proper budget and managers who know how to administer resources. We need a clear law to control the autonomy of the Dicasteries. Although we still don't know what shape this law will take, it is fundamental for it to guarantee control over expenditures and guide the economic-financial strategy of the Vatican. We have to set priorities and define coordination. We need a clear, defined procedure, as the Pope himself has indicated.

On the subject of transparency of information, there's a lot of talk about maintenance and restructuring work, but where is any of this entered into the budget? Where is that work recorded? Was there competitive bidding? At the Vatican, contracts are awarded informally, to friends and acquaintances. But one of the basic criteria should be the available funds. And during a crisis we have to cut back on maintenance because there are other more urgent priorities.

All eyes turned to Monsignor Vallejo Balda, the only prelate in the room after the Cardinal President. His support was indispensable to holding off Versaldi, and he did not disappoint:

Competitive bidding is limited to 5–10 companies that have always worked with the Vatican. No public announcements are posted. When the works are being done there is no budgetary ceiling and no item-by-item cost estimate.

Versaldi tried to quell the arguments and reintroduce his criticisms:

Opening up the competition to everyone, without distinction, would create chaos. It's better to have accredited companies that are regularly updated.

Vallejo Balda had a ready reply. He pointed to the recent works at the Vatican library, a thorn in the side of the Curia because of the huge discrepancy between the estimated and the actual costs:

> It's impossible to analyze the documentation because of this style of operating. Who allocated the funds? How was the budget decided? Was an estimate drawn up? What criteria were used to choose the company? Who is responsible for management?

It was up to Zahra to bring the discussion to its lethal conclusion. For him it was not so much a question of introducing new rules. What was missing from the Vatican was the will to apply them:

> The fundamental problem is that the procedures exist but they are not applied, and people are acting on the basis of practice and not rules. In addition to defining the guidelines more clearly, we need concrete tools to be able to step in and sanction departments that do not follow the guidelines. The procedures have to be updated and the various entities have to be held accountable.

The budgets had to be rewritten. Some of the auditors wanted even harsher measures. Prato was one of the most intransigent, proposing an across-the-board cut of 10 percent from the previous year's budget. He was held back by Kyle:

> Considering how slowly things move at the Vatican, I think the priority should be to achieve concrete results. None of the companies for which I've worked has ever been a dictatorship: there's always teamwork but in the long run someone had to make a decision. It's not up to the employees to define the budget: it's up to the managers. Anyone who ignores the laws and deadlines has to be replaced. Allowing resources to be mismanaged is a scandal for anyone observing the Church from abroad, especially young people.

The auditors' move was audacious. Versaldi acted as if he was unperturbed. He stared at the professionals assembled in the room, the same men who a few months earlier had given Francis the ammunition he needed to go after mismanagement. For them to take such a tough stance had to mean the Pope was behind them. But then, the auditors might have been merely interpreting the *voluntas* of the Holy Father without involving him directly. So for his next statement the Cardinal performed a masterful balancing act:

> I sense within this structure a physiological and pathological resistance . . . I wish to reiterate the need to try to change the Curia without opposing it. If the correction is then ignored, the heads of administration will have to allow themselves to receive instruction. If they do not, then we can talk about malicious resistance. I urge you to be cautious not because I am afraid of taking responsibility but because I want to find the right way to pursue the much hoped for change.[4]

In the end, he was overruled. With such a large deficit the time for caution and mediation was over. The meeting was adjourned. The auditors refused to sign the 2014 consolidated budgets of the Holy See and the Governorate.

The climate now turned frosty, and relations between COSEA and the Secretariat of State were tense. For two months the Secretariat had been led by a new man, Pietro Parolin, the Pope's closest collaborator. The 2014 budget had been prepared in the Apostolic Palace, the same building that housed the managers who had been appointed by Bertone, who had ruled the Secretariat with an iron fist for seven long years.

The Losses at Vatican Radio

To find a precedent for what the Prefecture's auditors had just done, you have to go back twenty years, to when Secretary of State Sodano rejected the budget of Vatican Radio.[5] But this time around, the initiative was even more newsworthy: none of the budgets of the Holy See and the Governorate had been approved, which meant that most of the Vatican's finances were blocked. Still, this initiative was not necessarily enough to set a new path for Church government. The auditors knew this, as the aftermath of the historic precedent had made clear.

Vatican Radio is a glaring example of how things never change at the Holy See. The station and the whole telecommunications unit were still in the red, and every attempt to stem their losses had failed. This deficit was one of the many thorns in the side of the Curia's financial health, a situation that had long fed concerns and tensions—under both John Paul II and Benedict XVI—and today it was still provoking harsh comments from the auditors.

At the December 18 meeting, there was heavy criticism of the management of the radio station, particularly from Prato:

> The Radio's propensity for spending beyond its means has remained the same, as its 26–27 million in losses attests. At the Vatican Radio *nichil sub sole novi*—there's nothing new under the sun. It would be interesting to know what leads anyone to think we can expect a sizeable lowering of the deficit in the future. The negative trend is substantially unchanged for *L'Osservatore Romano*, the print shop, the bookstore and the television center.
>
> The number of employees and their costs have risen, and the reasons for the increase are unexplained. A hiring freeze is absolutely necessary. The consolidated deficit for 2014 is estimated at 25.1 million euros, following the estimated loss in 2013 of about 28 million euros, accelerating the progressive erosion of the patrimony.

If this were a European Union country the managers would probably have already brought their account books to bankruptcy court. Not to mention that these same criticisms had been voiced at the June meeting. Now it was Versaldi's turn to lower the boom on the budgets of both the Catholic radio station and of the *L'Osservatore Romano*:

> We can no longer argue that no expense should be spared in spreading the word of God. We can lower costs without affecting our

> institutional purposes. We'll decide what to do in a few days. For now it's clear that the Santa Maria di Galeria station has to be closed because its upkeep is particularly expensive[6] . . . The increase in personnel does not correspond to an improvement in production. Even the Photography Service of *L'Osservatore Romano*, which has the exclusive on sales of pictures of the Pope, closes the year in the red.

This well-known situation was frowned upon in the Curia, but for years nothing had been done to change it. As Kyle had pointed out at the June meeting, in the various working groups, "Not even one cardinal had supported the current position of Vatican Radio, not even the representatives of the developing countries. The Secretary of State had tried to intervene, but to little effect. The short-wave emissions had to be blocked and with determination." The heads of the radio station had always opposed any change. Versaldi often remarked sarcastically that the managers of the broadcaster tried to treat "the heads of the Prefecture as businessmen rather than as men of the Church."

With regard to personnel costs Monsignor Vallejo Balda was scathing:

> Some aspects of management clearly show serious failures, and the heads of the various Administrations, including Father Lombardi, are perfectly aware of this. The equipment at the Ponte Galeria Radio belongs in a museum. The costs of supporting the media sector make up 20 percent of the Holy See's expenditures. The equipment analysis also included the structures in Piazza Pia and Piazza Leo XIII. The heads of the media sector don't even know the square footage of their offices. Since APSA handles the expenses, there may not be a lot of attention to optimizing costs. These properties could be rented and become a source of income. But the most radical change has to be in personnel. About 84 journalists work at *L'Osservatore Romano*, but not all of them are needed. They could at least modify their contracts, but instead, everything continues passively from one year to the next.

> Although this year's budget is balanced, it's hiding some unconvincing elements, such as the constant increase in personnel costs.

In the fall of 2013, with the help of the McKinsey consultants, the COSEA investigation uncovered the reasons for the hands-off treatment of the account books. Four risks were identified and presented to the attention of the cardinals in the Curia:

> The off-budget resources go to covering various geographic areas. At Vatican Radio the same number of editorial resources are dedicated to France and Belgium (three people for about 53 million Catholics) and to Albania (the same number of people for about 0.3 million Catholics). *L'Osservatore Romano*: the copies printed in Poland do not fully recover the costs of printing and shipment (a loss of about 1.5 euros per copy). Operations management is insufficient (as are outsourcing policies and production planning): 70 percent of the copies of the Italian edition are returned by the newsstands. The rotary printer of the Vatican Print Shop is only used for two hours a day. There is a duplication of the main activities by the various media departments (news production, digital activities, etc.).

Francis insisted on a communications reform and the creation of the Vatican Media Center, prepared by COSEA advisor Francesca Chaouqui. In early January 2014, the Commission scheduled an intense series of meetings with the heads of the various editorial departments. This enabled the Holy Father to get the cardinals' endorsement of a new department that would streamline human resources, costs, and investments in the field of communications. It would be an essential tool of the Church's evangelical mission in the world. In June 2015, the Secretariat of Communications was established, to be headed by Father Dario Edoardo Viganò, director of the Vatican television center.[7] He would be assisted by Monsignor Adrian Ruiz, head of the Vatican internet service, who gave Francis the gift of an iPad—in regulation white, of course—the day after his election to the papacy.

The Counteroffensive of the Vatican Bureaucracy

Starting on December 16, 2013, COSEA and the McKinsey consultants, including Filippo Sciorilli Borelli, entered the office of the Secretariat of State to begin a series of inspections and audits. The climate they found was icy. To get their hands on the data they needed, they had to overcome distrust, reluctance, and resistance. Zahra, feeling isolated, turned to Xuereb for advice. The cardinals close to Francis were not taking a stand, and tensions were mounting between COSEA and the Secretariat of State. A dangerous fracture was opening up between Bergoglio's supporters at the very moment they needed to be most united. In a quick sequence of events, between the end of 2013 and the beginning of 2014, COSEA opened up a much broader series of investigations into twenty-five departments of the Holy See.

On December 4, 2013, COSEA had written to Parolin asking that the documentation requested for the audit be made available. On December 16 the audit began, but on January 3 another letter was sent to Parolin in which Monsignor Vallejo Balda hinted that the acts and documents requested be forwarded no later than January 10. The next day, in a two-page letter, Parolin told him to take a hike. And he explained why: for one group of departments, "this Secretariat does not have the documents requested; beside which, it would seem more correct to forward the request directly to each of the departments mentioned." For some of the bodies named in the COSEA letter, he recalled that "the documentation is also kept at the Prefecture." All the Commission had to do was search through the file cabinets in its own offices. Parolin could not conceal his irritation:

> Allow me to add that I felt it was my duty to bring to the attention of the Holy Father our correspondence on this occasion, so that everything may be done in loyal adherence to the *desiderata* of the Holy Father.

At the same time, the budgets that had not been approved by the Prefecture needed to be cleared. On January 3, 2014, the matter was brought directly to the attention of the Pope, who granted an audience to an increasingly distressed Cardinal Versaldi. After the meeting, Versaldi wrote an urgent letter to both Cardinal Bertello, President of the Governorate, and Calcagno, the head of APSA, with a copy to Parolin. They needed to find a way out of the mess, and the terms in which Versaldi chose to express himself were not reassuring:

> At the audience granted to me by the Pope in response to my request, the Holy Father delegated me to sit down with APSA and the Governorate before the mid-February meeting of the fifteen cardinals. The purpose of these encounters is to explain to these dicasteries the criticisms advanced by the international auditors and give the technicians involved the means to assess and absorb them. This will make it possible to unblock a situation that will otherwise create a crisis for the whole economic and administrative system of the Holy See and the Governorate. I will come to request that your dicastery quickly indicate its willingness to attend a meeting in the Prefecture designed to satisfy the Pontiff's instructions. For my part I can assure you that my intention is to have a serene and collaborative talk for the sake of mutual understanding and a solution to the problems that objectively exist and that this Prefecture has signaled for years but that have taken too long to overcome.

Calcagno tried to lift the tension and sent a prompt reply:

> We are always available to verify together whatever can be improved. My best wishes for your work.
>
> See you soon, D. Calcagno

The two sides were locked in a dangerous struggle. On the one side the Secretariat of State felt invaded by the auditors, with their pressing demands for information; on the other, the budgets of the Holy See had been blocked for weeks. At the Apostolic Palace the atmosphere was stifling. And the news of some unexpected expenses did nothing to lift the tension. The Brazilian press reported that the Holy Father had donated 3.6 million euros to the Organizing Committee of the World Youth Day held in Rio de Janeiro on July 22–29, 2013, to help cover the enormous 28.3 million euro debt it had left. The event had been managed by the local archdiocese, whose bishop, Orani João Tempesta, was in line to be made a cardinal by Bergoglio.

In the meantime, at the Apostolic See, there was meeting after meeting. Zahra realized that if the waters were not calmed it would only benefit the defenders of the status quo. On January 6 he requested and received an audience with the Secretary of State. The meeting had two objectives: to receive the requested information and to lower the tensions.

Parolin is a priest from one of the poorer parts of Latin America, and he had been the Apostolic Nunzio to Venezuela. He is a simple man, spontaneous and sincere. But he was in the stalwart offices of the Curia. Zahra is a businessman who understands numbers. Both of them shared Francis's policies, but their personalities could not have been more different and the series of misunderstandings and incidents made dialogue between them quite difficult. Zahra went in with a strategy. Barely forty-eight hours after the meeting he held out an olive branch to the Secretariat of State: he wrote to Parolin a long summary of their meeting so that it would remain on the record:

> Dear Monsignor Parolin:
>
> It was a pleasure to meet with you on Monday and I wish to thank you for finding the time to see me. It was an honor to be of assistance

to you in helping our Holy Father in this stimulating process of reform to benefit our Universal Church. I wish to provide you with some feedback on some of the various points we discussed during our meeting:

. . . 4.) Accounts of the Secretariat of State. We received your response to our request regarding the accounts only this morning. The contents of your letter definitely cut in half our efforts to consolidate the accounts. The Prefecture has confirmed that it does not have copies of these financial statements or other partial information on the dicasteries mentioned in point 1 of your letter, without which we are unable to do our work. In the case of the Bambino Gesù hospital, the last statement that the Prefecture received is dated 2006. I am attaching a letter that Mr. Profiti sent to the Prefecture regarding these accounts.[8] It seems like an endless carousel. We cannot close our assessment of these accounts, unfortunately . . . I repeat that we are working on these very inspiring reforms and it is normal to encounter severe opposition and resistance. I know that you and I are both determined to proceed in line with the will of the Holy Father in the most fluid way possible. It is clear that not everyone understands the seriousness and urgency of this task . . . and I entreat you to find a solution that will be beneficial to the delicate work we are both conducting. I will be back in Rome on January 20, and I can make myself available for a meeting should it be necessary. Rest assured that I support you fully in your difficult mission.

My best wishes, Joe[9]

The Color Purple

During this same period, Parolin received the auditors' request for an explanation of the budgets they had rejected. It was a seven-page critique of the financial documents: "There is a general sense of inertia, with no clear signs of change or responsibility for careful management of the patrimony of the Holy See and without concrete actions to contain costs." Regarding the patrimony, for example, the request was made for a "required, but missing, planning of property maintenance jobs, greater efficiency in the rental area, and clarification of the contract awarding process." The budgets had to be redone, particularly the line items on financials and human resources. Until then they would remain blocked:

> The redoing of the employee expenses line item, keeping in mind the freeze on hiring, turn-over, the replacement of retirees, overtime, promotions, and limitations on raises in 2013 (or 2012) to cost-of-living hikes.

The Secretariat of State, APSA, and the Governorate finally chose to collaborate. They responded to all of these questions and sent in the revised budgets just in time for the January 14 meeting of the group of cardinals in the Prefecture.

While data and information was coming in on the budgets, there was still little movement on the documentation requested from the Secretariat of State for the audit. On Saturday, January 11, Zahra was forced to approach Parolin. He asked once again for the financial statements of the bodies that report to the structure he headed. The Secretary of State was under pressure, but Francis remained undeterred. And the next day Parolin received important confirmation of the Pope's unconditional trust in him. During Mass, at the *Angelus*, Parolin was named as one of the nineteen prelates who would be made cardinals by Bergoglio at the Consistory of February 22. This marked a significant changing of the guard at various Congregations. As a new cardinal, Parolin wrote one of his first emails to Zahra:

> Dear Mr. Zahra, Dear Joe,
>
> Thank you for the congratulations you sent me on my appointment as Cardinal. It is one more responsibility and challenge . . . purple is the color of martyrdom . . . pray for me! I am very pleased to

send my regards and my blessings to your family. I have received your two earlier emails and I thank you warmly for them and for the meeting that preceded them. I wish to assure you of my complete willingness to work together in pursuit of the dispositions of Pope Francis. It seems to me that the most urgent questions are listed under points 4 and 5 [the request for financing of COSEA]. As for 5) tomorrow I will speak directly with the Holy Father and I trust that the thing can be quickly unblocked. As for 4), I am perplexed, because I do not know exactly how to recover the documentation you need (especially because of the tight deadline). Tomorrow I will bring the matter up again with the Substitute. If you have no objection, Mons. Balda can contact me directly to see how to proceed . . . We will try to find the time to meet on the occasion of your next stay in Rome and have an update on the situation. Thank you for everything. Let us place everything in the hands of God and ask him to help us to act always according to his will and for the greater good of the Church.

With my warmest regards, Pietro Parolin

But the situation was not as simple as the Secretary of State would have it. Forty-eight hours later, Zahra sent him this reply:

It seems that the question of gathering financial information from the Secretariat of State is far from settled. Last night I received the financial documents from Mr. Profiti, who to my surprise is saying in his letter (attached) that he had sent the communication to the Secretariat. I also refer to the dicasteries indicated in points (1) and (2) of your January 4 letter. The Prefecture of Economic Affairs does not have this information or else [the information is incomplete]. Now we are writing directly to these dicasteries even if we would not be surprised to find this information already available at the Secretariat.

I now refer to the items in my January 3 letter [regarding the bank accounts of the Secretariat of State]. Your reply to my letter does not refer to these two items. You are aware that we need this information to complete the whole financial picture of the Holy See. Naturally I respect the fact that there might be confidential accounts at the Secretariat, but what I am asking for is information on these other accounts. You can understand how difficult my job is and you are aware of the resistance I am facing in fulfilling the wishes and the mission of the Holy Father. Your intervention with the managers to help us in the work we are carrying on would be most appreciated.

With my best wishes, Joe

The only person who could break the stalemate now was Francis, as was stated nakedly in the weekly status report of the McKinsey consultants:

Secretariat of State, status:

- Received a letter from the Secretariat of State confirming that none of the financial information requested is available.

Next steps:

- Receive guidance from the Holy Father on the unshared accounts.
- Keep in touch with Mons. Parolin.

Parolin had never given too much credit to COSEA or to the Commission on the IOR. In an interview published in the daily newspaper *Avvenire* in February 2014, he stated:

The Curia is a reality of service, not a center of power or control. There is always a danger of abuse of power, large or small, that we have in our hands, and the Curia has not and does not escape from this danger. "But ye shall not be so," as the Gospel warns us, and on this Word, so demanding but so liberating, we seek to model our activity in the Roman Curia, despite limits and flaws. I would like to emphasize that while a reform of the structures is needed, it will not be enough unless it

> is accompanied by a permanent personal conversion. The commissions? They have a limited term and a job to "refer," that is to say, their purpose consists in submitting to the Pope and the Council of Eight Cardinals suggestions and proposals in the framework of their competence.[10]

It was only thanks to the intervention of Francis, at the urging of Zahra, that on January 30 the Commission received a twenty-nine-page file of answers—incomplete—regarding the Holy See's tangled financial web. Something had finally broken. The laypeople on the Pontifical Commission, in this last phase of their work, could sense a crumbling of the opposition thanks to the Holy Father's intercession. A harmful and mutual distrust began to insinuate itself among them.

In the meantime, Francis was reflecting. When he has to make painful decisions, he regroups in private to find strength and focus. He prayed in his room, a simple environment in its furnishings and decorations: a crucifix, a statue of Our Lady of Luján, an icon of St. Francis giving mercy and hope, and a statue of St. Joseph sleeping.

The Curia as a whole deserved to be admonished. Once the budgets were unblocked, the entire community had to share Francis's concerns over the financial future of the Church, and he would have to impose with force, if necessary, the longed-for changes that were only on paper so far. There was a growing risk that the erosion of the patrimony would become unstoppable. On the one hand the economic crisis was striking the richest Catholic countries, reducing their generosity to the Church. On the other hand, in the Vatican, despite the arrival of Francis, expenditures kept going up. And while all of this was happening behind closed doors, faithful pilgrims continued to fill St. Peter's Square, unaware of the hard work it would take to turn the Pope's dictates into reality.

Francis realized that he needed to act immediately, taking drastic measures if necessary. So he decided to intercede mainly on the question of personnel, not only because all of his appeals to take greater care in hiring and assigning jobs had been ignored, but especially because personnel measures more than any other would change the daily perceptions of the people who lived and worked inside the walls. Drastic human resource measures that would make everyone understand that the situation was serious and that the Argentine Jesuit meant what he had promised.

The Holy Father summoned Parolin and immediately ordered the application of emergency measures to the entire Apostolic See. It was a turn of the screw. On February 13, 2014, the Secretary of State sent a memo indicating all the cuts that had to be made. In the document, sent to all the cardinals who headed dicasteries in the Curia, Parolin referred to the crisis, and called for the following:

> The immediate adoption of measures that will help contain expense items concerning personnel so that in this difficult moment of economic crisis the application of these decisions will contribute, in general, to guaranteeing the maintenance of the whole community of work at the service of the Holy Father and the Universal Church.

Bergoglio urged greater mobility between departments, and he imposed a freeze on overtime, on the renewal of temporary contracts, on new professional positions, on promotions, and, of course, on hiring. When a person retired, "the employees in our work force"—Parolin advised—"will not fail to shoulder generously the activity no longer being performed by their colleagues." But the ultimate goal was still remote. "How I would like a Church which is poor and for the poor," Francis had said without guile on March 16, 2013, at his audience with the media. In the Curia there were many who now remembered those words and contrasted them to the notorious remark of Monsignor Marcinkus, the head of the IOR during its worst scandal, who often quipped, "You can't run the Church on Hail Marys." With that he dictated a mind-set that would dominate a dark chapter in Vatican history, a mind-set that persists in some corners of the Curia today.

10

The War, Act II: The Revolution of Francis and the Rise of Cardinal Pell

The Revolution of Francis

ON FEBRUARY 21 AND 22, 2014, FRANCIS CELEBRATED HIS FIRST Consistory, where he appointed nineteen cardinals. Meanwhile, during moments of reflection and prayer, he defined the final details of the reorganization of the state. Among the papers he brought with him into his room at Casa Santa Marta, there was a six-page document that the COSEA Commission had prepared and delivered on February 18. The title was "Proposed Coordination Structure for Economic-Administrative Functions," and it contained a series of suggestions for revolutionizing the small state.

It was a tense and difficult moment. Earlier in the month, on February 3, Francis had also received the final report on COSEA's works, with observations on the critical failures and major risks they had come across. The tone of the report was unsparing:

Final proposals to present to the Holy Father . . .

1. A lack of governance, control and professionalism lead to high risks at APSA. 92 recommendations for addressing those risks have been identified . . . COSEA proposes to involve the adequate juridical authorities wherever particular findings require this.
2. A concrete recommendation for each commercial activity and a proposal for the future organization of the Governorate have been prepared. The summary report will also include a qualitative analysis of the benefits and downsides which a tax on income and sales (VAT) in the Vatican State would bring about.[1]

On the morning of Sunday, February 23, St. Peter's Square was filled with pilgrims. The cardinals who had gathered here less than one year earlier—at the Conclave that beneath Michelangelo's frescoes in the Sistine Chapel had elected an Argentine Jesuit as the next Pontiff—were back in Rome. Francis had carefully prepared the homily that he would read during the Mass at St. Peter's Basilica, where he would be facing the nineteen brother cardinals he had just appointed.

He spoke to them forcefully: "A Cardinal enters the Church of Rome, my brothers, not a royal court . . . May all of us avoid, and help others to avoid, habits and ways of acting typical of a court: intrigue, gossip, cliques, favoritism and partiality." A brief pause, and then the successor of Peter repeated his exhortation for an end to the infighting: "May all of us avoid intrigues . . . May we love those who are hostile to us. We are required not only to avoid repaying others the evil they have done to us, but also to seek generously to do well by them."

His message of peace was meant to ease tensions as well as to introduce the dramatic move he would be presenting the next day to the Council of 15 (C15), the body created by John Paul II to audit the Vatican's finances. It was a touchy situation. Once the Consistory was over, the cardinals of the Council would stay behind in Rome to discuss the 2014 budgets that had been blocked by the auditors. The documents had just been revised, and the Pope in person had ordered the elimination of unnecessary outside consultants and imposed a hiring freeze to reduce personnel costs. If the cardinals did not approve the budget now, the Holy See's activities could grind to a halt. While they were well aware of the situation, not everyone realized that a new super-dicastery was about to be created and that they themselves would be pushed aside. Bergoglio had prepared this new development along the lines indicated by both COSEA and the C8.

The confidential meeting of February 24 would go down in history and I was able to hear it documented in a digital recording. After decades of stalling, the most important reform of the Curia in many years was about to be announced by the Pope. The cardinals were sitting in the room, waiting to hear the news.

The Establishment of the Secretariat and Council for the Economy

Francis was the first to take the floor, making his big announcement immediately in his typically blunt and direct manner:

> During the Consistory I decided to make this dicastery for finance, the Secretariat of the Economy, and today I left the establishing document with the Secretary of State. This morning I signed the *motu proprio*, I spoke with Cardinal Pell, whom you know, and I asked him if he would be the head of this dicastery. The head, I said . . . I don't know if he will be a Secretary or President, the terminology has to be studied, it's written down but I don't remember it . . . I am aware that for him this is a *deminutio capitis* [reduction of power], because he is the head of a church. He is leaving that church to be a banker, which is a *deminutio capitis*, but he said without hesitation that he would do it. I thank him very much. I signed it with today's date, in collaboration with the Secretariat of State and bearing in mind the unique nature of the administrative bodies. For example, the Governorate is not the same as the dicastery for the

> Causes of Saints, and Propaganda Fide also has a special nature because of the donations it receives . . . I wanted to say personally to the members of the Council of 15 that now there will no longer be 15 cardinals but rather 8 bishops and cardinals and 7 laypersons.

After the Holy Father's statement the cardinals applauded, but Parolin silenced them with a gesture of his hand. A new dicastery, the Secretariat of the Economy, was being created and the Council of 15 was being suppressed. Or rather, it was being replaced by a twin body that would be called the Council for the Economy, on which seven of the fifteen participants would be qualified experts from the professional world who would serve not as simple consultants but as voting members, on equal footing with the religious members. Francis was now making concrete and clear to the Church hierarchy the rebalancing of religious and laypeople that had been studied for months by COSEA and the consultants of Promontory and McKinsey. This was a radical change: for the first time a group of lay officials was being allowed into the closed and inviolable world of Vatican finances.

Parolin slightly raised his right hand again, asked for everyone's attention, and thanked the Pope:

> Thank you, Holy Father for coming, thank you for the communication you have brought to us, and we are here to assure you of our collaboration.

And Francis:

> Of that I am certain, I have seen how you have collaborated with COSEA and I am certain.

An Exceptional Secret Document

Here are excerpts from this groundbreaking meeting, transcribed from a digital recording to which I was given exclusive access. We are thus able to enter for the first time into the secret council of cardinals and get a better understanding of the financial issues afflicting the Church:

Parolin: Thank you, truly. The Holy Father has announced and offered his best wishes to Cardinal Pell. We join the Pope in congratulating him on this appointment, also if it means, as the Pope said, a *diminutio*. Nevertheless he accepted, in the spirit of service, the exercise of this new responsibility.

Question from a cardinal: Will the new dicastery be made public immediately?

Parolin: It is not public, the Pope has told me. I myself did not know about it . . . I imagine it will be made public in the next few days. Perhaps Cardinal Pell knows something more . . .

A cardinal's joking remark in a low voice: . . . Of course . . . Pell knows everything . . . (*laughter*)

Pell: I think it will be made public maybe today or tomorrow. Seeing as the announcement has been made, like all of us I would say that it is already public . . . But the Holy Father told me the official announcement will be published today or tomorrow in the *Osservatore* and then we'll move forward.

Parolin: Thank you. I think it will be tomorrow because it takes at least a day for all the procedures, but the Pope told me that he sent the Chirograph to the office today. It'll take a minimum amount of time to process it, to send it up to the Secretariat of State and prepare the press release, etc. . . .

Wisecrack by a cardinal: Better today . . . otherwise Tornielli will tell all tonight [Andrea Tornielli is an Italian Vaticanologist who writes for the newspaper *La Stampa*].

Pell: Yes, it would definitely be better today. A press release has already been prepared, now we're in a new world, there's all the collaboration, but this press release has to be issued by the new dicastery . . .

Parolin: Fine, no problem. But I have to go out to make sure that everything is proceeding, because I imagine that it will be there waiting for me on my desk, perhaps, while you're presenting the budget. Let me go have a look . . . seeing as there's . . . this rush. I'm wondering if our meeting should continue . . .

Cardinals' voices: No . . . No.

Parolin: . . . Or whether at this point we can consider our work concluded for now . . . That is what I wanted to ask. If you have some thoughts . . .

Pell: Thank you, Eminence, I don't think there's much point in continuing now, but I think we have to define the policies for at least the next two or three months. I would suggest that some regulations remain valid for now and we hope there will be a meeting of this new council, consisting of cardinals, bishops and laypersons before the summer, in June or July. This council has to be established and the Holy Father is ready to do it as quickly as possible. It think it would be advisable for things to remain as they are until then. I am open to suggestions.

The cardinals were disoriented and becoming more and more confused. If the Pope suppressed the Council, what would happen to the bedeviled budgets which, now that they had been revised, needed to be approved urgently? There was a risk that everything would be paralyzed. On the one hand, the new dicastery had upset the arrangements of all the other entities. On the other, the Council called upon to approve the 2014 budget was expiring and thus had no power or prerogatives. The economic and financial life of the Holy See had to go on: construction work needed to be approved, suppliers established, consultancies reconsidered. The cardinals didn't know how to behave or even who was supposed to make the decisions.

The Clash Behind Closed Doors of Pell, Parolin, and the Cardinals of the Curia

The Council of 15 meeting was brought under control not by Parolin but by Pell, the ambitious bulldog from Sydney, who had arrived quietly in the Holy See in the spring of 2013 with the intention of playing an important role on Francis's team. He had a large personality and authority. He didn't trust anyone, tending instead to focus on every decision and responsibility himself. Today he was the leader of the assembly and for the moment, at least on paper, he was the new chief of Vatican finances, by the will of the successor of Peter.

Few would have bet on the brilliant career of this priest, who in his home country had survived accusations of covering up for pedophile priests, at least until April 2013, when Francis, indifferent to criticism of the man, appointed him as one of the eight cardinals to advise him on the direction of the Universal Church and the reform of the Roman Curia. Day after day, Pell prepared the change with the goal of taking command of the Curia. Hardly what you would call a *diminutio*! Everyone knows, also at the Vatican, that the person in charge is the one who holds the purse strings. Pell's stature had risen. He had achieved his goal.

At the meeting of the Council of 15, the Prefect of the newborn Secretariat for the Economy, fresh off his appointment, now had to face down cardinals whose concerns and distrust were growing by the minute because of the changes just announced. There was a tense power play between the Australian Cardinal, the old guard—represented by the Head of the Prefecture, Versaldi, and the President of the Governorate, Bertello—and the new Secretary of State, Parolin. The cardinals were hoping to approve the budgets and finally close the book on this chapter. But Pell did more than resist. In what might have looked like a slight skirmish, and using that soft tone of voice practiced by some members of the Curia, "the ranger"—as Bergoglio often described him, in appreciation of his tenacity—reprimanded Parolin with a rap across the knuckles:

> Versaldi: We have to be careful about taking steps, even if formally necessary, that might produce not so much a *vacatio* as a form of lawlessness . . . Each of us has to know if he still has the authority,

the autonomy . . . For example, does the Prefecture still have autonomy to audit accounts? In the meantime . . . shall we continue?

Parolin: We have to see what the Chirograph says in this regard, we don't know, so it is impossible to answer this question, but it seems logical to me that, until the new body starts its operations, things should continue as they do now. I deduce this based on the principles of logic . . .

Pell: The Chirograph will say that the world has changed. We obviously have to move forward through dialogue, gradually. There have been many discussions that have to continue, no one wants to do all this as some kind of revolution. But it would be a mistake to think we could go on exactly as before: the world has changed. The life of the Holy See must go on, and we are obviously seeking your collaboration, without which it is impossible to achieve the good of the Church. And this is what we all want, the good of the Church.

Parolin: There was Cardinal Cipriani, who wanted . . .

Background voice: But I wanted to ask you something . . . Free me from Calcagno, I would gladly go back to being a professor, as long as you don't [kill] me, too . . .

Cipriani: The only doubt is whether our only reason for doing so is to avoid blocking this budget . . . if there is some way that Cardinal Pell thinks we could approve it for two or three months or something of that kind, why isn't anything approved now? We have to go forward today. Otherwise what are they going to do tomorrow? I don't know . . .

Pell: It seems to me, Eminence, that one thing must be clear: an approval *ad interim* for three months would be not only useful but necessary, because life must go on . . .

Versaldi: I would propose we have a look at this separate sheet of paper that was given to us, which is the revision of the unapproved budget, and compare it to the letter that the Secretariat of State sent with the Pope's criteria for reducing personnel costs. If we could, on Cipriani's suggestion, render an opinion of possible approval so as to say that the unapproved budget, which provided for a 25 million euros deficit, has been revised down to 10 million, and therefore reduced by 15, it could be provisionally supported, with the criteria of the Secretariat of State.

Pell: . . . For the moment I think there's little, almost nothing we should change so that we can make sure of where we are. We don't want big revolutions in the next three months . . .

Calcagno: Thank you. First I'd like to assure His Eminence that our collaboration will be as full as it was with the visits of Promontory and COSEA in past months. Having said this, I think that if the budget for the ordinary activities of the Holy See is approved today, it should be valid not only because APSA continues to exist or not exist, but for the very fact that the Holy See has to be able to go forward. There the new structure that you will head will certainly have to make its maneuvers, its proposals . . .

Ironic remark by a cardinal: . . . Maneuvers . . .

Calcagno: . . . variations. But as a fundamental basis in my opinion the budget should be indicated as valid in the framework of the current year, because the year has already begun!

Pell: . . . We are not in a position today to approve something for a year. Something *ad interim*, okay . . .

Vallini: . . . The new dicastery will have time to equip itself with the tools that we here today are at least familiar with . . . unless Cardinal Pell can tell me that all this work has already been done and that in the Holy Father's Chirograph *motu proprio* a statute is coming out that regulates the competencies of the new body that we have only just learned about this morning.

Meisner: Distinguished brothers, first of all my best wishes to Cardinal Pell, who has been seated with us for many years. We have worked hard together and I am happy that we have found a new solution. The road from Sydney to Rome should not be a way of the cross but rather a Triumphal March. My simple question is: we have been given a newly revised budget. And I want to ask: our work today—and tomorrow—is not to discuss the new dicastery but rather to discuss these budgets, and then to draw the consequences . . .

Pell then quoted the *motu proprio*, whose title included a phrase from the Gospel according to Luke, *Fidelis dispensator et prudens*—the faithful and prudent administrator:

> The responsibility of the economic and financial sectors of the Holy See is intimately linked to its own particular mission, not only in its service to the Holy Father in the exercise of his universal ministry but also with respect to how they correspond to the common good in light of integral human development.

The Secretariat of the new dicastery would handle financial planning, and from now on would be preparing the budget. It would be in charge of economic management and vigilance over the agencies of the Holy See and Vatican City. These were competencies that had previously been assigned to the Secretariat of State, which from now on would deal only with diplomatic relations. The Secretariat of State and the Secretariat for the Economy were placed on the same level: both would answer directly to the Holy Father, but Parolin and Pell would have to work together. But the two men would never get along, and there would be no follow up to the Pope's motion to expand the Council of Eight Cardinals, on which Pell served, to include Parolin.

The establishment of the Secretariat for the Economy sent shock waves that would be felt not only in the Secretariat of State but also in the economic dicasteries. Through the creation of an auditor general with control over all the accounts, the Prefecture had been effectively voided. From July 2014 on, APSA would be split in two, losing jurisdiction over the ordinary section, where Pell would take over. It would thus exercise the functions only of a central bank, losing its power over the immense real estate holdings in houses, offices, and palaces. But this proposal did not get off the ground, either.

As for the IOR and its scandals, Francis preferred not to get involved for the moment. It remained outside the perimeter of the Secretariat for the Economy, which did not have full control over internal accounts. Father Lombardi would explain, feigning serenity, at a press conference, that the IOR would thus "not be touched by this reorganization, which has a much broader horizon, but it will continue to be an object of study and reflection."

Approval of the Budgets

The meeting was nearing its end, but someone had to break the stalemate over the unapproved budgets. The most realistic proposal came from Cardinal Angelo Scola, the Archbishop of Milan:

> Scola: Here we cannot give approval for one year or two months or three months. When the new reality is able to redo the budget it will redo it and submit it: this is my opinion. Let me add that unfortunately I will not be present from tomorrow afternoon on because Milan is not a small diocese, and I have been away for eight days . . .
>
> Parolin: I don't think anyone will be here, Eminence, rest assured.
>
> Scola: Well then, I commend the efforts that have led to a saving of 9,612,000 euros and I don't want to hold up the discussion. I approve the modified budget that was prepared for the Holy See.
>
> Tong: I, too, congratulate my classmate George Pell. I only wish to propose that the new structure pay attention to two things: the first is to try to gradually establish a series of standards for the staff and . . . a pay scale . . . You can't expect everyone to work for free . . .
>
> Pell: . . . In order for the people in the congregations to learn how to do a budget, there might be arrangements to send some of them to Paris, Oxford and Madrid for short-term or long-term courses on administration and economics. We will do many things in terms of efficiency and savings but we will not enter into religious or spiritual matters. As the Pope said, we are simple bankers.

Parolin: The Cardinal has inspired others to speak. Cardinal Scherer . . .

Scherer: Now I understand more clearly that we as a council have nothing to say because our work is over. As for the budget and whether or not to approve it, we've waited this long, we can wait another two months if necessary . . . But I wanted to make an observation. I think it would be very useful to set down some rules, some general principles that apply when you are drawing up a budget, otherwise everyone will do their budget as they please . . .

Pell: We will sit down with a congregation and we will say: this year you have such and such amount of money and you can only have this many workers, but then inside this congregation the responsibility for the decisions will be yours . . . And if you spend more, much more, the next year we will cut your budget and you'll have to find the money in your reserves. In many, many places the reserves are adequate, thank God . . . Thank God, because there are many challenges for the Holy See. But here and there, there is a lot more money than we ever knew about and that has never appeared in the balance sheets. And we thank God for these buried treasures.

Parolin: Good, we can consider our meeting adjourned . . . We'll carry on with the revised budgets until the new structure has produced a new budget.

The meeting concluded with two solid points. The first was the reorganization of the Curia hierarchy in matters pertaining to the economic and financial structure. The second was the budgets: they would have to be approved by the new Council for the Economy. Pell had won the battle: for months the budgets would remain in limbo, waiting to be approved, leaving the Holy See in a kind of financial purgatory: they would carry on with the budgets corrected by the auditors—this was Parolin's policy—until the new Council ordered by Bergoglio kicked into action.

The stalemate would last until March 21, when Father Luigi Mistò, the right-hand man of Calcagno, would send to all the departments that reported to APSA the guidelines for rewriting the 2014 budget with "corrections and modifications to the expenses initially planned, thereby incorporating the observation of the international auditors."

Pell made it clear that he was very familiar with the Curia's secrets. At the conclusion of the Council of 15 he gave his cardinal brothers advance notice of what the COSEA experts had discovered in their analysis of the Holy See's finances: namely, that many administrative bodies had "buried treasure" that was not recorded on the balance sheets. Do not fool yourself—the Australian Cardinal intimated—those mysterious off-budget reserves are providential today, in the midst of the crisis: they will become indispensable as we move forward, given the constant revelations of deficits in the account books, which are only destined to get worse.

Starting in March 2014, Pell dedicated himself to his new assignment. He met often with Francis on a confidential basis to come to an agreement on the new members of the Council for the Economy, and he flew to Malta to meet with Zahra, who would be one of the five COSEA commissioners chosen to be a lay member of the new Council. The other two laypersons included a friend of Zahra, the Italian Francesco Vermiglio. The selection of Vermiglio sparked discontent and criticism because of a potential conflict of interest. According to an investigation by the Italian magazine *l'Espresso*, Vermiglio was Zahra's partner in Misco Advisory Ltd., a joint venture created to stimulate Italian investments in the small Mediterranean island of Malta.

Seven of the cardinals who had served on the preceding C15 were also confirmed. The only new religious faces were Cardinal Daniel N. DiNardo from the diocese of Galveston-Houston, and Reinhard Marx, the Archbishop of Munich. The Secretariat's offices would be in the St. John Tower, a medieval structure located in the highest part of the Vatican gardens, generally used to receive important guests. In practice, it was the only free building in the whole state.

Logistics would be handled by Xuereb, who asked Calcagno and

Monsignor Fernando Vérgez Alzaga, Secretary of the Governorate, to order "20 computers, 6 printers, 21 landline phones, a loudspeaker for sending and receiving calls," so that all the work stations distributed over four floors and their relative internet connections would be immediately operative.[2] He also asked that the most important offices be equipped with shredders to guarantee the confidentiality of the most sensitive files.

The new Council had four important appointments on the calendar for 2014: the first was on May 2 in the Sala Bologna of the Apostolic Palace, then there were others in July, September, and December. The seating arrangements for these first meetings already gave a sense of the change under way. Religious and laypersons would alternate, a visual demonstration of how power is distributed. But unfortunately that didn't happen. The community chosen by Francis, made up of strong personalities from different cultures and backgrounds, was riddled with venom, malicious gossip, and traps. And month after month, its initial ambitious project would be downsized.

The Rise of Pell, Survivor of the Pedophile Scandals

Pell had been promoted to cardinal in 2003 by John Paul II. His controversial past deserves the appropriate attention. In 2010 Benedict XVI had mentioned him as a possible prefect of the powerful Congregation for Bishops, to succeed Giovanni Battista Re, who had reached the age of retirement. But when Francis arrived at the Vatican he didn't know Pell, or at least they weren't friends, although they had met in 2012 when the Australian was appointed Father of the XIII Ordinary General Assembly of the Synod of Bishops.

At the Vatican, immediately after the election of Francis, Pell became one of the Councilors on the C15. The Council is a venerable body but without great power. Yet by increasing its functions through an internal audit, it had the capability of becoming the operative arm of the Pope's soft revolution.

In the spring of 2013, Pell was trying to envision the pathway to change and to identify the councilors closest to the Pope. He guessed correctly the new climate that the Pope wanted to bring into the Curia, and he wanted to play a central role in the project of restructuring the Vatican. In particular, he started to spend time with Cardinal Santos Abril y Castelló, Francis's good friend and the next President of the IOR. He also approached Monsignor Vallejo Balda, the Secretary of the Prefecture and later the Coordinator of COSEA. (Vallejo Balda was the prelate who had immediately reported many critical flaws to the Pontiff, starting with the embezzlement he had discovered at the St. Mary Major Basilica.) Finally, the Australian Cardinal developed a solid relationship with Óscar Andrés Rodríguez Maradiaga, the Archbishop of Tegucigalpa, the capital of Honduras, and the coordinator of the then C8.

Pell's detractors claimed that the Cardinal had a single objective in those weeks: to obtain for himself a post in the Apostolic Palace and leave Sydney behind, thereby fleeing the aggressive investigation being conducted by the Australian Royal Commission into Institutional Responses to Child Sexual Abuse. There had been many reported cases of pedophilia in the diocese of Melbourne from 1996 to 2001, when Pell was Archbishop. It was suspected that the new Prefect had not cooperated with the investigators and had concealed the dramatic stories of minors who had been abused by priests in his diocese.

There was also the time, in October 2012, that Pell himself had been cleared of accusations that he had abused a twelve-year-old catechism student at a camp for altar boys in 1961. Or the accusations against him by a former altar boy, John Ellis, shortly after his appointment as Prefect. Ellis named the Church responsible for the violence he had suffered between 1974 and 1979, when he was abused by a priest who has since died. The former altar boy lost the first lawsuit in 2007. During the investigation his physical scars verified the abuse but the diocese was not found legally responsible for the appalling incidents.

Pell was left legally unscathed by these various accusations, which he had always rejected, but they did land him in the headlines of newspapers throughout the world. His biggest accuser was Peter Saunders, a victim of abuse during his childhood in Wimbledon and as of December 2014, handpicked by Bergoglio to be a member of the Pontifical Commission for the Protection of Minors. Saunders had repeatedly demanded that Pell be fired. During an episode of the Australian edition of 60 *Minutes*, Saunders accused Pell of dodging the work and the questions of the Australian Commission of Inquest. "He is making a mockery of the child victims of sexual abuse. He is a dangerous individual, almost sociopathic. He acted with callousness and cold-heartedness."

Nor should we forget the criticisms of the "Melbourne Response," the 1996 protocol approved by Pell that provided for modest damages to the victims of pedophile priests. The document put a cap on damages of $50,000, whereas in court the victims were being awarded even six times that amount. The Cardinal had a ready response: "Many of the people we helped through the compensation panel would have received nothing or very little if they had gone through the courts." But the findings of the Australian Royal Commission in its preliminary report were truly negative:

> The high prelate did not act fairly from a Christian point of view. The archdiocese over which he presided preferred to safeguard and protect its own resources rather than provide justice.

Pell was also famous for some of his particularly unfortunate public statements, starting with his remarks about Islam being "an essentially bellicose religion, the Koran is studded with invocations to violence." Another incident was on August 22, 2014, when, during a hearing of the Royal Commission on videoconference, Pell argued that "pedophile priests are like truck drivers who molest hitchhikers: neither the Church nor the trucking company can be held responsible," sparking outrage in the courthouse and in public opinion. Yet it should also be mentioned that during his testimony, the Cardinal confessed that his archdiocese had not "acted fairly."

The Commission's Costs

But nothing seemed to slow down the career of this cardinal, who now had an agenda filled with appointments, for the purpose of rationalizing the Curia's accounts once and for all. The action would be planned and developed over a three year period, from 2014–2016. The roadmap would create conflicts and enemies but it could also count on sizable resources.

The Secretariat had a surprisingly large budget: 4.2 million euros. To understand how it was used, let's take a look at its ledgers. First, there were the expenses of COSEA, which cost 2.5 million euros. Much of this amount went to consultants' fees, since the Commission's members all worked pro bono.

Thanks to my access to the documentation, I am the first who can specify who was paid what. Promontory received 980,000 euros for its audit of APSA, McKinsey 420,000 for the Vatican Media Center, Oliver Wyman 270,000 for its analysis of the pension funds, Ernst & Young 230,000 for its inspections of the Governorate, and KPMG 110,000 for accounting procedures. Although the official amounts would never be released by the small circle of the Pope's loyalists, the consultancy fees were the basis for one of the first attacks on Francis: how could the Holy Father balance the budget if he was spending such large amounts of money on a new round of consultants?

The Secretariat for the Economy would not become operative until March 2015, when its rules and regulations were approved. But in 2014, according to the reconstructions of newspapers, more than 500,000 euros were spent on travel, computers, clothing, and consultancies. Danny Casey, an economist and longtime friend of Pell, reportedly received 15,000 euros a month for his services:

> For Casey the Secretariat of the Economy even rented an apartment for 2,900 euros a month on Via dei Coronari and paid for top-quality office and home furnishings: under the item "wallpaper" the table indicates 7,292 euros; more than 47,000 for "furniture and cabinets," including a kitchen-sink cabinet for 4,600 euros, in addition to various jobs for 33,000 euros. The Cardinal added in a handwritten note expenses also for purchases at Gammarelli's, the historic tailor shop that since 1798 has dressed the Curia of the eternal city: in general the cardinals pay out of pocket for their cassock and cap, but this time the Secretariat received a bill directly of 2,508 euros for clothing.[3]

Despite his controversial past and expensive tastes, especially at a time of budget cuts and austerity, Pell was a frightening figure, and for many in the Curia this was the main reason behind the attacks on him. Cardinal Maradiaga would brand these reports as "slander: it's like Marxism that attacked the person since it couldn't attack the idea. Pell is a frugal man and he does not like luxury."

Poisonous Rumors

From the day of his installation at the Secretariat of the Economy, poisonous rumors had been spread about Pell in an effort to isolate, discredit, and exhaust him. The consolidation of all the economic departments under a superdicastery was behind schedule. For months there was no movement on the transfer of competencies, such as placing the Secretariat of State's personnel office under a single unit directed by Pell. Key staff members had still not been appointed. All of this left the situation of the economic dicasteries exactly as it had been before: apart from public announcements, nothing had changed. For example, although there was an announcement of the transfer to Pell's jurisdiction of APSA's ordinary section—which handles the real estate—nothing was done.

Although the Prefecture was supposed to be closed as early as possible, it was still open for business throughout the summer of 2015. The position of auditor general had been authorized in February 2014, but there would not be an appointment until sixteen months later, on June 5, 2015. The man selected was Libero Milone, a professional with thirty-two years of experience at Deloitte, a consultancy company in which he had also served as CEO (for Italy). Into the summer of 2015, there was still friction between the Secretariat for the Economy and APSA over who should keep the archives, since they shared jurisdiction over real estate: one handled management, the other supervision.

Vatican managers opposed and obstructed Pell and Bergoglio's plans, in the conviction that they could stop innovation and discredit the Pope through a war of attrition. "They used to say," a cardinal confided in me, "that the Church is two thousand years old and will survive even the priests. Today they might regret to admit that some bad apples in the Curia will survive even the pontiffs of change."

The Cleaning Crew

To accelerate the reform and disempower the opposition, on both the theological and financial fronts, Francis began to replace en masse the members of the old guard still in command at many of the offices that controlled the activities of the small state. But first he equipped himself with the means to make it easier. In the fall of 2014 he enacted regulations that would set the retirement age at 75 for directors of dicasteries. He also introduced a measure allowing him to request early retirement for members, "after having made known the reasons for the request" to the person affected in the context of a "fraternal dialogue"—as can be read in the document signed by Parolin on November 5, 2014.

In this manner many cardinals in the Curia were shown the door. And at the same time as he was drafting the new regulations for Pell, the Holy Father removed the American Cardinal Raymond Leo Burke from his position as Prefect of the Supreme Tribunal of the Apostolic

Segnatura. Burke became patron of the Sovereign Order of Malta, a largely honorary post. This conservative cardinal, once described as "a harpsichord playing in the desert" by some of Francis's loyalists, was one of the most vociferous opponents of the Pontiff. "Many of the faithful"—he stated after the Synod—"are feeling a bit seasick because they feel the church's ship has lost its way."

In March 2015 another member of the Curia, Cardinal Versaldi, President of the Prefecture, was transferred to the Congregation for Catholic Education. Monsignor Mariano Crociata was demoted, from the powerful Secretary General of the Italian Bishops' Conference to Bishop of the small diocese of Latina. Crociata was famous for his gaffe on the day of Bergoglio's election, when the Italian Bishops' Conference that he headed issued a press release welcoming the elevation to Peter's Throne of Cardinal Angelo Scola. He was replaced by Monsignor Nuncio Galantino, who in August 2015 openly attacked Italian politics as "a harem of cronies and con artists: the people are not just a flock of sheep to be guided and sheered." He also took aim at the hardline anti-immigration policies of the Northern League: "Do not seek votes on the backs of others."[4]

Jessica and the Others

For months Francis was in a silent tug of war with the Dean of Papal Protocol, the powerful Francesco Camaldo, who had been demoted to Canon of the Vatican basilica. Camaldo is the prelate who, on the evening of March 13, 2013, after the white smoke, could be seen in the second row to the left of the Pope on the balcony overlooking St. Peter's Square. This picture went around the world and was a source of no small embarrassment for Francis.

For many years Camaldo had been the Secretary of the former Vicar of Rome, Cardinal Ugo Poletti. The names of both men appeared in an investigation into the disappearance of Emanuela Orlandi, the teenage daughter of a clerk at the Prefecture of the Pontifical house, who on June 22, 1983, after her classes at a music school in Rome, was never seen again. The Italian prosecutors had long connected her disappearance with the odd burial place of Renatino De Pedis. The alleged cashier of the Magliana gang—an organized crime group that controlled the capital's drug market in the 1980s—De Pedis had for mysterious reasons been laid to rest in the crypt of the Sant'Appolinaire Basilica. This strange burial had been authorized by Cardinal Poletti while the investigators believed that the practical details had been left to his travel secretary, Camaldo.

Francis might also have received word of the nickname by which Camaldo was known in certain corners of the capital as emerged during the prosecutor's investigations: Jessica. It was hardly fitting for a man of the cloth, especially one so close to the Pope. He was not the only prelate or cardinal with such a unique sobriquet. There was also "Mother Superior," a Sicilian monsignor with a penchant for champagne and novices; "Peacock," a vain cardinal from northern Italy who enjoyed being "pampered" by a handsome young entrepreneur who did business with the Vatican; "Monica Lewinsky," and many more. The associates of the so-called gay lobby had nicknames that identified them by their origins or sexual proclivities. They would allegedly procure the services of laymen with criminal records who at night, after work, would cruise the Roman bars and nightclubs in search of young boys to satisfy the vices of the senior prelates who protected them. As compensation, the panderers would apparently receive tips, protected careers in Vatican offices, or government jobs, and higher pay than normally accorded a person with their job description or skill set.

I should specify, however, that Francis did not find a "gay lobby" in the Vatican. That is to say, there is no structured homosexual organization that determines appointments, assigns contracts, or controls dicasteries, money and people's lives and careers. But the reality is actually worse. In the clergy being gay is experienced as a secret, an unspeakable weakness, a broken taboo, and an easy target for blackmail. "Many cardinals cultivate a secret vice"—explains a banker, a Vatican consultant who preferred to remain anonymous—"some like boys, some like models, some are passionate about food and wine, some are greedy for money. If a con artist is looking for a mark, once he's pinpointed a cardinal's weakness he's on easy street. He satisfies the cardinal's itch and he'll be compensated handsomely." But doesn't this happen in every bureaucracy of the world? "No, at the Vatican they live with the hypocritical fear of causing a scandal, which conditions their choices, their reactions, and is unequaled in other parts of the world. They worry that the truth will alienate believers from the faith, which is why they keep everything hidden. At a very high cost. It's a shame that all these secrets foster pressure and blackmail. Francis is trying to end this situation but he is running into strong resistance."

The consultant then related the story of a monsignor who had been tailed on his visits to gay massage parlors on Via Merulana and in the Parioli district. A few choice photographs and the priest was a goner. Anyone who doesn't want to end up being blackmailed has to search for friendships and hookups on special gay websites that guarantee absolute anonymity. But sometimes these encounters lead to tragedies, like the case of a cardinal's young lover who years ago jumped off the building in Rome where he worked, tired of the pressures and the blackmail to which his beloved cardinal was being subjected.

Immediately after his election, Francis read the notes left for him by Benedict XVI, the report on the leaked documents, and he realized that the situation—also in terms of the morality and habits of his collaborators—was out of control. He asked for the files of the stipends and monthly salaries of the main advisors, where he discovered that there were secretaries being paid as much as 15,000 euros a month. "These sums"—as one of Bergoglio's collaborators commented—"are proof of friendship for sexual purposes." The reaction of the Pontiff is not known, but he is certainly aware that on this front, from the times of Benedict XVI to today, the situation shows no sign of improving.

Epilogue: Will Francis Resign, Too?

An Incomplete Revolution

I HAVE DESCRIBED HOW FRANCIS, UPON HIS ELECTION, FOUND THE Curia in disarray, characterized by inertia, scandals, thefts, wrongdoing, and opaque interests. An unreliable Curia had led Benedict XVI to resign and alienated many of the Church's faithful. To change that dynamic Francis had invested the best minds in the Vatican and spent millions of euros on consultants, hiring lay professionals from outside the walls and inviting them to comb through the accounts of the Holy See. This was an unusual gesture of trust but also a necessary path. Only in this way could the Pope defeat the old power centers that had taken root during the Cold War and grown in the shadows for decades. Only in this way could he restore full credibility and a future to a Church suffering from a chronic crisis in vocations, followers, and offerings.

Of all the reforms contemplated during the first year of his pontificate, very few managed to get off the ground. This unfortunately meant one thing: Bergoglio's plan to drive out the merchants from the temple was still unfulfilled some three years after his election. The only project that did become concrete was the communications hub, through the establishment of the new Secretariat for Communications. All the other projects and changes announced remained in the drawer or were only partially realized. This situation was a source of discontent all around. More and more cardinals were criticizing the Holy Father, some quite openly, like the Slovenian Franc Rodé, the former Archbishop of Ljubljana.

"Without a shadow of a doubt"—Rodé stated to the Slovenian national press agency—"the Pope is a communications genius. He communicates quite well with the crowds, the media and the faithful." He then added, "A great advantage is that he seems likeable. On the other hand, his opinions, on capitalism and social justice, are too far to the left. You can see how the Pope is marked by the environment from which he comes. In South America there are great social differences and lively debates on this situation take place every day. They are people who talk a lot but solve very few problems."

There was also the Guinean Cardinal Robert Sarah, the Prefect of the Congregation for Divine Worship. In March 2015, upon his return from a trip to France, he said, "Inside the Catholic Church there are signs of a certain confusion on fundamental doctrinal, moral and disciplinary questions."

Some cardinals made their dissent even more explicit, such as Gerhard Ludwig Müller, Prefect of the Congregation for the Doctrine of the Faith, who did not participate in a Mass because he did not share some of the Holy Father's interpretations of theology. Or Camillo Ruini, the former President of the Italian Bishops' Conference, who in October 2014, out of disagreement with positions on the remarriage of divorced persons, refused to shake Francis's hand after the Synod.

There were open manifestos, such as the book *Remaining in the Truth of Christ*, written by five cardinals—Müller, Raymond Lee Burke, Velasio De Paolis (former leader of the Prefecture), the Italian Carlo Caffarra, and the Austrian Walter Brandmüler—disputing the idea that divorced people can partake of the sacraments.

For a progress report, let's start with the Secretariat for the Economy, where Cardinal Pell was supposed to achieve the goal of consolidating all the Vatican's finances. This was Francis's wish, but so far it hasn't happened. Its twin, the Secretariat of State, continues to hold full control over the resources that it managed in the past—starting with the Peter's Pence, the generous flow of money from dioceses all over the world that is meant to support the pastoral mission of the Church and instead ends up being used to cover the deficits of the dicasteries.

Management of the Peter's Pence was supposed to be transferred to the Secretariat for the Economy, but there was huge resistance from Parolin's offices. For that matter, Pell and Parolin never managed to establish a true collaboration and have sometimes clashed bitterly. One example of this occurred in December 2014 and February 2015, when Pell spread the word that the investigations of previous months had turned up hundreds of millions of euros not reported in the Vatican's balance sheets.

"At the Consistory I explained that to date [February 13, 2015], there are 442 million euros in additional assets in the dicasteries, in addition to the 936 we had identified in an earlier moment." In the end it was found that a total of 1.4 billion euros had not been entered into the balance sheets. Then came Parolin's cutting reply: "The Secretariat of State also did not know it was not the only one to have set aside so much money for a rainy day." Some Vaticanists interpreted these statements as an attack by Pell on Parolin, and corrections and rectifications were quickly issued by the Vatican press office to clarify that the euros had been kept in reserve, off the books, and not in a slush fund. But the most significant fact was that the revelation of such a huge amount of money off the books had taken away both resources and discretionary power from those who, until recently, had managed those sums with complete autonomy.

As for the other dicasteries, the Governorate remained autonomous, as did Propaganda Fide and APSA. While it is true that APSA had to give up management of rental income, which was handed over to Pell, it still controlled the properties themselves. Here, too, there were daily tensions between Team Pell and Team Calcagno. The latest news that I can relate before this book goes to press took place in July–August 2015, when there was yet another tug of war between APSA and the Secretariat for the Economy over who should keep the archives for the Holy See's immense real estate holdings. These files contain the secrets on the sales and leases of palaces and houses to friends of friends. Who did the archives belong to? To APSA, the owner of the assets, or the men of the Australian Cardinal, who were trying to make better use of rental income? This was another occasion for infighting and misunderstandings.

A census and estimate of the artistic patrimony was in the works but still hadn't gotten off the ground. The reform of employee pensions was still in the planning stages, although it was a matter of urgency to prevent the more than 800 million euro deficit predicted by COSEA. All of the projects regarding health insurance and creating a single office for human resources were at a standstill. Secretary of State Parolin had taken upon himself the job of coordinating the various personnel offices, but centralization was still a distant dream, despite the fact that it would prevent the many fiefdoms and feuds that foster private interests and privileges.

The Auditor's Office—the control tower for all the Vatican's finances—would open for business after a one year delay. It reports directly to the Pope but the roles and responsibilities will not be defined until approval of the regulations enabling the office to become fully operational. So there has been some progress on accounting procedures to obtain standardized and, above all, credible, financial reporting.

Resistance, Sabotage, and Fake Bugs

Francis may never have imagined that he would encounter such entrenched and tenacious resistance. It was no easy matter to uncover dirty business dealings, not even for a pope. The evidence was hard to collect: at the Vatican no one reports wrongdoing, and few trust or confide in one another. The reform juggernaut of Francis was always at the center of misinformation campaigns and acts of outright sabotage—not only anonymous letters, burglary, and veiled threats like the forwarding of letters to Michele Sindona, but also criminal operations, such as various illegal wiretaps.

Stories like this pop up periodically like underground springs, leaving the small Vatican community aghast. The latest case was in March 2015 and it took place at the Vatican, but as usual, no news of it leaked outside the Leonine Walls. Hidden microphones had been discovered in some offices of the Prefecture. "Unknown hands" had planted a system of bugs in the cars, offices, and homes of some of the priests who work there. They were not just ordinary priests and monsignors. The Prefecture is the control center for the whole financial system of the Holy See. During those weeks the astonished cardinals and monsignors could not stop wondering who would have planted those bugs, and why. The news also landed on the desk of Francis's personal secretary. One detail made the mystery even more complicated: not all of the hidden microphones worked. Some of them might have been bluffs, rudimentary electronic devices put there to send a message, a warning, to the Pope's collaborators that no secrets were safe.

Another mystery was that the Gendarmerie, as far as anyone could tell, had not been involved in the investigation. Whose job was it to identify the culprits if not the small state's internal security forces?

These questions troubled the men who had chosen to collaborate with Francis and believed in his message. And they forced greater caution on this Pope who had arrived in Rome from the ends of the Earth. Perhaps it was no accident that the whole block of Italian cardinals considered responsible for the Vatican's woes had managed to resist the Argentine Pope with such determination. Many of them were removed from office, it is true, but not all of them. Bertello remained at the helm of the Governorate. Calcagno was leading APSA. Versaldi had left the

Prefecture, but only recently, for the new job of Prefect to one of the most important congregations, the Congregation for Catholic Education.

Francis's actions are never crude. He is waiting patiently for the majority to step down when they are forced to, at age eighty. In the meantime, he is monitoring them through the figures of men he trusts, like Monsignor Fernando Vérgez Algaza, a Spanish bishop. Promoted to Secretary of the Governorate, for many years he was close to the Argentine Cardinal Eduardo Francisco Pironio. Pironio was one of the cardinals whom Bergoglio used to see at the Vatican with pleasure during his trips from Buenos Aires in the 1980s and 1990s. Francis didn't seem to mind that a monsignor or cardinal belonged to an organization like Opus Dei, the Legionnaires of Christ, or the Focolari. What he valued above all was the independence, reliability, and consistency of various cardinals. And those who erred were cast out.

The story is told that Francis once met a monsignor with positions of responsibility behaving in a manner unbecoming the cassock he was wearing. Without batting an eye, Francis said: "I want you out of here by tomorrow. Later we'll decide where." Only Francis knows if the story is truth or legend. Whatever the case, it is certainly plausible, and it captures his character perfectly.

Divide and Conquer

It would be simplistic and misleading to reduce the conflicts to a division between two worlds: on the one side the reformers, Francis together with Pell, Zahra, and de Franssu, who since July 2014 has been the number one man at the IOR; on the other, the "Italian" curia that obstructs and resists him. The situation is much more complex and muddled. The clearest example of this may be Vatican Asset Management (VAM), the project realized by de Franssu to better handle the assets of the Vatican.

There were fundamentally two versions of VAM. In the first, the project was meant to gather under one roof the real estate patrimony of the Vatican by creating a kind of sovereign fund. Then the proposal was made to manage part of the IOR investments in a SICAV (*Société d'Investissement à Capital Variable*—Investment Company with Variable Capital), similar to an open-ended mutual fund in the United States. As a member of COSEA, de Franssu had already heavily promoted this plan in January 2014, for the purpose of building alliances. There were many dinners and meetings with Monsignor Wells of the Secretariat of State and Ernst von Freyberg, who at the time was the head of the IOR. De Franssu found an ally in Zahra, whom he had known ever since their days of working together at MISCO, the Maltese company that Zahra had founded to create incentives for Italian investment into the small island state. In this way COSEA was giving its endorsement and de Franssu presented the VAM project for the approval of the IOR board, chaired by Cardinal Santos Abril y Castelló. But the elderly Cardinal vetoed the idea. De Franssu considered the project fundamental to his future, however, and he refused to give up, so he decided to involve the Pope directly.

The VAM project ended up on the Pope's desk, in his small suite in the Santa Marta guesthouse. At the end of May, the Pope also rejected the idea, confirming the decision of his cardinal friend. The Holy Father did not want to put too much power in the hands of so few people. *Divide and conquer* as the ancient Romans used to say: in this case, divide the power among the subordinates and command. In 2015 trust in de Franssu was declining, but not so much because two years earlier Bertone himself had indicated de Franssu as a candidate for the leadership of the IOR, to replace Ettore Gotti Tedeschi. It was more because of the information finding its way into Santa Marta. A very thick and detailed file was delivered to the Pope in June 2014 on the relations between de Franssu and Zahra, and on relations between Zahra and the Vermiglio law office of Messina, for which the Maltese economist had done some work. These relations were completely transparent and above board, but they forced the Pope to reflect on the risk of placing too much power in laymen's hands.

Another thorn in Francis's side came from the selection of auditing companies in 2013 and 2014 to redesign the structure of the Curia. Some of the most delicate tasks had been assigned to the American company Promontory Financial Group, including oversight of the IOR's accounts. Promontory was supposed to be a guarantee, considering the prestige of its founder and CEO. He was Eugene A. Ludwig, a friend and law school classmate of former U.S. President Bill Clinton, with whom he had worked from 1993 to 1998. Many of the company's managers had been hired after cutting their teeth in federal agencies, to such an extent that the wags in the Vatican and conspiracy theorists saw Promontory as the long hand of the CIA.

In the Holy See there was a torrent of criticism of the powerful American company for its contradictory practices. A prelate who shall remain anonymous was interviewed in June 2015 for the television weekly news magazine *Report*. In his words, "To be considered transparent you need an independent consultant to certify your accounts. Today the IOR's accounts are being audited by the American company Promontory, which is paid by the IOR, so it will say whatever the IOR wants it to say. Not to mention that de Franssu's son was given a job at Promontory." He was referring to Louis Victor de Franssu, who after studying at Notre Dame in Indiana, had been an intern in London at Goldman Sachs and a parliamentary assistant at the House of Commons before entering Promontory, where he deals with risk management and regulatory compliance.

As if this were not enough, a few weeks later American newspapers reported that the Department of Financial Services was investigating Promontory for its alleged role in the transfer of funds to Iran from the New York branch of the English bank Standard Chartered, back in 2011, when the country was under embargo. This was a source of embarrassment for the Vatican, considering all the sensitive information the Promontory advisors had viewed during their audit of the IOR. Consequently, a thorough control of all outside consultancies was ordered in the summer of 2015 with the instruction to suspend operations with any auditing companies that were not irreplaceable.

The attempt to reform the IOR was another unresolved issue. I have only hinted at it here because the IOR was not a target of the wide-ranging investigation conducted by the COSEA Commission that is the focus of this book. Today the Vatican bank is still impenetrable in many respects, and a world unto itself. It is hardly as opaque as it was during the pontificates of John Paul II—when it didn't even present a financial report and its clients laundered money from government kickbacks—and of Benedict XVI, but the Vatican bank is still far from trustworthy. The international auditing bodies have expressed positive assessments of the transparency measures introduced, but Francis still has profound doubts about it, though he has said or done nothing decisive about its internal structure. Various old-guard officials and directors have kept their prominent positions. And there are fears of a recurrence of the situation under former President Gotti Tedeschi—worries that money will continue to be misused without the leadership knowing about it.

Will the Pope Win the Battle?

It is hard to answer this question with any certainty. I believe that his project cannot be deferred or avoided, but it is hard to argue that he will succeed in bringing to completion his ambitious mission. There are too many interests at stake, both inside and outside the walls. The Mafia has always fought anyone who tried to destroy criminal systems that were able to launder huge amounts of money, and to turn dirty money into apparently normal legal financial realities. It is no accident that Italian prosecutors who are experts in organized crime, such as Deputy Prosecutor Nicola Gratteri, have repeatedly expressed their fear about threats to Pope Francis's safety. But he is following the path that he must take, and he will not allow himself to be intimidated—unless the pressures ultimately become so unbearable that he will feel forced to resign, as he slyly insinuates every so often. Francis—the great, singular Pope—has to count the number of his friends every day to make sure he will not be left alone.

Notes

1. Pope Francis Issues a Shocking Accusation

1 From the Pope's press conference on July 28, 2013.

2 Of the eight cardinals, only one, Cardinal Giuseppe Bertello, President of the Governorate, resided in Rome. The others came from Chile (the Archbishop of Santiago, Cardinal Javier Errázuriz Ossa); Honduras (the Archbishop of Tegucigalpa, Cardinal Óscar Andrés Rodríguez Maradiaga); the United States (the Archbishop of Boston, Cardinal Sean Patrick O'Malley); India (the Archbishop of Mumbai, Cardinal Oswald Gracias); Germany (the Archbishop of Munich, Cardinal Reinhard Marx); Congo (the Archbishop of Kinshasa, Cardinal Laurent Monsengwo Pasinya); and Australia (the Archbishop of Sydney, Cardinal George Pell).

3 The chair of the new structure was Cardinal Raffaele Farina, the archivist/librarian emeritus of the Holy See. The Coordinator was the Spanish Bishop Juan Ignacio Arrieta Ochoa de Chinchetru, the Secretary of the Pontifical Council for legislative texts. The Secretary was Monsignor Peter Brian Wells, Commissioner for General Affairs of the Secretary of State. The members also included Mary Ann Glendon, former American Ambassador to the Holy See, and Jean-Louis Pierre Tauran, Chair of the Pontifical Council for Inter-religious Dialogue, who on the previous March 12 had announced to the world the election of Jorge Mario Bergoglio as the new head of the Church in the traditional *habemus papam* oration from the balcony overlooking St. Peter's Square.

4 In the letter the auditors underline the huge conflict of interests they have come across. "In many offices there is no clear separation of financial duties. This means that, in general, the same individuals are responsible for the financial decisions,

implementing them, recording the transactions and communicating them to the higher authorities. In the best of cases this results in limited oversight of irregularities, identification of errors, and identification of opportunities for improvement, not to mention ways of increasing efficiency." The examples are abundant: from the management of the immense real estate holdings to the pension fund. "These failures are quite visible"—the auditors go on to say in their letter to Francis—"in the real estate sector, where for several years now the Vatican's outside auditors have criticized the (non-existent) system of oversight, the difficulties in collecting rent, and other related questions. We are also worried about the pension fund, on which no professional actuarial analyses have been carried out."

5 The auditors suggest that Francis move gradually to prevent a spike in irregularities. "We would be quite concerned," the document continues, "if this consolidation were to take place before improvements have been made in planning, budgeting, and oversight and accounting processes, because otherwise even more serious losses would be possible because of irregularities. This is even riskier in the management of cash flow and investments, not to mention procurement, in which a more centralized management structure would be advantageous but could also involve risks so large as not to argue against centralization. In other areas there seems to be a simple reluctance to change the traditional style of operating, despite the huge potential in terms of savings."

6 Domenico Calcagno, Bishop of Savona from 2002 to 2007, and Secretary of APSA since July 2007, appointed by Benedict XVI as the successor to Cardinal Attilio Nicora. He is a controversial character, from the old guard of Bertone, and the protagonist of some rather singular events, as we shall see later.

7 Tarcisio Bertone would keep his post as Secretary of State until October 15, 2013, when he reached the mandatory retirement age of eighty and was replaced by Cardinal Pietro Parolin.

8 From 1973 to 1980 Jorge Mario Bergoglio was the youngest Provincial Superior of the Society of Jesus in Argentina.

9 The Commission for Reference on the Economic and Administrative Structure of the Holy See is the third commission that Francis created, after the eight-member Council of Cardinals to advise him on an overhaul of the Curia (April 2013) and the Pontifical Commission for Reference on the IOR.

10 The Rules and Regulations of the Prefecture for Economic Affairs of the Holy See dictate the following: "Art. 10. The Prefecture shall be headed by a Cardinal President, who is assisted by a specific number of cardinals, with the aid of the Secretariat, which is normally one prelate, and by a General Accountant, with the consultancy of the Advisors . . . ; Art. 20. The Prefecture shall make use of the collaboration of Advisors, Experts, and International Auditors. They shall be selected according to the criteria of competency and universality, and shall lend their efforts free of charge; Art. 23. The International Auditors, numbering five, are professionals who are particularly skilled in auditing accounts and analyzing financial statements. They are appointed by the Supreme Pontiff for a three-year period. The post can be renewed for a maximum of up to three terms."

11 The discrepancy between estimated and actual costs is huge. At the meeting Salvatore Colitta, an auditor from RB Audit Italia, gave a few examples. "There are weaknesses in the formulation of the budget"—according to the minutes—"that show discrepancies, in the planning stage, of up to 100 percent. I would recommend a revision of the budget at least every six months. The procurement process has not yet been completed. There are no referenced suppliers; there are no agreements with the senior officials . . . the management of real estate has unbelievable levels of arrears, which often exceed the credits. There is something wrong with the system. There are also anomalies that need to be understood by conducting an investigation tenant by tenant. With regard to laid-off personnel, we should increase the number of units in the legal and real estate offices."

12 The losses from the Banca Popolare di Sondrio can be blamed on the decisions of a single cardinal. General Accountant Fralleoni explains it clearly as the auditors' minutes show: "The year in which the Governorate purchased these shares, Cardinal Szoka [Edmund Casimir Szoka, 1927–2014, President of the Governorate from 2001 to 2006] wanted to centralize some activities of the Governorate through this bank. He thought that the stocks would guarantee benefits, but the relationship with the bank did not turn out as expected, so in those years there were cumulative losses that led to an overall devaluation of the original investment equivalent to 1,929,000 euros." The minutes of the meeting convey the drama that surrounded each thorny question, such as that concerning the American Patrons of the Arts in Vatican Museums (formed shortly after the American tour of the traveling exhibition *The Vatican Collection*, to support and finance the restoration of various pieces in the Vatican collection). "Cullell," the minutes record, "raised the problem of the American Patrons who help the museums with their projects. The fund for the collection is in dollars. How is this income recorded in the account books? Is it divided up by year? Fralleoni explains that these funds were used to pay temporary personnel working at the museums. This is one of the reasons why these funds were kept in cash and not invested in other activities. According to him, they should be recorded in the books not as income but as capital that gradually decreases." But Cullell would hear nothing of it: "If the donations of the Patrons are not recorded as a single entry, our general financial statement will have been falsified."

13 The Kingdom of Taifa refers to the small states established in Spain after the breakup and subsequent abolition of the Umayyad Caliphate in 1031, which inaugurated a period of complete anarchy.

14 In March 2013, the Cardinal discovered and reported to the newly elected Pope Francis that something was wrong with the budget for the basilica. He set his sights on Monsignor Bronisław Morawiec, the basilica's *camerlengo*. An investigation by the Vatican's chief prosecutor, Gian Piero Milano, found that Morawiec had withdrawn 210,000 euros from an IOR account held by the basilica, claiming that he had to pay for real estate brokerage services provided by "Integrate Trade Consulting SA," a Swiss company that proved to be nonexistent. "There emerged in an incontrovertible way," Milano wrote, "serious bookkeeping irregularities, false accounting transactions, and the total lack of a protocol for registering incoming and

outgoing correspondence." Morawiec was sentenced to three years of imprisonment on the charge of embezzlement and forgery. The Basilica of Santa Maria Maggiore is one of the richest, with holdings of thousands of apartments, lands, and other properties. The disappearance of 210,000 euros is not the only crime he was suspected of. The prelate was reported for publishing an illustrated volume at a cost to the basilica of almost 1 million euros.

2. The Saints' Factory

1 Monsignor Peter Brian Wells was, among other things, the Secretary of the New Commission of Reference on the IOR established in June 2013 at the wish of Pope Francis.

2 Joseph F. X. Zahra is a Maltese economist, the founder of MISCO, a financial and management consultancy that operates in Malta, Cyprus, and Italy. Former director of the Central Bank of Malta (1992–1996), former president of the Bank of Valletta (1998–2004), he led the Committee that was supposed to introduce the euro to Malta in 2008. He entered the Vatican in 2010 as a member of the board of the Centesimus Annus Pro Pontifice Foundation. He came to the Prefecture in 2011.

3 Jochen Messemer, born in 1966, received his degree Economics and an MBA in Business Administration. He lives in Düsseldorf, Germany. A former partner at McKinsey (1993–2003), during the same period he also worked for various institutions of the Catholic Church in Germany. In 2003 he became the senior manager of the Munich Re groups, one of the world's leading reinsurance companies. In 2009 he came to the Vatican as an auditor for the Prefecture of Economic Affairs of the Holy See.

4 Monsignor Lucio Ángel Vallejo Balda, Spanish, was born on June 12, 1961, in Villamediana de Iregua (La Rioja) to a middle-class family whose main activity was in the field of agriculture. He entered the seminary at the age of eight, and completed his studies in philosophy and theology. In September 2011 he was appointed Secretary to the Prefecture of Economic Affairs of the Holy See.

5 Marco Politi, *Francesco tra i lupi* (Roma-Bari: Laterza, 2014).

6 Born in 1954, George Yeo was active in the People's Action Party of Singapore, a local center-right political formation. From 1991 to 2011, he was the Minister for Information and the Arts (1991–1999), Minister of Health (1994–1997), Minister of Trade and Industry (1999–2004), and Minister of Foreign Affairs (2004–2011). In 2011, when the Center Left came to power, he withdrew from politics. He was a former senior officer of the air force, and former Chief of the General Staff between 1985 and 1986, as well as the director of Joint Operations and Planning of the Ministry of Defense from 1986 to 1988. Of Catholic background and education, he received his degree in Engineering from Christ's College of Cambridge. He was the man who pushed forcefully to computerize his country, although he was in favor of censoring the web. For Yeo censorship was little more than an "anti-pollution measure for cyberspace." In 2000 he stated to the *Wall Street Journal*, "Censorship is part of education . . . Through symbolic censorship, he put into the heads of the

youngest minds that some right and wrong standards of taste exist." (Source: affariitaliani.it.)

7 George Pell, the Archbishop of Sydney, is also one of the eight cardinals of the group created by Francis in April 2013 to reform the Curia, to break its over-centralization in Rome.

8 According to the biography that appeared when he came to the Vatican, he was "the President of Incipit, a consultancy company, and the former CEO of Invesco Europa, a member of the management committee for the whole Invesco world. Before entering Invesco, he was the director of the French Groupe Caisse de Dépots et Consignations. He received his degree from the ESC Business School of Reims, took a BA in European Business Administration from Middlesex University in the United Kingdom, and a post-graduate degree in Actuarial Studies from the University Pierre and Marie Curie of Paris. He is a former vice-president and president of the European Fund and Asset Management Association (EFAMA) and non-executive director of Tages Llip and Carmignac Gestion. He is also a member of the board of various charitable organizations in Europe and the United States." Since July 2014 he has been the leader of the IOR.

9 Evangelina Himitian, *Francesco. Il Papa della gente* (Milano: Rizzoli, 2013).

10 The preliminary document would be gradually perfected until the final draft of February 18, 2014, incorporating all the instructions Francis had given since the summer of 2013.

11 Excerpted from the document "Commission Meeting No. 1/13" of the COSEA Commission.

12 Congregation for the Causes of Saints, *Le Cause dei Santi*, LEV, 2011, 395ff.

13 This is a direct quote from the "preliminary document" of the Commission prepared for the cardinals and the Holy Father on February 18, 2014. COSEA would suggest that "a clear and consistent process be defined to manage the funds on behalf of the causes of saints and poor causes."

14 Ibid.

15 Ibid.

16 Ibid.

17 Ibid.

18 This was the number that Monsignor Vallejo Balda would give to various COSEA members at the September 14, 2013, meeting.

19 Rolando Marranci was appointed shortly after, on November 30, 2013, and with some opposition, Director General of the IOR. The new post was announced by Father Federico Lombardi, spokesman for the Holy See, as follows: "The appointment of Marranci brings to an end the interim of President Ernst von Freyberg after the resignations of Director General [Paolo] Cipriani and his deputy [Massimo] Tulli." Cipriani and Tulli had resigned in July 2013. Both had been implicated in a judicial inquiry by the Rome prosecutor's office for violations, on the part of IOR, of anti-money-laundering laws. The accusations regard the transfer of 23 million euros from the Credito Artigiano to JPMorgan Frankfurt (20 million) and to the Banca del Fucino (3 million). The trial is still underway as of September 2015.

20 This emerges clearly in the first point of the "Confidential Report on the operative decisions taken at meeting n.3" of the COSEA Commission.

3. The Secrets of the Peter's Pence

1 Marco Politi, *Francesco tra i lupi* (Laterza: Roma-Bari, 2014).

2 On May 19, 2006, after a canonical investigation that lasted more than one year, the Congregation for the Doctrine of the Faith sentenced Maciel to the penalty of having to renounce any public ministry, forcing him to withdraw to a private life of prayer and penance for the acts of pedophilia he had committed against seminarians of his congregation. The decision was personally approved by Pope Benedict XVI.

3 The other residents in the vicinity of the Holy Office are almost all high-ranking cardinals and monsignors: Cardinal Francesco Coccopalmiero, President of the Pontifical Council for Legislative Texts (265 square meters); the former secretary of Ratzinger Monsignor Josef Clemens (226 square meters); Cardinal Paul J. Cordes (259 square meters), head of the Disciplinary Commission of the Roman Curia; Bishop Giorgio Corbellini (204 square meters); and finally Cardinal Elio Sgreccia, one of the most famous bioethicists in the world. At the age of eighty-seven, he is living in 149 square meters.

4 In his speech to the members of the Circle of St. Peter on February 25, 2006, Benedict XVI went on to underline that the Peter's Pence is, "A gesture that not only has practical value but is also highly symbolic as a sign of communion with the Pope and attention to the needs of the brethren."

5 John Paul II was even more clear, if possible, in his speech to the Circle of St. Peter on February 28, 2003: "You are aware of the growing needs of the apostolate, the requirements of the ecclesial communities, especially in mission countries, and the requests for aid that come from peoples, individuals and families in precarious conditions. Many expect the Apostolic See to give them the support they often fail to find elsewhere. In this perspective the Peter's Pence Collection is a true and proper participation in the work of evangelization."

6 There was an endless list of entities, foundations, and companies who had still not sent in the requested documentation. In the letter to Monsignor Parolin, the following requests were made:

"The financial statements (or similar) and by-laws of the following entities:

- The Baby Jesus Pediatric Hospital
- The Home for the Relief of Suffering Foundation
- The Papal Basilica of St. Paul Outside the Walls
- The Basilica of St. Peter's / Fabbrica of St. Peter's (we do not have the *regolamento*)

Other entities for which financial/bookkeeping information was not found are:

- The Pontifical Missionary Works (all we have available is the book published on revenues)
- Funds of the Postulators of Causes of Saints (detailed IOR accounts/individual balances)

- Complete 2012 financial report of Pia Opera (an entity that reports to Propaganda Fide—we have only received specific financial information)
- Pontifical Parish of Castel Gandolfo
- Pontifical Parish of St. Anne in Vatican
- The Lateran Penitentiaries
- The [Liberian] Penitentiaries
- The Vatican Penitentiaries
- The Pontifical Seminary Romano Minor
- The Benedict XVI Foundation for Marriage and Family
- The John Paul II Foundation for the Sahel
- The John Paul II Foundation for Youth
- The St. Matthew Foundation in member of Cardinal Van Thuan
- The Santa Marta Independent Pediatric Dispensary Foundation
- The Pius XII Foundation for the Lay Apostolate
- The Foundation for the Assets and the Artistic Activities of the Church
- The St. Josephine Bakhita Foundation
- The St. Michael the Archangel Foundation
- The Cardinal Salvatore de Giorgi Foundation
- The Science and Faith Foundation
- The Ennio Francia Financial Fund"

7 The amounts indicated in the document refer to 2012.

8 The McKinsey consultant's questions also touched on other issues, such as expenses for the papal nunciatures: "Does the 5.5 million in special expenses also include the cost of purchasing the buildings of the nunciatures (for example, of the Russian Nunciature)? All the buildings of the nunciatures are held by APSA at the cost of one euro. How does this work from an accounting perspective if consideration is given to the amounts the Secretariat spends to purchase real estate? Was this another donation to the benefit of APSA? What happens when the property is sold, who gets the profits? Why do the names of the accounts for the 'Peter's Pence Fund' vary according to the institution that holds them (for example, in 2012 a 20-million-euro account is referred to as 'Peter's Pence'; a 264-million account is called 'Secretariat of State'; a 95-million euro account is given yet another name)?"

9 "This was the twin of the German publisher of the same name that opened in the fall of 2008 with offices in Munich and a bank account at Hauck & Aufhauser, a cryptic private bank with branches in Luxembourg, Switzerland, and Germany," as I wrote in *His Holiness*.

4. Handcuffs in the Vatican

1 According to a memo of October 23, 2013, from department head Paolo Mennini to Cardinal Calcagno, the road to APSA's becoming a central bank began in 1940 when: "In a letter of June 10, the then delegate of the 'special section,' Bernardino Nogara, requested—through the papal nunzio to Washington, Monsignor Cicognani—and obtained—thanks to the authorization of the Ministry of the Treasury of the United States—permission to open a custodial account for the gold reserves of the special

section that had previously been deposited in London. The processing of the gold transactions was handled by a commercial bank, JPMorgan of New York. On February 15, 1954, the Federal Reserve Bank denied APSA's request to open an account in US dollars, since Fed policies only allowed that facility for central banks. In letters of March 2, 1976, and March 8, 1976, the Federal Reserve Bank, following express approval by President Volcker and the Board of Governors of the Federal Reserve System, allowed APSA to open an account in US dollars with 'full account facilities,' including the possibility of investments and custody of stocks. Attached to the letters were the terms of treatment and operability reserved exclusively for Central Banks." With regard to the International Regulations Bank, "APSA sold the physical gold at the bank, while keeping its deposit active, and currently maintains a bank account in US dollars." Relations with the Bank of England go back to October 2, 1989, when APSA, "wrote to the Bank of England requesting the possibility of opening a gold custodial account as generally accorded to all central banks, indicating as a reference the relationship it already enjoyed with the Federal Reserve Bank of New York, the International Relations Bank in Basel, and the World Bank in Washington. The reply of the Bank of England, dated November 2, 1989, granted APSA the right to open a gold custodial account and a bank account in sterling pounds, attaching the relative terms and conditions. Recently the bank has sent us the updated conditions that regulate access of central banks to inspection of their physical deposit of the gold bars that they own, reiterating its recognition of this Department's status as a central bank."

2 *Corriere della Sera*, November 24, 2013.

3 Email sent to Cardinal Calcagno, President of APSA, on January 22, 2014.

4 From the preliminary document of February 18, 2014, on the work of the COSEA Commission, drafted for the meeting of the so-called G8, the group of eight cardinals who are helping Bergoglio with the reforms.

5 Ibid.

5. The Sins and Vices of the Curia

1 From the Pope's homily at the Mass for new cardinals at St. Peter's on February 23, 2014. http://w2.vatican.va/content/francesco/en/homilies/2014/documents/papa-francesco_20140223_omelia-nuovi-cardinali.html.

2 In his report Nicolini emphasized many "weak points" in the project. Because of "the almost total lack of adequate human resource management," various countermeasures had to be taken. Among these, he indicated, "the start of a mid- and long-term project for the purpose of significantly reducing human resources, creating incentives for personnel in order to combat growing absenteeism, recourse to overtime hours as a tool at the disposal of management and not as a means of supplementing an employee's salary."

3 Of the other Vatican-owned gas stations, three are located in the city of Rome, one is near the pontifical villas, and one is in the vicinity of the Vatican Radio.

4 The group was established during the October 12 meeting and was led by Enrique Llano and had, as members, Zahra, Monsignor Vallejo Balda, and Jean Videlain-

Sevestre, as can be seen in the document with the "operative decisions" taken at the meeting.

5 The final draft is dated February 18, 2014, and it gives a progress report on COSEA's investigations into thirteen different workstreams.

6 Ibid.

7 Ibid.

8 Nello Rossi made this observation during a conversation with the author on September 21, 2014.

9 Ibid.

10 The document goes on to say: "EY recommends the following actions to improve oversight and reduce the operative and/or economic risks of the commercial activities:

- With regard to buyer's cards: review the policy and the requirements for issuing the cards; verify the status of the temporary cards; regulate the limits on use.
- With regard to the sub-contracted operators/contracts: agreement for a temporary extension until a new partnership strategy and reliable procurement process have been defined. The commercial activities should address their attention to revenue and the generation of profit for basic supplies [in other words, without going overboard]. For this purpose, specific actions have been inserted for each activity:
- Supermarket: limit customer targets and reduce the assortment of products; also, assess an alternate path for the supermarket.
- Fuel: limit target customers; also, assess the number and position of sales points and consider the partnership with a third party.
- Pharmacy: limit customer targets and reduce the assortment of products.
- Clothing and Electronics: limit customer target and assortment of products; in the long term, the activity can be suspended.
- Tobacco: limit customer target, raise prices (bring Vatican prices to the level of Italian prices); in the long term the activity can be suspended.
- Fragrance Shop: raise prices (bring Vatican prices to the level of Italian prices), limit customer target and establish maximum amounts card-holders can buy; in the long term, the activity can be suspended."

11 The email is addressed to a Governorate manager and signed by a manager of the private company.

12 The President of the Governorate, Cardinal Giuseppe Bertello, has a project to reorganize the Governorate. This, too, is stalled. He had been pushing for "a new structure of the Governorate that would be more streamlined and functional, reducing an organization of 23 departments and central offices to only 10."

6. The Immense Real Estate Holdings of the Vatican

1 The letter that Monsignor Viganò wrote to Pope Benedict XVI, defending his actions and criticizing Secretary of State Bertone, is an eloquent document of the dramatic period I am describing: "*Most Holy Father*, I find myself constrained to make recourse

to Your Holiness because of an incomprehensible and serious situation affecting the governance of the Governorate and me personally . . . My transfer from the Governorate in this moment would cause deep dismay and discouragement among those who believed that it was possible to clean up the many situations of corruption and abuse of power that have long been rooted in the management of various departments . . . I place in the hands of Your Holiness this letter, which I addressed to His Eminence the Cardinal Secretary of State, so that you may dispose of it in accordance with your august will, having as my only desire the good of the Holy Church of Christ. With sincere sentiments of profound veneration, the most devoted son of Your Holiness." A few days later, Viganò would deliver to Pope Benedict XVI in person a confidential note describing his actions. Here is an excerpt from that note: "When I accepted the assignment at the Governorate on July 16, 2009, I was well aware of the risks I would encounter, but I never thought I would find myself facing such a disastrous situation. I mentioned this on several occasions to the Cardinal Secretary of State, pointing out that I would not be able to manage through my own forces alone: I needed his constant support. The financial situation of the Governorate, already gravely debilitated by the international crisis, had suffered losses of more than 50–60 percent, also because of the incompetence of the persons who administered it. To remedy the situation, the Cardinal President has assigned the management of two State funds to a Finance and Management Committee, consisting of some major bankers, who ended up acting more for their own interests than for ours. For example, in December 2009, in a single operation they made us lose two and a half million dollars. I reported this to the Secretary of State and to the Prefecture of Economic Affairs, which considered the very existence of this committee to be illegal anyway. Through my constant participation in the meetings, I tried to contain the action of these bankers, with whom I often had to disagree necessarily. More about the conduct of this committee can be related to you by Mr. Gotti Tedeschi, who was a member until his appointment to the IOR, and he is well aware of how much I tried to keep its conduct under control."

2 The Sacred Congregation for the Propaganda of the Faith (Propaganda Fide), as it was formerly known, is the pontifical dicastery that leads and handles the general governance of Catholic missionary activity in the world. It currently consists of sixty one members, including cardinals, bishops, and archbishops. The head prefect is currently Cardinal Fernando Filoni, who was appointed in May 2011 by Pope Benedict XVI.

3 This estimate is for the real estate assets of APSA (approximately 45 percent of the total value of the purchase), pension funds (about 17 percent), and Propaganda Fide (about 10 percent).

4 If a tenant wished to have his entire apartment renovated at the expense of APSA, he would have to pay a 15 percent surcharge, which would drop to 10 percent if the tenant opted for a partial renovation or if work had already been done by the previous tenant.

5 The data indicated in the RB audit refer to September 30, 2013.

6 The data indicated in the RB audit refer to May 21, 2013.

7 The document forwarded by Cardinal Calcagno highlights the gradual decline in APSA's power: "Consequently attention should be drawn to the gradual erosion and dilution of the institutional role of APSA, from which many duties have been removed, but even more, which has had (and will continue to have) cognizance of various realities gradually emerging in the Holy See that rob APSA of its administrative duties (art. 172 of *Pastor Bonus*). All of this has inevitably diminished the power of the Dicastery in those areas that could be granted to it as financial 'piazzas' and, above all, it has opened up areas of administrative management that received practically a waiver from any form of oversight and that at times were the source of occasions of 'hindrance' with investments also outside of the IOR."

8 This is also mentioned in an investigative report published in *Europeo* in January 1977: "On August 6, 1976, the Holy See accepted a substantial donation from the Mollari siblings: it is twenty-two hectares of land with rural buildings at the locale 'La Mandria' on Via Laurentina 1351. There are two novelties about this donation. The first, as in countless other cases, is that the appraisal of the donated assets is unreliable: only 500 million. The second is that the decree by Italian President Leone requires the Holy See to sell everything within five years."

9 "Un Vaticano da 10 miliardi," an investigative report published in issue 29 of July 24, 2014, by Emiliano Fittipaldi.

10 "Diversa SA was founded in Lugano"—Fittipaldi writes—"in August 1942, while the battles of Stalingrad and El Alamein were being fought. Today it is chaired by Gilles Crettol, a Swiss lawyer who manages the interests of the Pope on the other side of the Alps: his name appears at almost every Swiss company."

11 On July 31, 2013, Profima had to pay more than 98,000 Swiss francs for services contracted to third parties, such as PwC for account auditing (26,924 francs), and 70,000 to the accounting experts of If Sfg not to mention the cost for Diversa SA of virtual office services at the Jordan holding company. If the attendance paid to the six board members was zero francs, this means that Gilles Grettol must have been paid 36,000 francs in 2012.

12 According to the data collected as of January 31, 2014, it appears that the chairman, Robin Herbert, receives gross compensation of 12,357 sterling pounds, while the other four directors receive 8,240 each.

7. Holes in the Pension Fund

1 From the 2013 estimated budget, chart of pension fund contributions and post 1.1.93 pension chart.

2 When confronted by the crisis of the diocese of Berlin, the German Bishops' Conference agreed to let the consultants from McKinsey step in. According to the journalist Sandro Magister, the Conference, "asked the manager of the Munich branch, Thomas von Mitschk-Collande, to get its accounts back in order. He also drew up a plan for the German Bishops' Conference to save on costs and personnel." "La curia di Francesco, paradiso delle multinazionali," *Espressoonline*, January 17, 2014.

3 From the minutes of the auditors' meeting on June 21, 2012.

4 "If you look at the contribution of active employees (current average value of

contributions—presently active)," Messemer underlines, "it will bring in 494 million euros: this is about 288 million less than what is needed to cover the estimated liability of 782 million euros for active employees.

"It is presumed that this discrepancy is financed both by the net assets and by future employees and that it will be covered, for the most part, by a mathematical reserve of about 180 million euros in the profits and losses account. To put it simply, the contributions of future employees should amount to about 575 million euros, while liabilities for the same group of persons is estimated at only 395 million euros.

"To be more concise: contributions from future employees will finance about 180 million euros of the pension [liability] of current employees. If you look at the need to cut personnel costs, thereby reducing the financial base of future contributions to the pension fund, this would seem to be an unrealistic assumption . . .

"The most important analysis that must be done urgently is an analysis of the correspondence between assets and liabilities. We are unable to say whether earnings from current and future assets (from a prospect based on the rate of risk/profit) are stable enough to guarantee the profits needed to cover the liabilities. The current interest rate for the calculation is about 4.7 percent. I should mention that the current interest rate on German government bonds (10 years) is 1.3 percent.

"The IRS, the Swap interest rate (20 years) is about 2 percent, also indicates that we are seeing a dramatic drop in interest rates, within which a projected rate of about 5 percent is truly ambitious. Making things more complicated is the fact that one-third of the assets are real estate. What type of asset are we referring to? In what does it consist? Are there also investments that could, in the future, modify the budget structure?"

5 The auditor had been particularly harsh five months earlier, on June 21, 2012, as documented in the minutes of the meeting of the international auditors' board: "Mr. Messemer hopes that, in the space of a few years, we can have a holistic view of the economic and financial activity of the Vatican, avoiding unpleasant surprises . . . This is why it is important for the Pension Fund to have exact risk assessments and to undertake an accurate actuarial calculation. To this end, Mr. Messemer underlined several important needs:

1. Change the pension system for new employees (i.e., per contribution);
2. Understand that the Pension Fund is part of a scenario in which interest rates vary from 2–3%;
3. Verify the exact correspondence between assets and liabilities. There are models that could be used as reference;
4. Always assess the counterpart's risk. The top insurance companies never neglect this aspect. If an insurance policy is drawn up with a bank, first check whether the bank is solvent.
5. Try to respect promises made to employees. This regards both the Pension Fund and the Health Insurance Fund.
6. Address the media's skepticism in calm cool tones, trying not to sound too worried about what is happening."

The other auditors share Messemer's concerns: "Mr. Prato returned to the subject of the Pension Fund and the two systems, of payments and contributions, that should exist after the introduction of contributions for new employees. Considering, however, the rather low turnover rate of Vatican personnel, it would be better to schedule a set date for the full transition to a system of contributions, for all employees, to prevent any possible disorder due to the coexistence of the two systems. Mr. Messemer claims that the separation of the two systems is the most immediate solution. It is problematic to transition to the new system if the old one is still widely misunderstood. Another source of concern is tied to the flows from one system to the other to allow the new pensions to pay for the old ones."

6 The document continues by underlining the following:

1. All the personnel offices of all the administrative bodies that report to the Apostolic See, in any way and regardless of the de facto or legal autonomy they have so far enjoyed, will be unified in a single administrative structure that will perform all the functions in this area. Some of these functions could be delegated, in part or in whole, for a fixed term.

- This structure will be called "Personnel Office of the Apostolic See" and it will report to the Prefecture of the Economic Affairs of the Holy See.
- It will be headed by an appointed Director of Human Resources who will direct and coordinate all personnel who, at present, handle assignments in this field at the single administrative bodies;
- The structure will be divided into two sections: one for all full-time permanent employees and another for other types of collaborators of any type working for administrative bodies of the Holy See, including unpaid collaborators.
- All the existing regulations at the single dicasteries will remain valid, provided they are in compliance with regulations at the higher level and, of course, with the universal principles of equity and justice.

7 Minutes from the meeting of the board of auditors on December 12, 2012.

8 Risk-identification document drafted for the Council of Cardinals on February 17–18, 2014.

9 Ibid.

10 Ibid.

11 From the "Report on the 2013 YTD Budget and the 2014 Estimated Budget."

12 Subsequently, we find 35 million in ordinary bonds of Barclays Bank Plc, 25 million at the Commerzbank, another 25 at General Electric, 12.3 million in France (Govd. Of), and 8 million in Eléctricité de France. Among the stock bundles, the most substantial are at Snam Rete Gas Spa (38,326), for a value of 143,000 euros, BASF for 141,000 euros, Eni for 127,000 euros, Enel Spa (22,800) for 64,000 euros, and Royal Dutch Shell with stocks valued at 73,000 euros. A substantial amount of stocks: investments in bonds would increase for the pension fund, to 11.2 million in the 2014 estimated budget (10.6 in euros and 0.6 in dollars) by comparison to the 10.9 million in the 2013 YTD budget.

13 From the "Report on the 2013 YTD Budget and the 2014 Estimated Budget."

14 In the summer of 2014, Francis gave the OK to the reform of the assets of the Holy See. The Vatican's immense patrimony will be placed under a single office, on the basis of ethical and Catholic criteria, currently being defined. The main novelty of the reform will be the style of management for the IOR, APSA, Propaganda Fide, the Pension Fund, and the Governorate. All asset management will be assigned to a new entity, Vatican Asset Management (VAM). The transition process will be gradual. As the Pope sees it, a more central system means more oversight, which was always missing in the past. But too much power in a single entity and to a small number of cardinals also generates the risk of mismanagement.

8. Attack on the Reform

1 Maria Antonietta Calabrò, *Corriere della Sera*, July 11, 2014.

2 "Diario Vaticano / La nuova curia prende forma così," October 22, 2013. www.chiesa.espressoonline.it.

3 Antonio Spadaro, "Francesco." *La Civiltà Cattolica*, September 19, 2013. English translation from the Vatican website. In the interview Francis also underlines that, "The church's ministers must be merciful, take responsibility for the people and accompany them like the good Samaritan, who washes, cleans and raises up his neighbor. This is pure Gospel."

4 Eugenio Scalfari, *la Repubblica*, October 1, 2013. English translation by Kathryn Wallace.

5 Parolin assumed his new post in absentia, since he was recovering at the hepatobiliary surgery ward of the Padua hospital and would not be installed until November 18. In the meantime, his functions were performed by the office managers.

6 On several occasions—for example, at the Basilica of Our Lady of Tears in Siracusa on the day after the announcement of his replacement by Parolin—Bertone responded to the many "accusations" to which he had been subjected: "Of course there have been many problems, especially in the past two years, and many accusations have been thrown at me by . . . a cabal of crows and snakes . . . But this should not obscure what I consider a positive final balance." "I have had my flaws," he said, but "I have always given my all" and no one can say that "I did not try to serve the Church." "On the one hand it would seem that the Secretary of State decides and controls everything, but that is not the case. There are events that got out of hand because these problems were 'sealed' within the control of certain persons who refused to liaise with the Secretariat of State." (ANSA, September 1, 2013.)

7 Enrique Llano expressed a similar position: "I am strongly in favor of the establishment of a Ministry of Finance and of the idea that it should report to the supreme authority, that is to say, to the Secretary of State—if the idea of a prime minister were to prevail—or to the Holy Father—if the idea of a Ministry of Foreign Affairs were to prevail. The Ministry of Finance should have the ultimate responsibility for financial control of the Holy See and the Governorate."

8 Francesca Chaouqui also took the floor: "There are two questions that must be addressed: 1. How to reform the financial management to help the Holy Father

immediately; and 2. In the past the Rome of Bernini, Michaelangelo, et al. was the cultural fulcrum of the world and the Church was the matrix of civilization: how can we procure the means to become a wellspring of such talents that would enable the Church to spread the word of God and at the same time have a clean financial system? We must envision the creation of an exemplary financial system."

9. The War, Act I: Blocked Budgets and Bureaucratic Assaults

1 Marco Politi, *Francesco tra i lupi* (Roma-Bari: Laterza, 2014).

2 The General Accountant also identified problems in the Governorate: "A person might have the impression that they're in good health when that is not the case . . . Important projects are planned for the museums, which would justify increased costs, but the item for personnel is always higher and higher, both for the museums and for the gendarmerie."

3 Prato also criticized the Governorate's accounts: "The other burden indicated by the Prefecture concerns 'various services' for more than 11 million euros provided by highly-specialized professional figures. This underscores the extreme 'liberty' of the Governorate's style of management, which ignores the guidelines of the Prefecture and the critical weaknesses in the general context. With regard to cultural activity and scientific research, the estimated doubling in the costs of normal management—as thoroughly evidenced by the Office of the Prefecture—is particularly significant."

4 From the minutes of the meeting of international auditors on December 18, 2013, at the offices of the Prefecture.

5 The Vatican radio station was founded in 1931. Today it employs four hundred people of sixty different nationalities, broadcasting programs in thirty-one languages.

6 In early May 2014, the historic antenna of the Santa Maria di Galeria station was taken down for financial reasons.

7 In his *motu proprio* decree on June 26, 2015, Bergoglio wrote: "Within the established timeframe, the following organisms will be combined in the new dicastery: the Pontifical Council of Social Communications; the Press Room of the Holy See; the Vatican Internet Service; Vatican Radio; the Vatican Television Center; *L'Osservatore Romano*; the Vatican Printer; the Photographic Service; and the Vatican Editions Bookstore."

8 Giuseppe Profiti was very close to Bertone. For seven years he was the president of the Bambino Gesù hospital, and he was later implicated in a series of scandals. He was acquitted by the Court of Cassation of involvement in the so-called "mensopoli" case in Genoa, and he is currently under investigation for the bankruptcy of the Casa delle Divina Providenza in Bisceglie. He resigned in January 2015.

9 The other items in the long email regard concerns about 1) the Pension Fund; 2) the unification of human resources; 3) replacing Paolo Mennini on the various APSA boards of which he is a member; and 5) funding for COSEA's expenses.

10 Stefania Falasca, "Parolin: col vangelo diplomazia di pace." *Avvenire*, February 8, 2014.

10. The War, Act II: The Revolution of Francis and the Rise of Cardinal Pell

1 From the "Summary Report of COSEA Meeting No. 7 (February 21, 2014)," redacted in both Italian and English.

2 From the letter sent by Alfred Xuereb to Cardinal Domenico Calcagno in early April 2014.

3 Emiliano Fittipaldi, "I lussi del moralizzatore," *l'Espresso*, March 5, 2015.

4 *Lectio magistralis* on Alcide De Gasperi in Pieve Tesino (TN), August 18, 2015.

About the Author

Gianluigi Nuzzi is an Italian journalist, nonfiction writer, and TV anchorman. He is the author of two bestselling titles, *Vaticano SpA* and *Sua Santità*, which have sold more than one million copies in Italy, Germany, France, Spain, the United States, Brazil and the Netherlands. He lives in Milan.